HIGHER EDUCATION AND CIVIC ENGAGEMENT: INTERNATIONAL PERSPECTIVES

Corporate Social Responsibility Series

Series Editor:
David Crowther, Professor of Corporate Social Responsibility,
De Montfort University, Faculty of Business & Law, Leicester, UK

This series aims to provide high quality research books on all aspects of corporate social responsibility including: business ethics, corporate governance and accountability, globalisation, civil protests, regulation, responsible marketing and social reporting.

The series is interdisciplinary in scope and global in application and is an essential forum for everyone with an interest in this area.

Also in the series

Higher Education and Civic Engagement: International Perspectives

Edited by

LORRAINE McILRATH AND IAIN MAC LABHRAINN
National University of Ireland, Galway

ASHGATE

Published by
Ashgate Publishing Limited
Gower House
Croft Road
Aldershot
Hampshire GU11 3HR
England

Ashgate Publishing Company
Suite 420
101 Cherry Street
Burlington, VT 05401-4405
USA

Ashgate website: http://www.ashgate.com

British Library Cataloguing in Publication Data
Higher education and civic engagement : international
    perspectives. - (Corporate social responsibility series)
    1. Citizenship 2. Citizenship - Study and teaching (Higher)
    3. Political participation 4. Political participation -
    Study and teaching (Higher) 5. Responsibility - Political
    aspects 6. Responsibility - Political aspects - Study and
    teaching (Higher)
    I. McIlrath, Lorraine II. Mac Labhrainn, Iain
    323'.042

Library of Congress Cataloging-in-Publication Data
Higher education and civic engagement : international perspectives / edited by
Lorraine McIlrath and Iain Mac Labhrainn.
        p. cm. -- (Corporate social responsibility series)
    Includes bibliographical references and index.
    ISBN 978-0-7546-4889-5
    1. Citizenship--Study and teaching--Cross-cultural studies. 2. Civics--Study and
teaching--Cross-cultural studies. 3. Student service--Cross-cultural studies. I.
McIlrath, Lorraine. II. Mac Labhrainn, Iain.

    LC1091.H39 2007
    378'.015--dc22

                                                                    2006103130

ISBN 13: 978-0-7546-4889-5

Printed and bound in Great Britain by Antony Rowe Ltd, Chippenham, Wiltshire.

Contents

PART 3   EMBEDDING PROCESS AND PRACTICE

List of Figures and Tables

Notes on Contributors

Professor Ronald Barnett is Professor of Higher Education at the Institute of Education, University of London. He has gained an international reputation for work undertaken on the conceptual understanding of the university and higher education and has been awarded a higher doctorate (DLit(Ed)) by the University of London. He has considerable experience of senior management and leadership positions in the Institute of Education and beyond. He has served on a myriad of major committees including the Society for Research into Higher Education and the ESRC Teaching and Learning Programme. He has particular interest in bringing scholarly research to bear on practical matters of institutional change, especially quality enhancement and academic development. His publication rate is prolific and his books include *Realising the University in an Age of Supercomplexity* (2000) and (with K. Coate) *Engaging the Curriculum* (2004).

Professor Ahmed Cassim Bawa, a theoretical physicist by training, has served as the Deputy Vice Chancellor for Academic Affairs at the University of Natal before becoming the Programme Officer for Higher Education and Scholarship in the Ford Foundation (South Africa). After a brief return to physics as a Professor in Hunter College (CUNY) he is now Deputy Vice Chancellor of the University of KwaZulu Natal. He is a Fellow of the Royal Society of South Africa as well as the Academy of Sciences of South Africa and served as Vice President for the latter from 1999–2000.

Josephine Boland is a lecturer in the Education Department at the National University of Ireland, Galway, specialising in the areas of curriculum and assessment and qualitative research methods. As course director of the Masters in Education, she has responsibility for the design of continuing professional development programmes for education professionals. Josephine also contributes to the Certificate in Teaching and Learning in Higher Education programme in the areas of course design and assessment. Prior to joining NUI Galway, she was Senior Development Officer with TEASTAS, the body responsible for advising the Minister for Education and Science on a legislative framework for a new national qualifications framework for Ireland. She worked for a number of years with the National Council for Vocational Awards and was part of a team responsible for the development of a national awards system for the further education sector. She had particular responsibility for curriculum development, assessment and certification processes in the business area. In the earlier stages of her career, she spent over ten years teaching within the further education sector.

Mark J. Doorley earned a B.A. in Philosophy from St. Alphonsus College (1984), a MDiv from the Washington Theological Union (1988) and a PhD in Philosophy from Boston College (1994). He received an appointment in the Core Humanities Programme at Villanova University in 1997 and was later appointed to the Ethics Programme (1999). Prior to his appointment at Villanova, Doorley taught at St. John's University in New York and St. Joseph's University in Philadelphia. In 2002 he was named the Assistant Director of the 'Ethics Programme' becoming Director since August 2005. Doorley has published one book *The Role of the Heart in Lonergan's Ethics* (University Press of America, 1996) and co-edited a volume of essays with Jim Kanaris entitled *In Deference to the Other: Lonergan and Contemporary Continental Thought* (SUNY Press, 2004). Since the spring of 2000 he has been using service-learning pedagogy in his introductory ethics courses and his research explores the notion of authenticity in ethical reflection and the value of service-learning in the pedagogy of ethics.

Andrew Furco is a professor in the Graduate School of Education at the University of California-Berkeley, where he also serves as Director of the campus's Service-Learning Research and Development Centre. Established in 1994, the Service-Learning Research and Development Centre is the first university-based research centre for service-learning in the USA. The centre has produced more than two dozen research studies on service-learning in primary, secondary, and tertiary education and it currently houses the National Service-Learning and Civic Engagement Research Directory. Professor Furco has published more than thirty journal articles and book chapters, and has co-edited two books on service-learning research: *Service-Learning: The Essence of the Pedagogy* and *Service-Learning through a Multidisciplinary Lens.* He is the recipient of the 2003 Award for Outstanding Contributions to Service-Learning Research and the first John Glenn Scholar for Service-Learning.

Michael Edwards is the Director of the Governance and Civil Society Programme at the Ford Foundation in New York, (one of the world's largest philanthropic trusts, with assets exceeding $10 billion). Prior to joining the Foundation in 1999 he was the World Bank's Senior Advisor on Civil Society (Washington DC), and before this spent 15 years as a senior manager in international relief and development ngo's, including periods with Oxfam-UK (as Regional Director for Southern Africa), and Save the Children-UK (as Director of Research, Evaluation and Advocacy). His many books and articles have helped to shape our thinking about ngo's, civil society and international cooperation. Michael is the author (most recently) of *Civil Society* (Polity Press/Blackwell 2004), The *Earthscan Reader on NGO Management* (Earthscan/Stylus 2002), *Global Citizen Action* (Lynne Rienner 2001) and *NGO Rights and Responsibilities: A New Deal for Global Governance* (Foreign Policy Centre 2000). A revised edition of his award-winning *Future Positive* – dubbed 'the book that revolutionised international cooperation' has just been published by Earthscan/Stylus. Michael was awarded a congratulatory double-first from the University of Oxford and a PhD by the University of London for his work on low-income housing markets in Colombia. For more information about Michael and his work, please visit the Future Positive website at www.futurepositive.org

Jennifer Iles is a Senior Lecturer in Sociology at Roehampton University in London. She convenes the Service Learning course in the School of Business and Social Sciences and directs the London programme of the International Partnership for Service-Learning and Leadership. She also teaches courses in tourism, the heritage industry, death studies and the family. She holds at PhD in sociology from Roehampton University and her research interests include battlefield tourism, death studies and experiential learning in higher education.

Elizabeth Hollander, in 2006, is the outgoing Executive Director of Campus Compact. Prior to her appointment to this position in 1997, she served as Executive Director of the Monsignor John J. Egan Urban Centre at DePaul University, which works with the university to address critical urban problems, alleviate poverty, and promote social justice in the metropolitan community through teaching, service and scholarship. She also was the President of the Government Assistance Programme in Illinois and the Director of Planning for the city of Chicago under Mayor Harold Washington. While in Chicago, Hollander served on the Boards of Trustees at Chicago State University and the Illinois Institute of Technology. From 1992 to 2004, she served on the Truman Regional Scholarship Committee. Hollander also serves on the Advisory Board of the online Journal of College and Character, the American Committee of the International Consortium on Higher Education, the Advisory Board of the Centre for Information and Research on Civic Learning and Engagement (CIRCLE) at the University of Maryland, the Board of the National Civic League. Hollander received an honorary doctorate from Millikin University in 2001, and DePaul University in 2003 and is a fellow of the National Academy of Public Administration.

Nan Kari was educated as an occupational therapist, and was one of the founding partners of Project Public Life (the Centre for Democracy and Citizenship). She co-directed the Lazarus Project action research effort at Augustana Nursing Home in Minneapolis, which sought to change the culture into a more participatory, civically engaging environment for residents and staff alike. She later developed what came to be known as an organising approach to faculty development, while serving as the Director of Faculty Development at the College of St. Catherine. She is co-founder of the Jane Addams School for Democracy in St. Paul and senior associate of the Centre for Democracy and Citizenship at the University of Minnesota. She has worked on civic engagement projects in nursing homes, settlement houses, religious institutions, higher education and neighbourhood settings. Nan has written extensively on citizenship and public life, including co-authoring *Building America: The Democratic Promise of Public Work*, with Harry Boyte.

Lorraine McIlrath is the Coordinator of the Community Knowledge Initiative (CKI) at the National University of Ireland, Galway and an Academic Staff Developer (Service Learning) based at the Centre for Excellence in Learning and Teaching. She is responsible for supporting the development of the service learning component of the CKI. She has a BA in European Studies (University of Limerick) and attained a scholarship from the Institute for Peace and Development Studies to pursue the MA programme in Peace and Conflict Studies at University of Ulster, awarded in 1997. She has worked on a number of major citizenship education projects, including the framework for 'Local and Global Citizenship' for Key Stage 3 in Northern Ireland and the development of the 'College of Multicultural Education in Sochi, Russia with the British Council. While in post as a Lecturer in Education at the UNESCO Centre at the University of Ulster she developed an academic programme on the Northern Ireland conflict peace process which underpinned service learning. Further information on the Community Knowledge Initiative can be access at http://www. nuigalway.ie/cki

Iain Mac Labhrainn is the Director of the *Centre for Excellence in Learning and Teaching* (CELT) at the National University of Ireland, Galway since 2002. He is a member of the Higher Education Academy (UK) and the American Association for Higher Education. With a PhD in Physics and working as a researcher, lecturer and Reader in this subject, he has spent the last ten years working and researching on student learning and the purposes of higher education. A committed volunteer (with the National Association for the Care and Resettlement of Offenders, Newcastle-Upon-Tyne and the Community Education service in Glasgow) his Centre currently hosts the *Community Knowledge Initiative*.

Timothy Murphy is a graduate of Teachers College, Columbia University, New York, where he received his doctorate in education in 2001. He is a member of the Service Learning Pilot Group for the Community Knowledge Initiative (CKI) at the National University of Ireland, Galway, where he has also worked as a Lecturer in Education from 2002–2005. He is currently attached to the Centre for Excellence in Learning and Teaching at NUI, Galway as a Researcher looking at teaching and learning issues within the context of higher education. He is particularly interested in exploring the extent to which participation in Service Learning activities can impact on the role identity of educators, especially concerning their capacity for civic engagement.

Nan Skelton is co-director of the Institute's Centre for Democracy and Citizenship at the University of Minnesota. The centre seeks to renew American democracy as a commonwealth created and sustained by the public work of its citizens. Skelton works on youth policy, citizen education, and community development through three major projects: the Jane Addams School for Democracy and Public Achievement, the Neighbourhood Learning Community, and Public Achievement. Skelton has research interests in youth development and immigration policy. Integrating civic perspectives with these fields has led her to raise important questions about much of contemporary scholarship that focuses on young people and immigrants. Prior to joining the Humphrey Institute, Skelton was an assistant commissioner with the Minnesota Department of Education from 1983–1990. As assistant commissioner, Skelton provided leadership on youth development legislation, AIDS education, school-to-work initiatives, and dropout prevention research with the National Governor's Association. She has been a programme officer in the Lilly Endowment's Education Division. During the 1970s and 1980s, she founded and directed several community-based non-profit organisations in the Twin Cities. Skelton has a bachelor's degree in education from the College of St. Catherine.

Paul Smyth is the Director of Public Achievement in Northern Ireland. He has extensive experience in the practice and development of community relations youth work with the University of Ulster, the Youth Council for Northern Ireland and, since 2003, in his current role. He has worked extensively with partners in conflict regions around the world, particularly in the Middle East, Balkans, South Africa and the USA. He has taught at the University of Ulster, Queen's University Belfast and at the University of Minnesota.

Richard Taylor is Professor and Director of Continuing Education and Lifelong Learning at the University of Cambridge. He was previously Professor of Continuing Education at the University of Leeds, where he had been Head of Department and, subsequently, Dean of the Faculty of Business, Law, Education and Social Studies. His PhD was on the history and politics of the British Peace Movement in the 1950s and 1960s and he has published widely in politics and peace studies. He has worked in university adult education for many years and has published several books on adult education and higher education, and comparative studies on the politics of post-compulsory education in North America and India. His most recent works are (with David Watson) *Lifelong learning and the Universities: A post Dearing agenda* and (with Jean Barr and Tom Steele) *For a Radical Higher Education: After Post-Modernism*. He is currently researching the evolution of British Labour Party's Higher Education Policy since 1945 and has published several recent articles in this area. He was Secretary of the UK's Universities Association for Continuing Education (UACE) from 1994–98 and has been Chair of the National Institute of Adult Continuing Education (England and Wales) since 2001.

Ross VeLure Roholt is an Action Research Officer for Public Achievement in Northern Ireland and has also worked as the external evaluator for Public Achievement in the USA. He is responsible for the development and testing of the practice model and linking with international partners (Palestine, South Africa Yugoslavia) in the development of an international learning community.

Marshall Welch has been at the University of Utah since 1987 as a faculty member in the Department of Special Education. Marshall was department chair for the last two years of his faculty appointment before being appointed Director of the Lowell Bennion Community Centre in May of 2001. Marshall began teaching a service-learning course addressing issues of children and became involved with the Bennion Centre. He served on several advisory committees of the Bennion Centre and was named the Borchard Service-Learning Faculty Fellow in 1996–97, providing assistance to other faculty across campus interested in service-learning courses. His scholarly interests are in the area of service-learning, civic engagement, and community-based research. He earned his doctorate in Special Education from Southern Illinois University in 1987.

Edward Zlotkowski is a professor of English at Bentley College and Senior Faculty Fellow at Campus Compact. From 1995–2004, he served as general editor of the American Association for Higher Education's 20-volume series exploring the relationship between service-learning and academic disciplines/disciplinary areas. He has also designed and facilitated professional development opportunities in service learning for provosts and deans as well as a series of summer institutes for engaged academic departments. He has written and spoken extensively on a range of service-learning topics, and regularly uses service-learning in his own teaching. In 2002, he edited *Service-Learning and the First-Year Experience: Preparing Students for Personal Success and Civic Responsibility*, and in 2004 served as lead author of *The Community's College: Indicators of Engagement at Two-Year Institutions*.

Acknowledgements

The following publication would not have been possible without the support of the twenty esteemed authors who have enabled this collection of international perspectives. Complex and significant insights are offered through a myriad of lenses, including that of communities partnering the process, students engaged in the activity, academics creating civic engagement initiatives and reflecting on the civic purpose of higher education. The chapters within this book are original, however one has been reprinted with the permission of *The Journal of Public Affairs,* entitled 'Institutionalising Service-Learning in Higher Education' authored by our colleague Andrew Furco at the University of California Berkeley (Supplemental Issue 1: Civic Engagement and Higher Education) in 2002 Vol. VI, 38–67, and we wish to acknowledge their support.

The opportunity to develop and publish this collection emanated from an international teaching and learning conference held at the National University of Ireland, Galway in June 2005, on the theme of 'Civic Engagement and Higher Education: Universities, Students and Community'. The conference marked the first phase of a major civic engagement initiative, the Community Knowledge Initiative or (CKI), based at that institution and enabled the evolution of a national debate in Ireland on the civic purpose of higher education which continues to gain momentum. The CKI has thrived at the National University of Ireland, Galway under the guidance of the CKI Board which includes Professor Jim Browne, Registrar and Deputy President of NUI Galway, who has been instrumental in terms of enabling a successful initiative, and the Chair, President (An tUachtarán) Dr Iognáid G. Ó Muircheartaigh. Also success has been enabled through the CKI International Advisory Board whose expertise spans a number of sectors from community development to service learning from Ireland to South Africa. The CKI is presently being mainstreamed across the university though the vision and commitment of academic staff embedding community based learning opportunities at the programmatic level, enthusiastic students availing of volunteering and service learning opportunities and the genuine commitment of community to our endeavours.

The CKI would not have been possible without generous support from Atlantic Philanthropies (Ireland) who have enabled this initiative though a generous donation since 2001.

The editors would also like to thank the CKI dynamic team and the work undertaken to create original work within the context of higher education in Ireland. In particular we would like to acknowledge Mary Bernard, CKI Administrative Assistant, for her patience and expertise in terms of formatting, and preparing the final version of the text.

We would like to thank Ashgate and their support staff in terms of enabling the production of this publication.

Foreword

Elizabeth Hollander

This foreword offers the perspective of someone with a decade of experience in the movement to reassert the civic purposes of higher education. As the Executive Director of Campus Compact,[1] I have been in a position to gain a broad view of the progress that has been made and the challenges ahead.

The movement to *reassert* higher education's public purposes, in the United States of America as in most other countries, recalls the bases on which institutions of higher education were founded. For example, American colonial colleges were founded to train the next generation of leaders to guide the new nation. In the late 1800s, public land grant colleges were founded to serve the agricultural and technical needs of a growing nation. In the 1960s, the USA saw an explosion in the creation of two-year community and technical colleges with the purpose of training a more diverse labour force. In his 1876 inaugural address as the first president of Johns Hopkins University, Daniel Coit Gilman described the burgeoning of higher education as the embodiment of a wish for 'less misery among the poor, less ignorance in the schools, less bigotry in the temple, less suffering in the hospitals, less fraud in business, less folly in politics'.

Over the past several decades, however, the role of higher education in educating the next generation of active citizens has been overshadowed by a focus on the transfer of disciplinary knowledge and preparation for professional life. The recent desire to reassert the public purposes of higher education has sprung from concern over decreasing levels of 'social capital' and over whether the next generation is willing and prepared to take up the responsibilities of democracy. In the early 1960s, more than two thirds of American students thought it important to be knowledgeable about current events, and most said that the key purpose of higher education was to develop a philosophy of life. Now just one third of students say that knowledge of

---

1 Campus Compact, established in 1985, is a coalition of more than 1,000 institutions of higher education across the United States of America and elsewhere, with one member institution based in Ireland at the National University of Ireland, Galway. Campus Compact works to build civic engagement into campus and academic life by influencing education policy, providing training and technical assistance, developing extensive print and online resources, creating opportunities for ongoing discourse, and making available grant opportunities. The coalition has a national office at Brown University in Rhode Island and 31 state offices across the USA. The organisation serves presidents and chancellors, academic and student administrators, faculty members, service learning and community service directors, students and community partners. Further information on Campus Compact can be accessed at http://www.compact.org.

current events is important, and more than two thirds describe the primary purpose of their education as enhancing their employability. Voting rates during the 2000 national election within the eighteen to twenty-four year-old grouping was barely above a third; while that figure increased to fifty per cent in the 2004 elections, it remains distressingly low.

Another precipitating factor in the civic education movement in the USA has been the institutional role that higher education can play to enhance challenged local communities. Many communities are facing increasing need in a time of decreasing aid. As repositories of knowledge, resources, and labour, colleges and universities can play a role in strengthening communities while advancing their civic and academic missions.

Much progress has been made in fostering higher education's public purposes in the USA and around the world. Evidence includes the growth of membership in Campus Compact as well as the proliferation of other efforts to foster civic engagement. Accreditation and classification standards in the USA now include measures of engagement, and many campuses (including eighty-six per cent of Campus Compact members) have centres to coordinate service, service-learning or civic engagement efforts. Although we have made a great deal of progress, we need to be vigilant about maintaining the momentum of this movement. I believe that there are three essential ingredients for doing so: rigour, real-world problem solving and raising awareness.

Rigour

In the 1980s, Campus Compact began with the conviction that if students were given an opportunity to be involved in extra-curricular volunteer work, this work would subsequently lead them to other civic behaviours, such as addressing policy issues and voting. However, it became apparent that if the desire was to instil in students civic behaviours such as a sense of *agency in their democracy,* they first needed to understand the systemic causes of the conditions they were seeing in disadvantaged communities and be given time to reflect on what that meant for their own civic engagement.

Service learning seemed a very good vehicle to achieve these aims. By embedding community experiences into academic work, higher education institutions could better prepare students to understand and address community problems and help them reflect on the impact of their work on the community and on their own lives. One example of this is a course in chemistry instrumentation in which students take samples in lead-contaminated homes, analyse them and give the findings to the city authorities. As well as deepening their understanding of chemistry instrumentation, students learn about a widespread social problem, its impact on children, and the ways in which chemistry can be used to help ameliorate the problem.

Thus a well taught service learning curriculum involves academic rigour and in addition will feature civic learning outcomes as well as course content outcomes. Assignments should require students to think deeply about their experience within the community through structured reflection. Service learning opportunities should also include community-based research, as well as community-based problem solving and community volunteerism. It should not encompass periodic volunteerism without guided preparation and opportunities for deep, collaborative reflection.

Real-World Problem Solving

One of the principal criticisms from community members working with the academy is that they are studied, like rats in a laboratory, so students and faculty can gain knowledge that is not shared back with the community. Genuine civic engagement should be powerful for all those involved in the process, including the community. One example is the 'Saturday Academy' for fifth graders on the campus of Johnson C. Smith University, an historically black institution in North Carolina, USA. This Academy has measurably increased the reading and math scores of the children who attend, and has also exposed these children to the college campus and its students, raising their capacity to imagine higher education for themselves. The college students who volunteer at the Academy learn what it means to educate students from disadvantaged backgrounds and see first-hand the impact that economic disadvantage has on students' self-esteem, hopes and dreams.

How can institutions of higher education promote more powerful real world problem solving? One focus is on developing a team of 'bridge builders' or 'world spanners' – personnel who can transcend the boundaries of the campus and the community and help construct powerful experiences for both the student and the community. In the USA at the state level, a funded volunteer corps of nearly 300 college graduates known as Volunteers In Service To America (VISTAs) have successfully been deployed to enable campuses to make powerful community connections and deepen relationships with local communities.

Raising Awareness

Higher education in the USA is currently facing a serious decline in public investment at both the national and, in particular, the state level. This is partly due to competing demands for health care and other social provisions, but it is also because there is a belief that those who 'learn more, earn more' and are therefore in a position to repay the high costs involved in third level fees. Education has increasingly moved from being a public purpose to a private right.

Many in the civic education movement are deeply troubled by these trends, and are using their social capital to express these concerns to those with influence on the funding of public education. There is a need to gain powerful allies for civic education who are not in the academy, such as government ministers, business and philanthropic leaders, and even parents. Campus Compact is due to celebrate its twentieth anniversary, and as part of that effort the organisation is gathering an influential 'Leadership Circle' of business, government, foundation, and other leaders from every political perspective who have supported this work.

A powerful tool to respond to this pertinent issue has been to deploy students to talk to legislators and others about their civic engagement experiences through service learning in institutions of higher education. Campus Compact has created a state and national student campaign entitled 'Raise Your Voice' that encourages students to visit their state houses and the Congress, as well as to host many activities on their own campuses. State offices provide training for student leaders on their member campuses and offer small campus grants. The national office provides an action framework in addition to technical assistance materials on a web site called Action for Change.[2] The state offices also work directly with government leaders, including legislators and governors' offices, to explore the importance of civic education throughout schooling, which has included elementary, secondary and post-secondary education. The national office also undertakes this process with federal agencies, the Congress and other relevant leaders.

It is essential that presidents and chancellors within higher education articulate their commitment to education's civic mission. One of the most successful ventures in this regard is the *Presidents' Declaration on the Civic Responsibility of Higher Education,* which has been signed by more than 500 presidents across the USA. Those who have endorsed the Declaration pledge to educate the next generation of active citizens and model good citizenship within their own communities.

Finally, it is important to remember that civic engagement and service learning are not just pedagogical techniques or tools; they are key elements in advancing higher education's role in developing and maintaining civil democratic societies. The great US educator John Dewey, in 1907, said 'Democracy has to be born anew in every generation, and education is its midwife' (Campbell 1995, 215). This work is about the future of our nations and our world, and this publication will go far to raise international interest in enabling institutions of higher education to embed and mainstream civic engagement opportunities and become, in the words of the Declaration I just cited, 'agents and architects of a vital democracy' (Campus Compact 2005).

References

Campbell, J. (1995), *Understanding John Dewey: Nature and Cooperative Intelligence* (Peru, IL: Open Court Publishing Co.).

Campus Compact (2000, 2005). *Presidents' Declaration on the Civic Responsibility of Higher Education (*Providence, RI: Campus Compact).

Kenny, M. et al., (eds.) (2002) *Learning to Serve, Promoting Civil Society through Service Learning* (Massachusetts: Kluwer Academic Publishers).

---

2   Further information can be assessed on http://www.actionforchange.org.

Introduction

Iain Mac Labhrainn and Lorraine McIlrath

This collection of articles developed from a conference held in Galway, Ireland in June 2005 at which almost 200 participants from around the world met and shared their ideas, experience and knowledge of issues on the civic role of higher education and how it might be pursued through service learning, volunteering and community-based research. From the US, we heard of service learning programmes that have been well established for many years; from South Africa the issue was how universities and communities can build a new nation from that hugely diverse population; from the UK, issues at the heart of what citizenship means and how universities reconcile such; and from Ireland of a range of small scale but growing programmes that seek to redress the 'disconnect' that many sense is happening in our communities, through harnessing the passion, energy and idealism of youth.

A number of very distinguished keynote speakers, well-established in their field, mixed and discussed with practitioners from students' unions, volunteering organisations, service learning centres, university management and NGOs. Those who helped to organise the event saw immediately the value in trying to capture at least a fraction of the spirit and atmosphere of the event through a publication. This is not a traditional conference proceedings volume, however, in that a number of the articles are reflections on what was said, enhanced through discussion. In addition, we also have excellent contributions from a number of key authors who could not be at the event itself but who share our goals and vision.

The event itself was one of the first major activities of the *Community Knowledge Initiative* (CKI),[1] a project based at the National University of Ireland, Galway which seeks to nurture greater levels of civic engagement, student participation as active citizens and to bring community issues to the heart of the university. Funded, largely by a major philanthropic donation and guided by an International Advisory Board, CKI since its inception in 2001 has grown, its goals being championed by enthusiastic academic colleagues and students from across the institution. There are four strands to the CKI, which include student volunteering, research, service learning and knowledge sharing. The service learning dimension has grown substantially over the last three years, with the piloting and embedding of a number of academic programmes, at undergraduate and postgraduate levels, across the institution supported by a seed funding scheme, the formation of a service learning support group and regular seminars and meetings. Also of particular note has been the rapid growth of student volunteering under the ALIVE (A Learning Initiative and

---

1   See http://www.nuigalway.ie/cki for more details.

Volunteering Experience) scheme, which provides personal and civic skills training in parallel to work undertaken in local community organisations as well as through a variety of volunteering pathways available on campus.

Contested Language

Before we can even begin to consider the development of practical programmes to embed service learning and promote student engagement with the wider community we really do need to have some clarity of what we mean (or at least what we think we mean) by terms such as 'community', 'citizenship' and 'engagement'. Each of these terms is contested in both the academic literature and in the public/political sphere. *Community* is particularly problematic in that it can be used for exclusionary purposes as well as with more positive connotations (for example, Delanty 2003; Bauman 2000). 'Social Capital' is another 'buzz-phrase' that rears its head in many such discussions and once again the term has different connotations in different parts of the political spectrum. Popularised by Putnam, but originated by Bourdieu, it potentially provides a useful framework for exploring the nature of our social networks and their contribution to the construction of civil society. The range of definitions currently in play, however, causes some difficulty when attempting to measure its extent and value (Field 2003).

In these times of troubled international relations, immigration and multiculturalism, the nature of 'citizenship' is also, of course, hotly debated and we in academe cannot stand aloof. Indeed, it could be argued that the natural tendency of much of university research is to disengage, or decouple, from contemporary social debate, keeping a low profile to avoid controversy (as perhaps is illustrated in the historical background described in the contribution here by Velure Roholt and Smyth). Whilst this may perpetuate the notion of objective enquiry, it doesn't fit well with the concept of democratic participation.

The nature of these definitions and how such ethical challenges can be reconciled with the purposes of higher education are discussed by Richard Taylor and Ron Barnett. Michael Edwards in some senses goes further and, more fundamentally, poses the question as to motivation. What is it that drives us to seek social justice, to reach out to help, to seek a better world? Placing religion, faith and politics to one side he expands on his earlier suggestion that it might be 'love' and that its combination with reason provides a powerful force for change.

Pedagogy

The value of experiential learning has been well established and much extended since Kolb's early publication of the 'learning cycle'. Apprenticeship is perhaps one of the oldest forms of training, yet for many centuries its separation from more academic forms of learning and teaching created a perception of irrelevance to 'higher learning', despite the fact that most scholars can be considered as undergoing just such an apprenticeship at the hands of supervisors and mentors by the time they enter postgraduate study. For undergraduate courses, the tradition has been lectures, tutorials and examinations, with a particularly strong separation between the affective and the cognitive domains. Yet, in recent years, this has begun to become more and more of a stereotype, insofar as newer approaches have begun to make, in some cases significant, inroads into university education. Take for example *problem* or *enquiry based learning*, a set of approaches that has its enthusiastic proponents (and detractors – but such is the nature of higher education) and in some cases (Maastricht, McMaster, Aalborg and so forth) even is the predominant, institutionally sanctioned approach to teaching. On a more modest scale, the value of project work, case studies and peer-discussion has been well appreciated and most academic staff would point to pressures of timetabling, resources and workload as being the reasons why such methods are not more widespread, rather than any intrinsic intellectual or ideological opposition. Such engaged, active forms of learning are also endorsed by the educational research literature and supported by professional bodies whose membership requires graduates with critical thinking skills and the ability to become reflective practitioners.

However, there is a subtle but important distinction to be made between what Ron Barnett has described as critical 'being' and critical 'thinking', and which is described in detail in terms of the potential impact on curricular design in a recent publication (Barnett and Coate 2004). Perhaps, this is where service learning can seek its opportunity. Service learning, after all, is meant to be about more than simply experiential learning, as many authors in this volume (Zlotkowski; Welch; Boland and McIlrath) discuss. The additional dimension is that of *civic awareness*, an ability to see beyond the mechanics of the current situation and appreciate, with a view to challenging, the wider social context within which the experience is situated (see Doorley).

Marshalling the fundamental academic attributes and skills of research, analysis and an ability to distinguish the critical factors in any given situation, it is possible to move beyond mere experience and begin to outline the nature of the challenge, if not the solution, of societal and civic issues. It is, then, clear also that there is a distinction between *service learning* and *volunteering*. All too often, both are casually conflated together. Service learning is a specific pedagogical approach, it is not about voluntary contribution to a community organisation for 'charitable' purposes; it is about benefiting from such experience through reflection and academic critique and providing, ultimately, recognition through academic credit and, ultimately, helping also to build capacity with community organisations. However Furco, in his chapter, points out that the literature offers over two hundred definitions of service learning, however it is essential within the institutionalisation process that each institution arrives at its own definition and understanding. As Furco and Holland (2004) put it, 'service learning is an academic strategy that seeks to engage students in activities that enhance academic learning, civic responsibility and the skills of citizenship, while also enhancing community capacity through service' (Furco and Holland 2004, 27).

Perhaps, Barnett's ideas of *being* and Edward's conception of *love and reason* can help extend this definition a little further by focusing on the transformative potential that can be unleashed through the combination of 'being', action and engagement.

Much of the literature in the field of service learning emanates from the US, where the concept finds its roots in the early ideals of a 'liberal education' and resonates strongly with the ideas of John Dewey and others of his ilk; more recently supported by Boyer's (1990) conception of the 'scholarship of engagement'. In this volume, Zlotkowski outlines the fundamental pedagogical strength of the concept whilst many authors indicate some of the key factors that need to be addressed in institutionalising service learning. Marshall Welch and Mark Doorley take this discussion into the area of practical matters, exploring both 'best practice' and the nature of the student-teacher relationship and the trust on which it is founded. Murphy also makes an additional plea to appreciate the opportunity to embed a service learning pedagogy in the initial formation of school teachers, whilst Kari and Skelton speak passionately about their work within a community education organisation. Andrew Furco highlights the complexity surrounding the strategic institutionalisation of service learning across diverse higher education institutions in the US and presents findings from a three-year exploratory study. While this chapter has been written from experience gained in the USA, the lessons and insights presented have important ramifications for the mainstreaming of service learning across higher education internationally.

Universities in the Global Twenty-First Century

The historical role and cultural attributes of universities, however, varies quite considerably across the world. In some cases they serve to maintain tradition and are still seen as the preserve of an elite, whilst in others, they are accessible to all and are strongly coupled with programmes of industrial and economic modernisation. A 'translation' from the American context, therefore, is going to be essential if service learning and civic engagement are to find their opportunities in each national system. Indeed, in some cases, similar types of community engagement with higher education have long been in existence but perhaps haven't been formally identified or labelled.

Ahmed Bawa, for example, provides a fascinating insight into the situation in South Africa, where the challenge is also one of nation building and of the opening of academic minds to the lived reality of alternative knowledge systems that have a hold on the popular imagination and civil society. His examples of the challenges of seeking 'truth and reconciliation' are echoed in the Northern Ireland experience described eloquently by Ross Velure Roholt and Paul Smyth. Lorraine McIlrath and Josephine Boland write from the perspective of a small but dynamic European country (Ireland), which seeks opportunities to build on its traditions of community and volunteering, and in which there is recent government and public focus on a perceived decline of 'engagement'. Jennifer Iles' chapter describes one of the first programmes in the UK, at Roehampton University, where service has been part of the general undergraduate programme since 1993.

In most national systems (and in many private institutions) the notion of the university fulfilling some, often unidentified, civic purpose is long established. The important issue, however, is the extent to which this 'mission' is actually pursued, rather than existing at the level of aspiration. Furco highlights, that for successful institutionalisation, the process of embedding service learning must be bound to the overall mission of the institution.

Indeed, globally, in recent years, we have seen increased government involvement in the shaping of higher education strategy, with a clear focus on the perceived economic needs of the 'knowledge economy' (Wolf 2002). Employers' organisations have become more vocal in their opinions of both course content and 'transferable skills'; parents and students themselves have become more concerned about issues of quality in terms of organisation of classes, provision of support services etc; whilst much of university management is suspected by some at least of having adopted the language of 'managerialism' (Wynyard and Hayes 2003). The introduction of student fees and the growth in part-time student employment in some countries and an increased sense of commodification of education (through the GATTS framework for example) has led to a fear that the university experience is becoming, for many students, more narrowly focused and culturally and socially impoverished. Attention has been drawn to many of these issues recently through, for example, the NBC documentary (and associated collection of essays), *Declining by Degrees* (Hersh and Merrow 2005).

Some have gone a little further in their personal 'critique' of contemporary higher education. Robert Zemsky (2003), in the *Chronicle of Higher Education*, wrote:

> In the 1960s and to a lesser extent the 1950s, campuses were public arenas –platforms for political theater, recruiting grounds for social activists, and often the places public officials turned to for judicious expertise when sorting out vexing issues. While certainly not every idea discussed in collegiate settings really mattered, rare was the social, political, or economic movement that did not consider the college campus as a critical venue for the airing of viewpoints and perspectives.

> Today, however, colleges and universities are seen principally as providing tickets to financial security and economic status. Few people worry about higher-education institutions leading young people astray. If anything, the lament is that they have, in their pursuit of market advantage, become dispensers of degrees and certificates rather than vibrant communities of educators who originate, debate, and promulgate important ideas (Zemsky 2003, B7)

The challenge for those of us that are concerned with the ideals of a university education, is to demonstrate its wider merits and benefits to the individual and society in non-monetary terms, whilst at the same time ensuring that our academic colleagues are as convinced as we are of the intellectual and academic integrity of endeavours such as service learning, community-focused research and greater civic and democratic participation. In their chapter, Ross VeLure and Paul Smyth from Public Achievement (Northern Ireland) describe their experiences of promoting participatory democracy, highlighting many of the real-world practical challenges when universities and community organisations meet. Nan Kari and Nan Skelton, also share a vivid picture of forging links between local community and the academy, whilst the transformative impact of the experience on student participants is expressed clearly in the reports of Whitney, McClure, Respet in their shared chapter with Patti Clayton.

Clearly, however, the issues of community, citizenship, democratic participation and the public role of intellectual endeavour are fertile grounds for research, debate and discussion and we hope that the articles gathered in this volume make some contribution to initiating this much neglected dimension and continue the exploration of what Davies (and Paterson) calls the 'democratic intellect'. Finally, also, in the discussions and contacts built up during the editing of this book and the associated conference and seminars it is clear that we have much to learn from each other and that progress can only be made locally by sharing experience, knowledge and ideas internationally. This is particularly true if we are to solve the greatest problem of all: bridging the gap between theory and practice.

References

Barnett, R. (1997), *Higher Education: a Critical Business* (Buckingham: Open University Press and Society for Research into Higher Education).

Barnett, R. and Coate, K. (2004) *Engaging the Curriculum in Higher Business* (Buckingham: Open University Press and Society for Research into Higher Education).

Bauman, Z. (2000), *Community: Seeking Safety in an Insecure World* (London: Polity Press)

Davies, G. E. (1961), *The Democratic Intellect: Scotland and her Universities in the Nineteenth Century* (Edinburgh: Edinburgh University Press).

Delanty, G. (2003), *Community* (Oxfordshire: Routledge)

Field, J. (2003), *Social Capital* (Oxfordshire: Routledge)

Furco, A. and Holland, B. (2004), 'Institutionalising Service-Learning in Higher Education: Issues and Strategies for Chief Academic Officers', in Langseth.

Hayes, D. and Wynyard, R. (eds.) (2003), *The McDonaldization of Higher Education* (Westport, CT and London: Greenwood Press).

Hersh, R. H., Merrow, J. (eds.) (2005), *Declining by Degrees: Higher Education at Risk* (New York: Palgrave Macmillan).

Langseth, M. and Plater W. M. (2004), *Public Work and the Academy – An Academic Administrators Guide to Civic Engagement and Service-Learning* (Boston: Anker Publishing Company).

Paterson, L. (2003), 'The survival of the democratic intellect: academic values in Scotland and England', *Higher Education Quarterly*, 57:1, 67–93.

Wolf, A. (2002), *Does Education Matter? Myths About Education and Economic Growth* (London: Penguin Books).

Zemsky, R. (2003), 'Have we lost the "public" in higher education?', *The Chronicle of Higher Education*, 49:38, B7.

PART 1
Higher Education and Civic Engagement: Conceptual Issues

Chapter 1

Concepts of Citizenship in the Context of Political Education

Richard Taylor

Introduction

The argument in this chapter is essentially three-fold. First, in the history of western civilisation, the concept of citizenship and its practice have been central to the development of a healthy politics and, in the modern period, central to the creation of a healthy democracy. The elaboration and development of citizenship have not only acted as a means of informing the people of relevant public policy issues but, more importantly, have provided a context for the involvement of the enfranchised. Of course, the nature of this enfranchisement and of the wider structures of western societies have varied tremendously, but the concept of citizenship has always been central. In its more radical forms, citizenship has been the vehicle for imagining, discussing and reinventing visions of the 'good society'.

Secondly, in our own times it can be argued that citizenship is more important than ever. With patterns of migration and multi-culturalism accompanying increasing globalisation, both socially and economically, social identity has become of crucial importance. Part of this, of course, relates to phenomena which are not directly political: for example, radical changes in family structure and the rise of secularism in most western countries. Politically, the volatility and rootlessness of social and political identity in most western societies have been of considerable importance in the last twenty or thirty years. Citizenship education can therefore be seen as a crucial element in the development of lifelong learning – crucial that is not only for the creation of a fully rounded educational provision, but also central to the maintenance and development of a vibrant democratic structure. Citizenship education should thus become a high priority for policy makers and for lifelong learners across western societies.

Thirdly, citizenship as a concept has been highly contested. Like most key ideological concepts, there is no clear-cut and universally accepted definition and articulation of citizenship. Broadly speaking, definitions of citizenship have been dependent upon dominant ideological forms at any given time.

This chapter has three principal aims. I begin with a typological delineation of the classical concepts and forms of citizenship from ancient western societies through to the present day. This is not an attempt at an overall history, which would be far too big a task in this context, but rather a highlighting of some contrasting conceptualisations in different historical periods. I then move on to discuss some of the contested definitions of citizenship in the age of the nation state and, more recently, in globalised and multi-cultural society. Finally, I hazard some suggestions of the appropriate perspectives we should have as advocates and practitioners of lifelong learning on the development of citizenship education in the context of late capitalism. These perspectives are based on a series of radical and progressive arguments, and in the realisation that such views are counter-cultural in an age dominated by neo-liberal, individualist and generally right-wing ideology.

As a footnote, it is important to add that, as is so often the case, in this context the United States of America is something of an exception to the general pattern of ideological development in western society and this 'exceptionalism' is discussed briefly towards the end of the chapter.

Historical Forms of Citizenship

In ancient Greece, citizenship was the preserve and privilege of a small minority: democracy and citizenship were the domains of a small, organic but, above all, exclusive inner circle. David Held has characterised Aristotelian concepts of citizenship as essentially 'developmental republicanism' (Held 1996). For this small minority, citizenship was wholly democratic but, of course, it excluded all women and all slaves. Citizens were the elite in every sense. They ran their own affairs as legislators and executors and took responsibility for defending themselves against attack from external forces. Indeed, military obligation was given a high priority and citizens took pride in defending both physically and ideologically what they perceived as their superior culture against invaders. For Aristotle, to take no part in governing the community in this democratic context was to be either a beast or a god (or, one might add, a woman or a slave). Therefore, to be fully human was by definition to be a citizen, and obligations to the polis took precedence over everything else. In fact, it has been argued that there was no question of 'private morality', in ancient Greece: everything was vested in the polis (Jordan 1989).

Roman concepts of citizenship, by contrast, were both more inclusive but also more centralist and authoritarian. Citizenship was seen in some ways as an agency of social control and became detached from any notions of participation and democracy; increasingly, citizenship was seen as a legalistic construct to undermine and control sources of discontent. Within a relatively short period, therefore, citizenship came to be seen as one of the devices for maintaining through the legal system the power of the ruling class in Roman society (Faulks 2000).

With the rise of mediaeval Christianity in Europe, the importance of the concept of citizenship in society declined. Christianity emphasised obedience and salvation and these replaced notions of civic virtue. The Church, rather than the political community, became the moral reference point. Moreover, although the structure and ideology of the Roman Catholic Church and its parallels in the Eastern Orthodox tradition were extremely hierarchical and authoritarian, theologically Christianity was based very much upon the relationship of the individual with the church and, through the priesthood, to God. Institutionally, as Perry Anderson has noted, 'the most important institutional effect of religious change was the social promotion of a large number of "service Christians" who had made their administrative careers by loyalty to the new faith, to the ranks of the enlarged "clarissimate of the fourth century"' (Anderson 1974a, 91). The stranglehold of the Roman Catholic church upon political life continued virtually unbroken until the French defeated the Papacy in the fifteenth century, which resulted, amongst other things, in the development of the Northern Italian city states, leading to the Italian Renaissance. The Renaissance was driven by an intense desire to move away from the Philistinism and 'darkness' of the Middle Ages. Italian city states, such as Florence and Venice, attempted 'the deliberate revival and imitation' (Anderson 1974b, 149) of the civic and cultural life of classical civilisation.

As is often the case, however, the position was very different in Britain. In the seventeenth century, Thomas Hobbes was in many ways an authoritarian political philosopher with a highly pessimistic view of human nature and the potential for progress of human society. Only through a strong legal framework and a powerful and centralised state could the natural, inevitable tendencies of human beings to behave selfishly, greedily and, by conventional standards, immorally, be curbed and controlled and civilised society be protected. For Hobbes this meant that the individual had no rights, with the important exceptions of self-defence and self-preservation, and should be subject to the will of the state, as expressed through a strong sovereign. On the other hand, Hobbes can be seen as something of a half-way house between John Locke's subsequent social contract system, based upon rights and law-based theories of citizenship, and the thraldom of the religious system of earlier centuries. Hobbes did believe in a contract, albeit one-sided, between the individual and the state; and he did believe in the equality of 'ordinary men' so that, despite individual differences of character and ability, he maintained that these differences were in reality, remarkably small in relative terms.

Locke built a rights, law-based theory of citizenship involving a social and legal contract between the State and the individual citizen, which became the legitimation of the bourgeois liberal conception of the capitalist state and the infrastructure which underpinned it thereafter. Locke's importance in the development of the British legal and parliamentary constitutional system can hardly be exaggerated. For Locke, economic freedom, construed effectively as facilitating the development of bourgeois society and its accompanying economy, was combined with a real concern for rights and justice. Locke thus articulated the appropriate ideological structure for the rapid development of bourgeois society, which in turn led to the creation of the world's first industrial economy and society. Definitions of citizenship, and its centrality conceptually, were a central part of this whole edifice. Of course, the restrictive definition of who was eligible for citizenship within this system was a matter of political contention for the next two hundred years, and until the twentieth century was based upon Lockean notions of property ownership and the argument that such ownership was linked indissolubly to enfranchisement.

It was the French Revolution of 1789 that first began to fuse legal citizenship with the nation state. However, fascinating though the radical conceptualisations of citizenship were in the French Revolutionary period, the heady political radicalism of the period was relatively short-lived. According to Faulks, since then conceptions of citizenship in western Europe have been 'largely subordinate to market principles and the intentions of the political and economic elite' (Faulks 2000, 10). However, it would be quite erroneous to see citizenship entirely in terms of the hegemonic subordination of the lower classes to the ideas and values of the dominant class, even though this may be the essential foundation of concepts of citizenship in industrial and post-industrial societies. As Marx and others have pointed out, modern societies are characterised by contradiction, tension and conflict between various social and economic interests as represented through social class structures. Ideological formulations reflect these fundamental differences. Thus liberalism's ideology, particularly as articulated by John Stuart Mill in the later part of the nineteenth century, had a strong egalitarian element, albeit within the confines of an assumed free-market capitalist structure. Mill laid particular emphasis upon the importance in a civilised, democratic society of the rights of minorities and the primacy issues of free expression and free belief within a state system which should be only minimally constrictive (Mill 1859).

The contested nature of liberalism in the nineteenth and early twentieth centuries is a good example of the tensions within the rapidly developing capitalist system. On the one hand, liberal ideology articulated the necessary free market economics and liberalised state structures, which were essential for capitalist investment and development. At the same time it gave expression, through Mill and others, to the desire to create a more humane and radical liberalism and a democratic society where all people could feel full citizens of a radically transformed social order.

The forces of Labour, which grew increasingly strong through the nineteenth and early twentieth centuries, also had a major impact on the development of citizenship ideology. The pressure of trade unions to secure workers' rights, as well as increased security of employment and better material conditions, co-existed uneasily with the ruling class' need to incorporate consensually the working class and its organisations into the economic and socio-political system. At one level, the social and economic history of the twentieth century can be seen as a series of conflicts and subsequent resolutions between class forces over the control of capitalism and its resources and power structure. The place of workers and all 'ordinary' people in the new, fully enfranchised social and political system has been a continuing matter of debate. As Faulks notes 'there is a contradiction … at the heart of the modernist project: the tension between the State as an exclusionary community and citizenship as a universal status' (Faulks 2000, 30).

Citizenship and the Nation's State

In Europe, since the sixteenth century and especially since the nineteenth century, the nation state as a concept and as a reality has been dominant in political discourse. At times this has been construed in almost mystical terms as an entity rising above more prosaic material concerns of the populous in any society at any given time. The concept of 'the nation' offered an identity for people who spoke the same language, who lived in settled communities and who had an identity with a national culture. At a more intangible, and obviously at times dangerous level, it was also a unifying factor for people who were 'of the same blood'. The concept and actuality of the

European nation state thus form the bedrock of the system of rights, duties and obligations and the parallel social solidarities that went with this.

A good example of this phenomenon and its immense power within the political framework is provided by Disraeli in late nineteenth century Britain. Disraeli used his great oratorical and political skills to construct a visionary rhetoric and conceptualisation of the British nation which transcended class differences and accomplished the transition of the Conservatives from a party based almost wholly upon the landed interest with a system of highly restricted franchise, to the most powerful and long-lived political organisation in the very different circumstances of a mass democracy and an industrial society. In particular, Disraeli sought to unify the British people around the concept of the nation and the British Empire, and thus in effect 'transported' potential conflict to other regions of the world. This engendered a high degree of solidarity and conformity in what was objectively a deeply hierarchical, class-structured and exploitative society.

During the later twentieth century this concept was considerably reinforced in modern liberal, western states by social integration through the creation of a welfare state. After the Second World War, secular state structures across virtually all of western European and north American societies, and parallel developments in societies elsewhere, extended social and material rights to all people. (There is, however, considerable evidence to show that the contributory nature of welfare state systems in effect had little impact upon the social and economic hierarchy and upon differential access to medical, educational and other social benefits for the richer and more privileged sections of society. (Gough 1979)) This system underpinned a continuity and pattern of general social stability in most western European states, despite a number of countervailing factors. Chief amongst these were the proven horrors of extreme nationalism during the 1920s, 1930s and 1940s, the rise of fascism, particularly Nazism, and the subsequent Second World War; the rapid ending after 1945 of European colonialism in Africa and Asia; and perhaps most important of all in the longer term, the growing multi-culturalism and globalising tendencies of late twentieth and early twenty-first century society which have seriously undermined conceptions of discrete nationhood.

Another crucial element in this jigsaw is the fact that gradual and continual improvement in welfare state provision and services were predicated upon stability and economic growth. After 1945 this was largely a realistic assumption and was based on Keynesian or neo-Keynesian economic assumptions and practices. For a whole variety of reasons, which are not relevant to enter into here, this stability ended abruptly from the 1973 oil crisis onwards. There has been a volatility in most western economies and in the international economic and financial structures of multi-national capitalism, which have resulted, amongst many other things, in cutbacks in welfare policies and the abandonment of the post-war mixed economy welfarism by neo-liberal governments in many western societies. Perhaps the most dramatic examples of this phenomenon originally were articulated and put into practice by Margaret Thatcher in Britain and Ronald Reagan in the USA. Thus, the combination of welfarism within a new conceptualisation of the social contract and a revitalised pattern of citizenship has been consistently undermined by authoritarian, neo-liberal ideology and particularly by the baleful influence of the United States, particularly in the current era.

The cataclysmic effect of the collapse of communism and the resultant chaotic state of most post-communist societies have led to the undermining, as Habermas claims, of the universalistic core of republican politics. For example, neo-Nazi groups now parade openly and often violently in many formerly communist countries, and right-wing political parties, with an overtly nationalistic and aggressive ideology, regularly command a significant percentage of votes. Equally, there is to an extent a turn away from liberal secularism, which characterised earlier social democratic politics, with some ethnic minority groups embracing authoritarian ideologies that dismiss equal rights for women, are intolerant of other minorities, and adhere to what seems, at least to secular Western eyes, a primitive, fundamentalist religious belief. This is paralleled, it should be added, by the crude fundamentalist Christian ideology of a large section of the population of the USA.

Perhaps the nation state, therefore, has come up against its limits, given the unpromising current context: and with this potential demise, maybe liberal conceptions of citizenship can be argued to be fatally undermined. For Habermas, the solution resides in vesting increasing significance in the growth of international political and legal institutions, such as the United Nations, the European Court of Human Rights and ensuing legal agreements between the majority of nations to counter international crime and restrict the traditional immunity of national elites from prosecution and commercial regulation. From this essentially liberal prescription – which has interesting parallels with Bertrand Russell's equally passionate advocacy of such internationalism in the 1950s and 1960s (Clark 1975; Russell 1969). Habermas tentatively opts for a future notion of 'global citizenship' which would overcome some of these problems and embrace wider and more democratic conceptions without the restrictions and reactionary tendencies of the nation state concept. Through such international agreements, practical and grave problems, such as tackling drug trafficking, internationalising the campaign to eradicate AIDS, and beginning to tackle the potentially catastrophic ecological issues which dominate much political and policy discussion in the early twenty-first century, may be resoluble.

The Role of Lifelong Learning in this Context

The prospects for the maintenance and enhancement of democratic conceptions and practices of citizenship thus appear to be somewhat gloomy. There seems little alternative other than to support Habermasian, liberal prescriptions, at least for the time being. How, in practical terms, do we redefine the theory and practice of citizenship education in this context? The work of Martha Nussbaum is instructive in this respect (Nussbaum 1997). Nussbaum is a strong advocate of a rearticulated classical liberal humanism, which is, she argues, inherently pluralistic. She rejects post-modernist romanticism and insists that all particular forms of humanity are underpinned by a common core, which in itself can be discovered through dialogue and analysis. Her position is that cultural traditions are not monolithic and unitary, but are subject to internal as well as external rational criticism.

> Since any living tradition is already a plurality and contains within itself aspects of resistance, criticism and contestation, the appeal to reason frequently does not require us to take a stand outside of the culture from which we begin. The Stoics are correct to find in all human beings the world over a capacity for critical searching and a love of the truth ... In this sense any and every human tradition is a tradition of reason. (Nussbaum 1997, 63).

She supports both the Enlightenment view – that ethical enquiry requires encouraging a critical attitude to habits and conventions, rather than an unqualified acceptance of authority – and the assertion that the recognition of the virtuous life in all cultures is discernible. This, however, is hampered on occasion by local group loyalties which frustrate the broader, internationalist view, minimising commonalities and prioritising 'group identity politics'.

Rather than advocating programmes of multi-cultural education, which can often degenerate into uncritical recognition or celebration of difference, as if all cultural practices were morally neutral or legitimate, Nussbaum prefers the term 'inter-culturalism'. This connotes a comparative searching for common human needs across cultures and of dissonance in critical dialogue within cultures.

Such inter-culturalist programmes should embrace a number of principles, including the following. First, it should be multi-cultural in the sense of examining objectively and with empathy all the major religious, ideological and cultural facets of the society in question and similar societies, and this should be accompanied by critical understanding of one's own traditions, habits and conventions with the inculcation of the capacity to question the seemingly inevitable naturalness of our own ways and assumptions. Nevertheless, there are certain values and certain cultural beliefs which cannot be viewed in such a liberal way and, indeed, cannot be tolerated. Examples include racism, either overt or implicit; the systematic subjugation of women and women's rights within certain cultures; and any ideology or philosophy which either entails or implies authoritarian practices which would limit unjustifiably freedom of expression, or assembly, and private morality. Secondly, as with all liberal education, such programmes must centre on the engagement of a critical, sceptical intelligence which analyses rationally, but also emotionally and empathetically, all positions within the legitimate cultural sphere. Thirdly, local and national identities should be discussed and analysed within a globalised context. This is not quite the same as a multi-cultural approach because it needs to take account of both the negative and the positive factors inherent in the globalising process. Finally, such educational programmes should be designed flexibly according to the educational levels of those concerned and, not least, the age of the participants. The Labour Government in Britain has accepted, at least in principle, that such citizenship education programmes need to begin at an early stage of schooling and continue not only through school but throughout life as an important and developing learning experience.

Currently, in almost all developed societies, such programmes are difficult both to construct and to implement and do not yet receive the high priority which they deserve. As lifelong learning advocates and practitioners, we should be finding all ways possible to proselytise on behalf of this agenda and the rationale underlying it.

I turn finally to the exceptionalism of the United States of America. It is clear that the emergence of the USA as the single global super-power, following the collapse of Soviet Union in 1989, has created a new world order, at least temporarily, in a variety of ways. Indeed, it is quite clear that the USA has been the underlying global super-power since at least the end of the Second World War. It is commonly acknowledged that the USA is a special kind of imperial state, with huge military and civil bureaucracies, flanked and underpinned by massive business organisations, many of them multi-national in their operations. Whilst there have been recent devastating analyses of the underlying economic non-viability of the USA's economy in the longer term, and it seems reasonable to suppose that its days as the world's superpower are numbered, it is equally clear that the USA exercises a huge influence over other parts of the developed world, not only economically but socially and ideologically.

In this context, it can be argued that globalisation is an extension of an old strategy with a new name, a euphemism for USA economic expansionism and, certainly under neo-liberal American Presidents, a marauding free-market capitalism that takes little if any account of ecological, humanitarian, or indeed any other moral issues. The sole motivating factor under Bush's presidency has been the drive for an ill-defined, evangelical Christian crusade to protect the USA economic and political interests and 'way of life', ignoring cultural difference, social and political mores and much else besides. As Chomsky has pointed out, one key to the hegemony of this bizarre ideology is that the USA public is kept on permanent alert to potential threats, real or imagined, by an 'economy of fear'. This is invaluably supported by a virtually closed and both trivialising and neo-liberal mass media. In Orwellian parody, American administrations systematically undermine civil liberties, suppress minority opinions, and ensure 'patriotic' obedience, all in the name of protecting American freedoms. The 'war on terror' (so called) serves as an admirable blanket for the invasion of privacy, the silencing of criticism, and a marauding and catastrophic interventionist foreign policy. Nor is this consciousness and practice confined to the Bush period, though this has been the most dramatic, crude and extreme example. USA imperialism, and the ferocious suppression of democratic and popular movements, have characterised the whole of post-1945 history, as Harold Pinter so graphically recounted in his Nobel acceptance speech in 2005 (Pinter 2005).

Despite all this, it is remarkable that the USA has been the base for so many of the important radical social movements of our time. The articulation of a vociferous citizenship agenda through the Women's Movement, the Black Consciousness Movement, the Gay Pride Movement and some disability groups, have all developed into significant social forces and have exercised considerable influence throughout the developed world. Of course, all such movements have been culturally conditioned by the peculiar mix that makes up American radical social theory. The collective rights that Habermas talks about will have to be enshrined in a way that leaves individual freedom from group oppression, or State authoritarianism, unmolested. Thus, the very process of 'Americanisation' may well produce a rise in political consciousness which centres on just those rhetorical expressions, American freedoms and human rights, which have been so callously disregarded in practice by American administrations.

Programmes of education in the citizenship arena and broader political education can play a significant part in this radicalising process in many different contexts. Some evidence of these phenomena is already available from experience in Latin-America (Kane 2001). There are embryonic movements for similar radical developments in some western societies.

Whatever the rights and wrongs of economic analysis predicting the collapse of the American economy, and whatever the geopolitical forces which may anyway undermine the American 'empire', what is undoubtedly true is that the American ideological structure exemplifies the contradictions inherent in the whole society. In this particular respect, the United States is not an exceptionalist case: the same point can be made about Britain and other newly industrialised societies around the turn of the nineteenth/twentieth century. Radical and progressive ideas have always been attacked by the ruling order in any given society. This is the nature of the beast. Whilst there exists global capitalism, there will exist exploitation, economic and moral irrationality and a whole series of other negative characteristics. This very process gives rise to an ever growing demand from the mass of the people for a better society, a better way of living, and an imagined future.

Educational provision, facilitating discussion of these important issues, constitutes an important part of this radicalising process. As for the importance of citizenship and education in this respect, I can do no better than conclude with a quotation from Rosa Luxemburg, one of the great libertarian revolutionaries; 'Without unrestricted freedom of press and assembly, without a free struggle of opinion, life dies out in every public institution.'

Finally, to return to a perhaps more parochial point, universities and their managements would do well to heed Luxemburg's words, given the current dominance of neo-liberal ideology and the consequent drive towards exclusively 'bottom line' criteria, combined with the marketisation of higher education and the closing down of vigorous ideological debate. (Taylor, Barr and Steele, 2001; Delanty, 2001; Coffield and Williamson, 1997).

References

Anderson, P. (1974a), *Passages from Antiquity to Feudalism* (London: Verso).

Anderson, P. (1974b), *Lineages of the Absolutist State* (London: Verso).

Clark, R.W. (1975), *The Life of Bertrand Russell* (London: Jonathan Cape, and Weidenfeld and Nicolson).

Coffield, F. and Williamson, B. (eds.) (1997), *Repositioning Higher Education* (Buckingham: Open University Press).

Delanty, G, (2001), *Challenging Knowledge: the University in the Knowledge Society* (Buckingham: SRHE and Open University Press).

Faulks, K. (2000), *Citizenship*, Key Ideas Series (London: Routledge).

Gough, I. (1979), *The Political Economy of the Welfare State* (London: Macmillan).

Held, D. (1996), *Models of Democracy* (Oxford: Polity Press).

Jordan, B. (1989), *The Common Good* (Oxford: Blackwell).

Kane, L. (2000), *Popular Education and Social Change in Latin America* (London: Latin America Bureau).

Nussbaum, M.C. (1997), *Cultivating Humanity, A Classical Defence of Reform in Liberal Education* (Cambridge, MA: Harvard University Press).

Pinter, H. (2005), Address on receipt of Nobel Prize in Literature, represented in *The Guardian* (9 December 2005).

Russell, B. (1969), *The Autobiography of Bertrand Russell*, Vol.3, (London: Cape).

Taylor, R., Barr, J. and Steele, T. (2002), *For a Radical Higher Education: After Postmodernism* (Milton Keynes: Society for Research in Higher Education and Open University Press).

Chapter 2

Love, Reason and the Future of Civil Society

Michael Edwards

Introduction

In this chapter, I want to look at the role of universities from the perspective of a civil society enthusiast rather than the other way around. Therefore, I will focus my remarks, not on service learning per se, but on the context in which service learning programmes take on more, or less, significance. Other contributors to this book, in my opinion are far more knowledgeable than I about the details of service learning, so perhaps the most useful contribution that I can make is to help locate these ideas in a broader discussion of the role universities might play in building civil society, a task which I believe is becoming more important, but more difficult, as a result of a range of forces that I will describe in brief. As a result, and while there are some pioneering exceptions (many of which are represented in this volume), universities are failing in this crucial task. The stakes are very high.

One major caveat is that most of my examples come from the USA where I am based, though I'm sure there are equally good cases in other parts of the world. My remarks may therefore be unrepresentative of other contexts and experiences.

What is Civil Society?

Situating the university in the context of civil society requires me to be clear about the meaning of this term. I'm well aware of the increasingly slippery usage of 'civil society', the appropriation of this term by politicians and ideologues on all sides of the political spectrum, and the confusion that characterises the contemporary civil society debate. According to whose version one prefers, civil society means 'fundamentally reducing the role of politics in society by expanding free markets and individual liberty' (The Cato Institute, USA[1]), 'the single most viable alternative to the authoritarian state and the tyrannical market' (The World Social Forum, Brazil[2]), or the missing link in the success of social democracy (central to 'Third Way' thinking and 'compassionate conservatism'). In academia, civil society has become the 'chicken soup of the social sciences', and in the world of foreign aid the

---

1 Additional information on the Cato Institute can be accessed at http://www.cato.org.

2 Additional Information on the World Social Forum can be accessed at http://www.wsfindia.org.

key to 'good governance', poverty-reducing growth, and even the underlying reason for war against Iraq – to kick-start civil society in the Middle East, according to administration officials in Washington DC (Edwards 2004a).

Is civil society one of three separate sectors or intimately interconnected with states and markets? The preserve of groups predefined as democratic, modern, and 'civil', or home to all sorts of associations, including 'uncivil' society and traditional associations based on inherited characteristics like religion and ethnicity? Are families 'in' or 'out', and what about the business sector? Is civil society a bulwark against the state, an indispensable support, or dependent on government intervention for its very existence? Is it the key to individual freedom through the guaranteed experience of pluralism or a threat to democracy through special interest politics? Is it a noun – a part of society, an adjective – a kind of society, an arena for deliberation – the 'public sphere', or a mixture of all three? There is absolutely no consensus.

It is easy to become lost in the complexities of this debate, or captured by the ideologies of one side or another. One way out of this impasse is to look beyond the clash of theories to the underlying qualities or capacities that are necessary to fashion a civil society worthy of the name – recognising that interpretations, recommendations and priorities will continue to differ at any level of detail. For me, the most important of these capacities are love and reason, each essential both in and of itself and as a counterweight to an excess of the other. Love and reason make possible a principled negotiation of our differences, and although rarely described in these terms, I believe that universities have a central role to play in developing these capacities at both the private and the public levels. Service learning, when well constructed and consciously shaped in these directions, can help in this task in a number of important ways.

Developing and protecting the capacity for reason is something that is often identified with the role of the university, love much less so. Talk of love, at least in public, is embarrassing, 'flaky,' perhaps even faintly ridiculous. Nevertheless, I want to make the case that love should be a central topic of our conversation.

Reason

In its role as the 'public sphere', civil society becomes the arena for argument and deliberation, and the extent to which such spaces thrive is crucial to democracy, since if only certain truths are represented, if alternative viewpoints are silenced by exclusion or suppression, or if one set of voices are heard more loudly than those of others, then no genuine sense of the common or 'public' interest can be constructed. The concept of a 'public' – a whole polity that cares about the common good and has the capacity to deliberate about it democratically – is central to civil society thinking. The development of shared interests, a willingness to cede some territory to others, the ability to see something of oneself in those who are different and work together more effectively as a result – all these are crucial attributes for effective governance, practical problem-solving, and the peaceful resolution of our differences. All life, one might say, is negotiation, and the price of entry into civil society is the willingness to change one's mind through an encounter with the views of others. Like rocks in a stream, the sharp edges of our differences are softened over time as they knock against each other. A healthy civil society depends on the development of our collective capacities to learn, talk, argue, innovate and ultimately solve our problems together.

Jürgen Habermas, of course, has developed these ideas in a very complicated way, but John Dewey and others articulated them with more simplicity much earlier in the twentieth century, seeing active social learning writ large as the basis of democratic governance through deliberation and consensus building. Harry Boyte calls this the 'politics of freedom', in which no one has a monopoly over truth and everyone shares an obligation to negotiate their differences with each other (Boyte 2005b). 'Dialogic politics,' to use another descriptor of the same thing, are continually engaged in a search for better ways forward, animating democracy *between* elections and not just once in every four or five years. Democracies are 'long term experiments in the capacity of citizens to live without secure foundations. We are all required to practice daily the art of living on the edge' (Keane 2003). Only politics, as Machiavelli famously taught, creates the possibility for manoeuvre and forward movement. Democracy is also the weapon of choice for the 'public humbling' of all centres of concentrated power, whether armies, governments, ngo's, corporations or political parties, through the constant exercise of public monitoring, transparency, and accountability (Keane 2003).

The health and success of democracy in this sense obviously depends on the cultivation of critical thinking, social energy, and 'active citizenship' to use a phrase currently much in vogue. This phrase rolls comfortably off the tongue, but belies an exceptionally-challenging reality given the demands that are placed on us by the modern capitalist economy in which time is so constrained, citizenship is eroded, and public monitoring, or even authentic public conversation, are actively opposed by increasingly-powerful interests. I recently read of a test that is given to all potential employees by the Wal-Mart supermarket chain in America. 'Do you agree', asks the test, 'that rules have to be followed to the letter at all times?' The only acceptable answer, surprise, surprise, is 'very strongly'. So, while active citizenship may be the foundation of civil society there are many forces urging complicity, conformity, and silence.

Now, one might think that animating the public sphere is obviously the function of the university, but the context in which we live makes this function much more difficult to fulfil. Let me cite a couple of reasons.

First, the increasing commercialisation and responsiveness of the university to market-driven demands and interests rather than the common good, a trend that breeds individualism, insularity, over-specialisation and over-competition, driven by an academic star system worthy of Hollywood.

Second, the shadow of government interference over academic freedom and the independence of universities. Examples from the United States include the manipulation of federal funding for area studies to privilege certain approaches to the Middle East, and the use of universities as covert training grounds for CIA agents through the *Pat Roberts Intelligence Scholars Programme*.

Third, the injection of state-sponsored versions of the truth deep into the public sphere, and the deliberate erosion of public debate and scrutiny over government decisions. 'The new game', writes journalist Nicholas Confessore in a recent edition of *Washington Monthly*, 'is to dominate the entire intellectual environment in which officials make policy decisions, which means funding everything from think tanks to issues ads to phoney grassroots pressure groups' (*Washington Monthly*, December 2003). Reality can then be manufactured in the public mindset to suit the interests of those in power, Iraq being a good example. Regardless of whether you were 'for' or 'against' the war, the absence of a full and transparent discussion of the rights and wrongs of the case leading up to one of the most important decisions in recent history was something that should worry all active citizens.

Fourth, there is an increasing scepticism about reason and rationality as the basis for public policy-making, a tendency to look for external rather than internal sources of authority, revealed rather than negotiated truths, ideology rather than a moving policy consensus obtained through rational disagreement. Blogs replace journalism, stripped of the need to check facts and be held accountable. Complexity, nuance, choice and judgment are diminished in the face of supposedly god-given certainties. Politicians openly mock the reality or facts-based universe of their opponents. What matters is the power of the myths you seek to create, and the tactics used to cement these myths in the public imagination. So what if teenage pregnancy is at its lowest level in the US since 1940, people can still be persuaded that abstinence-only sex education programmes are required to halt the slide towards unmitigated promiscuity. Why not outlaw needle exchanges for drug users despite their proven effectiveness in reducing HIV/Aids? Global warming is a myth, despite the weight of scientific evidence to the contrary, and evolution is just another theory to set alongside Genesis and space aliens. In modern politics it seems, facts are for losers.

Fifth, political and religious polarisation and intolerance are on the rise, whipped up by unscrupulous politicians and their servants in the media, the pulpit, and the world of public relations. Politics has become a zero-sum game in which winning at all costs is the only goal. Once more in history, difference is something to be feared, controlled or suppressed, rather than celebrated and protected. A recent survey by Public Agenda (2005) showed conclusively that Americans were less likely to compromise their views on hot-button issues like abortion, gay rights and the death penalty if they approached these subjects from a religious grounding. So much for civil society as that place where we can 'meet as strangers and not draw the knife' as John Keane (2003) puts it. So much for civility as 'the capacity to recognize the other as the bearer of legitimate rights and values', a wonderful phrase invented by the Brazilian scholar, Evelina Dagnino (2002).

Publics are becoming more and more segmented, and less and less willing to negotiate the interests they hold in common. As scholars like Theda Skocpol (2003) have pointed out, the atomisation of civil society in America is destroying the bridges between interest groups that underlay all great social reforms in the post World War Two era. As she has shown through her research, it was nationally-federated mass-membership, cross-class groups like parent teachers associations, labour unions, and organisations of elks, moose and other forest creatures that used to provide strong linkages between citizens and government, and which created a mass-based constituency for reforms like the GI Bill of 1944. Broad-based reforms like these (think health care and social security in the US today) depend on the development of more independent patterns of thinking among voters so that they can escape the cage in which the traditional party system has imprisoned them, and signal their support for new solutions that cut across the divisions of Left and Right, religious and secular, immigrant and non-immigrant groups. Some university administrators see a greater willingness to do this among the current generation of students when compared with the baby boomers. Let us hope they are correct.

Overall, one can see a continued decline in the health and vitality of the public sphere, so what role can universities play, and service learning in particular, in reversing this situation? I would put my own suggestions into two categories: strengthening public reason, and protecting private reason.

Strengthening public reason means recognising that universities have an important role to play in facilitating public deliberation about the great issues of the day. They are 'bridging' institutions in the best sense of the term. The *Wingspread Declaration* sees universities as 'both agents and architects of a flourishing democracy, bridges between individuals' work and the wider world' (Campus Compact 2000, 2005). 'Public Square' in Chicago, for example, brings leading academics from local universities into conversations with the public in cafes and coffee houses, cinemas and bookshops, to debate social and political issues across partisan lines.

Strengthening public reason also means engagement with community groups and civil society activists in a joint search for new knowledge. Without those links, societies will miss out on forms of experiential knowledge and learning that are vital for solving the problems they face. Collective learning requires collective action, said Kurt Lewin, and vice-versa too. But despite twenty years of trying, I don't feel we have made much progress here. The tremendous gulf between higher education and the world of social practice is as wide as ever, beset by entrenched cultural differences on both sides. It is interesting to note that, until 2002, community colleges in the US were prevented from using the letters 'edu' in their Internet address. It's also significant that many of the best community engagement and action research programmes are run out of non-elite academic institutions.

Nevertheless, there are some good examples that show that any university can undertake this kind of work if they are committed. The Centre for Reflective Practice at the Massachusetts Institute of Technology, for example, the Institute of Development Studies in the UK (which has just started a new Master of Arts on Participation), and the Institute for Policy Alternatives at Sarah Lawrence College that links faculty, students, and participants in social movements. Service learning can make a real contribution to these experiments, but it has to move beyond 'hit and run' assistance by students who spend only short periods of time with community groups and non-profits, to long-term, sustained engagement.

Strengthening private reason is more traditional ground for universities, recognising their cherished role as protected zones of rational thinking and independent critique that underpin the exercise of accountability through the application of rigor to public policy problems. No one is better equipped to 'speak truth to power' than a tenured professor.

More importantly, universities are training their students for a life as active citizens, and a role as 'tempered radicals' in the jobs they will hold – individuals who are able to promote change in institutions despite the constraints they will invariably face (Myerson 2001). How well are universities doing in this sense? A recent survey of university education for community change in America conducted by Andrew Mott (2005) concluded that there are 'fewer than a handful of universities that offer the kind of interdisciplinary programme mixing classroom work and community-level experience that was offered forty years ago in Iran' when he taught courses at Pahlavi University.

> If poverty, race and community are such central issues for our societies, how come universities play such an insignificant role in training young people for careers in fixing these things, and training mid-career professionals to hone their skills? (Mott 2005)

There is great potential in building on the current wave of interest in service learning to foster innovation in university curricula. Seventy-three per cent of all college students in America volunteer for some form of community service according to Mott but most service-learning programmes are only weakly connected to learning (Mott 2005, 16). They are rarely linked to courses, peer group meetings and mentoring which might enable students to reflect on their experience, study the issues facing communities, and make the connections to an underlying analysis of causes. There is a continued disconnect between service and political engagement despite the well-known 'service politics' framework of Campus Compact. Research on the political impact of service learning is inconclusive, at least if measured by voting rates, but there is clear evidence that early involvement in concrete social action (that is sustained and authentic participation in social movements and community struggles) does feed through into higher levels of political engagement later in life (Galston 2001).

The worst service learning programmes ignore this fact, offering young people an escape route from a politics that, to be sure, often seems bankrupt, and seeing service as a security blanket for a life with all the hard edges and choices taken out. The best programmes build on it. Los Angeles Trade Tech, for example, is a community college at the edge of South Central Los Angeles that offers a two year Associate of Arts degree in Community Development designed specifically to attract people of colour from low income neighbourhoods. The University of Massachusetts at Boston teaches participatory action research as a key component of its service learning programmes. California State University at Monterrey Bay requires students to 'analyse and describe the concepts of power relations, equity and social justice' as part of their civic education. Colgate University in New York teaches all students active listening, conflict resolution, organising skills and negotiation. Tufts University is a well-known pioneer in aiming to prepare all of its graduates for lives of deep and sustained civic engagement through university-wide reforms in curricula and practice. 'But to effect these changes', concludes Harry Boyte in a recent article, 'has required a self-conscious challenge to the service paradigm that has taken hold in student affairs' (Boyte 2005a).

Hence, while there are many good examples, universities overall seem to have lost their way in supporting public reason, retreating more and more into the privacy of the campus and failing to support any broad based process of public engagement or debate around the great issues of the day. That is not a healthy sign for the future of civil society.

Love

It would be a very dry world if reason ruled unchecked by the life of the spirit, the imagination, the artist and the lover. It would also be unrealistic to expect the manifold problems I've just outlined to be resolved through the application of reason alone. When reason grows hubristic, it becomes another form of irrationality, even a form of insanity, leading in a direct line to the death camps of the Third Reich or the massacres of more recent memory in Rwanda, the Balkans or Darfur. 'Reason', as Terry Eagleton (2005) puts it in a recent book review on the Enlightenment, 'must somehow keep faith with the irrational forces from which it springs, acknowledging their power as the ancient Athenian State paid its dues to the terrible power of the Furies'.

What is this strange power that counterbalances the influence of reason in civil society? Some would say it is religion or faith, but these things are usually particularistic, attached to defined sub-sectors of humankind and agendas that are privileged, resulting in the 'segmentation' problems I talked about in reference to the United States, and beset by the prejudice that one finds in some religious communities – the consistent attacks on women's rights, the homophobia, the narrow-mindedness and reluctance to enter into community-wide activities and concerns rather than intra-congregational commitments, and the substitution of individual acts of charity or service for a full and complete understanding of the structural factors that lead to oppression. 'Pillar of the community, church deacon, wife beater' as a sign on the New York subway reads. Social conservatism is rarely more dangerous than when it cloaks itself in religious garb that cannot adequately be challenged by rationalist arguments for social justice because it assumes an-other worldly authority. Think of the unholy alliances that have formed throughout history between religious groups and authoritarian states – the Bulgarian Orthodox Church in recent times, for example, or the rise of Hindu nationalism in India. This is why so many people fear the penetration of the public sphere by religion.

More promising in my view is love. I am not talking here of romantic love, nor love in the infantile sense of being made happy, but what Martin Luther King called 'the love that does justice' (Edwards and Post 2006), signifying the deliberate cultivation of mutually reinforcing cycles of personal and systemic change. This is universal love, unconditional love, attached only to the equal and general welfare of the whole. 'The essence of love', says the wonderfully named Institute for the Study of Unlimited Love at Case Western University, 'is to affectively affirm as well as unselfishly delight in the well being of others, and to engage in acts of care and service on their behalf, without exception, in an enduring and constant way'. This is radical equality-consciousness, a force that breaks down all distance and hierarchy. This is a love that respects the necessary self-empowerment of others, eschewing paternalism and romanticism for relationships of truth and authenticity, even where they move through phases of conflict and disagreement, as all do. This is a love that encourages us to live up to our social obligations as well our individual moral values, connect our interior life worlds to public spaces, encourage collective judgments and create open networks of self-reflective and critical communication – all the things that are necessary for a healthy civil society.

This love is active, not passive, explicitly considering the effects of oppressive and exploitative systems and structures on the welfare of others, and not just focused on the immediate circle of family and friends – a deep and abiding commitment to the liberation of all. This is a love that seeks not to accumulate power, even in the face of oppression, but to transform it so that 'victory' can mean more than a game of revolving chairs among narrow political interests.

This love forms an essential counterbalance to an excess of reason, adding in the discrimination, humility, intuition, ethical commitments and emotional intelligence that are essential ingredients of wisdom. This love helps us to understand when and how to uphold and apply rationality even in the toughest of circumstances by increasing self-awareness of our biases, prejudices and blind spots, sustaining our objectivity about our own strengths and shortcomings. Love enables us to use our fine minds as the servant of a wider purpose, and not just as a weapon to protect and enhance our own individual power, knowledge and status.

Love releases us from fear and insecurity, and our diminished sense of self. Love gives us optimism and hope, an expansion rather than contraction of our critical faculties, openness instead of closure. 'Even when we cannot change ongoing exploitation and domination,' says bell hooks (2001), 'love gives life meaning, purpose and direction. Doing the work of love, we ensure our survival and our triumph over the forces of evil and destruction'. Yet the absence of love from the public sphere has become a defining characteristic of contemporary society.

This may sound wonderful, but what on earth can be done to nurture the 'love that does justice?' The answer is 'a great deal', with service learning at the centre. 'To take love seriously and to learn it like a task, this is what young people need... with their whole being, with all their forces, gathered closely about their upward beating heart'. (Rilke 1975). And if love is too challenging a concept to place in the context of the university as we currently know it, then at least think in terms of 'baby steps' that would lead slowly and incrementally in this direction, like encouraging compassion, altruism, and non-hierarchical engagement.

In the public sense, universities can research and teach what one might call the 'social science of love,' meaning a set of theories, models, methods and empirical cases that show how politics, economics, organisational development, social and international relations could be transformed through this radically-different form of rationality. From the perspective of change, all social systems rest on three bases: a set of principles that form an axiomatic basis of ethics and values; a set of processes – the functioning mechanisms and institutions that under gird the system; and the subjective states that constitute our inner being – our personal feelings and intuitions in the deepest sense (Edwards and Sen 2000).

However, the linkages that develop between these three bases of change are not immutable – they can be altered to produce a different set of outcomes, for example, by rebelling against the subjective state that is promoted by a particular set of institutions, or experimenting with new institutions that operate from a different subjective or axiomatic base. This is why love, as the most powerful subjective state we know, can have such a transformative effect when injected like a virus into economic, political and social institutions. These institutions are not simply floating somewhere out there in space, they constitute and are constituted by each one of us as active citizens, so when we talk of engaging with these systems and structures, we are really talking about engaging with ourselves and with each other. This is as obvious as it is neglected in public discourse.

Love does not generate ready made answers to deep rooted and intractable problems of economic and social life, codified according to the conventional logics of *left* or *right*, Democrat or Republican. Instead, it provides a different set of motivations from which alternatives can grow. Can public policies motivated by love really 'deliver the goods' in social, economic and political terms? Can they generate enough jobs and an economic surplus large enough to satisfy human needs at lower cost to producers and consumers in globally integrated markets, to the environment, and to the underlying values that hold societies together? Can they facilitate political decision-making that is fair and effective in mediating competing claims and interests without falling prey to the 'dictatorship of the majority' or the perils of special interest politics? Can they address problems of discrimination and exclusion in the social realm, which often require enforcement and coercion by state authorities, not just voluntary action? And can they resolve global conflicts and differences peacefully, but more effectively than at present, even in the most difficult of circumstances, like the task of unseating tyrants such as Saddam Hussein? I don't know, but I think it's worth a try, and that is why we need a new social science of love.

In the private sense, universities can alter academic training to focus much more on emotional intelligence and the other faculties that underpin the love that does justice – 'the intelligence of the heart' that Carol Gilligan (1993) has described in her writings. To be successfully scaled up and sustained, the *social* science of love requires *personal* transformation. Personal transformation opens us to accept new forms of knowledge that can complete the knowledge that we derive from more conventional sources (for example, knowledge generated by communities and others perceived as lower in the social hierarchy). Arthur Zajonc (2005), a physicist at Amherst College in Massachusetts, has developed what he calls an 'epistemology of love' organized around principles such as sustained attention, openness, an ability to hold contradictory views in one's mind without reaching a judgment too quickly, gentle yet rigorous methods of inquiry, and deep respect for the views of others. An increasing body of empirical evidence shows that love and altruism affect cognitive skills in significant ways. Stephen Post, Professor of Bioethics at Case Western University, summarises this evidence as follows: 'when people do and feel good, their thinking becomes more creative, integrative, flexible and open to new sources of information' (Post 2005, 5).

Service learning can play an important role here, but it must encourage the love that does justice and not just individualized acts of caring. The love that does justice signifies a willingness to care for the common good and address the structural barriers that stand in its way. But the moving force in this process must be love, since without it, we may never make the necessary commitments on an enduring basis, or if we do then we are likely to carry with us the 'thieves of the heart', the greed, ego, anger, fear and insecurity that will likely pollute or erode the success of our efforts to be a positive force for change. Great inner strength is required to confront the structures of power in the world unselfishly, without demonising one's enemies, alienating potential allies, or holding on too tightly to a particular vision of ends and means that can eventually become a prison. In the love that does justice, personal and structural change can reinforce each other. Only by operating from the space where we are joined together in some deep sense are we likely to find true common ground in facing up to the collective problems that confront us.

There are already some examples of universities that raise the tricky subject of love explicitly with their students. Case Western University is one that I've already cited, redefining, in its own words, 'liberal education for the twenty-first century by emphasising service to humanity throughout so that graduates will put aside self interest and dedicate their lives to helping others by practicing benevolent love'. Interestingly in view of my earlier remarks on reason, the other organising principle for this revolution at Case Western is that science and technology are also at the centre of university reform. Or take the Centre for Contemplative Mind in Society, based in Massachusetts, which has a whole programme dedicated to the conscious cultivation of love and compassion in the academy, built around the kind of contemplative practices that we know are needed to deepen personal change – practices such as meditation, prayer, silent reflection, nature walks and so on. Marrying a rich inner life dedicated to the cultivation of loving kindness and compassion with the practice of new forms of politics, economics and public policy is the key to social transformation.

Conclusion

To conclude, I want to end by calling attention to another phrase that I think is helpful in thinking about civil society as the coming together of love and reason: 'critical friendship.' In *Future Positive* I defined critical friendship as 'the loving but forceful encounters between equals who journey together towards the land of the true and the beautiful' (Edwards 2004b). It is the combination of those two qualities – love and forcefulness, rigor or reason – that defines the kind of relationships that are central to the democratic resolution of social problems. Toni Morrison (2003) puts it even better when she writes that 'the peace I am thinking of is the dance of an open mind when it engages another that is equally open' (Morrison 2003) In this sense, we can think of civil society as both the process and the outcome of lives lived in critical friendship. We may never share a common vision of ends and means in politics and economics, but we can all be committed to a process that allows everyone to share in defining how these differences are reconciled.

Although some of what I have written may seem abstract or distant from the day to day realities of service learning, I do think that critical friendship provides a framework that defines an exciting role for universities in the century to come. Here, on the boundary between love and reason, lies the future of the world. And here, at the intersection of love and reason, lies the future of the university, of that

I'm sure. The question that animates this volume is a simple one that cuts to the core of our own personal commitments: where *stands* the university in this regard, and where stand *we*? This is not a new question. As far back as 1962, the *Port Huron Statement* marked the launch of 'Students for a Democratic Society' with the following call to action: 'we are people of this generation, bred in at least modest comfort, housed now in universities, looking uncomfortably at the world we inherit. Social relevance, accessibility to knowledge, and internal openness, these together make the university a potential base and agency in a movement of social change'. That challenge echoes down the years to remind us that we must redouble our efforts to make our universities a more effective vehicle for developing the capacities of love and reason that are essential to the future of our planet. It is difficult to imagine a more important task than this. We must not fail.

References

Boyte, H. (2005a), 'Reframing Democracy: Governance, Civic Agency, and Politics', *Public Administration Review* 65:5, 536–546.

Boyte, H. (2005b), *The Politics of Freedom* (Unpublished mimeo).

Confessore, N. (2003), 'Meet the Press: How James Glassman reinvented journalism – as lobbying', *Washington Monthly* [website] (published online December 2003) http://www.washingtonmonthly.com/features/2003/0312.confessore.html accessed 24 November 2006.

Dagnino, E. (2002), *Sociedad Civil, Esfera Publica and Democracia*. (USA: Fondo de Cultura Economica USA).

Eagleton, T (2005), 'The Enlightenment is Dead! Long live the Enlightenment!', *Harpers Magazine* (March 2005, 91–5).

Edwards, M. (2004a), *Civil Society* (Cambridge: Polity Press).

Edwards, M. (2004b), *Future Positive* (Revised Edition) (London: James and James).

Edwards, M., and Post S. (eds.) (2006), *Essays on Love and Justice* (forthcoming).

Edwards, M., and Sen G. (2000), 'NGOs, Social Change and the Transformation of Human Relationships: A 21st Century Civic Agenda', *Third World Quarterly* 21:4, 605–16.

Galston, W. (2001), 'Political Knowledge, Political Engagement and Civic Education', *Annual Review of Political Science*, 2001:4, 217–34.

Gilligan, C. (1993), *In a Different Voice: Psychological Theory and Women's Development* (Cambridge, MA: Harvard University Press).

hooks, b. (2001), *All About Love: New Visions* (San Francisco, CA: Harper Paperbacks).

Keane, J. (2003), *Global Civil Society* (Cambridge MA: Cambridge University Press).

Morrison, T. (2003), *Love* (New York: Knopf).

Mott, A. (2005), *University Education for Community Change* (Washington DC: Community Learning Project).

Myerson, D. (2001), *Tempered Radicals. How People Use Difference to Inspire Change at Work* (Cambridge, MA: Harvard Business School Press).

Port Huron Statement (2004), *Progressive and Conservative Campus Activism in the United States* (Boston: Political Research Associates).

Post, S. (2005), 'Altruism, Happiness and Health: It's Good to be Good', *International Journal of Behavioral Medicine* 12:2, 66–77.

Public Agenda (2005), New Survey Shows Religious Americans Less Likely to Support Compromise – Press Release (New York: Public Agenda), January 23rd 2005.

Rilke, R.M. (1975), *Love and Other Difficulties* (New York: W.W. Norton).

Skocpol, T. (2003), *Diminished Democracy: From Membership to Management in American Civic Life* (Oklahoma City, OK: University of Oklahoma Press).

Zajonc, A. (2005), *Love and Knowledge: Recovering the Heart of Learning through Contemplation* (Unpublished mimeo, Amherst College: Physics Department).

Chapter 3

Recovering the Civic University

Ronald Barnett

Introduction

The university is now back 'in' society. If, once, the phrase 'the ivory tower' had any legitimacy, now the phrase has no prospect of its being a serious depiction of the academy's situation. Governments are busily shaping higher education if not in their own image, then at least to their own ends. Those ends are concerned with economic flourishing, knowledge transfer, and the enhancement of human capital and its mobility and continuing regeneration; and so the new terms of engagement are drawn in certain ways but this reflection does not dent the main point here. The academy is now drawn into the state's agendas whether it likes it or not.

We are witnessing, indeed, the emergence of a new compact (Gokulsing and Da Costa 2000); the state provides often quite generous support to the academy and in return extracts a high price in terms of the involvement it expects of the academy in the wider society. Certainly, these policy shifts take place within a context of the 'marketisation' of higher education and globalisation, but this wider context only serves to enhance the academy's new engagement with society, even if the society in question is a global society.

Under these circumstances, the idea of the civic university is in difficulty, but it may not be quite the difficulty that many envisage. The main difficulty turns out to be not so much one of re-engaging the university with society (Bjarnason and Coldstream 2003) but rather one of redrawing the terms of the engagement that are now emerging. The idea of the civic university speaks to agendas of enlightenment, public service and a generous sense of citizenship itself, both in the wider community and in the relationships between the academy and society. Now the university is perhaps more to be understood through concepts of money, position, and institutional and personal gain. Public service does not, it may seem, sit easily with entrepreneurialism or individualisation. The idea of the civic university is in difficulty not because the university is too distant from society but because it is too much bound into society on terms that run counter to the very idea of the civic university.

This, then, is the conundrum facing us in this chapter: that of teasing out the prospects for the realisation of the idea of the civic university in the contemporary age. Might the concept of the civic university still do work and offer a sense of a way forward?

Loss of Space or More Open Space?

Does the contemporary university have more or less space, as we move further into the twenty-first century? A trite answer is 'yes'. After all, the university is granted space by its host society to become itself, to identify its own mission and to secure the wherewithal to realise that mission. The world is its oyster; or so the rhetoric seems to imply. But the space in which the university is expected to find its own being has its own place; a universe of discourses and ideologies spelt out by the familiar stock phrases of our times: 'learning economy', 'globalisation', 'world-class', 'knowledge transfer', 'widening participation', 'skills', 'research'. In a slightly larger context, too, lies a set of commentaries, both endorsing and critical; and here we find terms such as 'entrepreneurialism', 'enterprise', 'academic capitalism' and 'corporate university'.

So the space in which the university now moves is very large. The university really is autonomous in ways that it could barely have dreamed of. But the pushes and the pulls, the pressure and the support, to which it is subject orient it towards worlds marked out by money, distinctiveness and competition. There is much talk in the critical literature of both 'performativity' and 'commodification'. The one speaks of activities (including knowledge production) only being valued insofar as they yield greater efficiency and an 'optimum return'; the other speaks of activities only being valued insofar as they can be rendered as objects that can be bartered and claimed privately. Where, amid such a space, is there space for a concept such as 'citizenship'?

'Citizenship', after all, occupies a different conceptual space from that marked out by competition, exclusivity and return on investment. Citizenship, whatever it might mean, speaks to a 'public service' role of the university; and public service is itself non-competitive, non-exclusive and altruistic. And so the matter as to whether there is space for the university to realise a mission around citizenship is open to doubt.

I said earlier that to the question as to whether the university has less or more space, the trite answer is 'yes'. We can now explain why such an answer would be trite. The university likes to believe that it has characteristically associated itself with public goods and that the slide to commodification and 'academic capitalism' is rather recent. A more balanced judgement would surely be that that set of self-beliefs is rather question-begging.

On the one hand, the contemporary shift whereby academic activities are prized in terms of their economic return and their private ownership is probably still relatively muted (even in countries such as the USA, the UK and Australia, where these trends are especially pronounced). On the other hand, and more pertinent still for our story here, the public service ideal is not necessarily incompatible – or so it would seem – with 'academic capitalism' (Slaughter and Leslie 1997). After all, it is the USA where the idea of a public service role for universities is strongest and where the academy is influenced most by private and corporate money. One way, I think, that we may explain this apparent inconsistency – where public and private interests coexist – is that the academy remains dominated by sectional interests across the disciplines. For the most part, the academy has been preoccupied by its own activities and has interpreted its activities as *its* activities.

So, the space in which the contemporary university moves is a wider space, indeed, wider set of space*s*. Universities vary, even within a unitary national system, but such curtailment of space is relatively limited. There are no national curricula in higher education and most staff still have discursive space to write and to speak out as they wish; it is rather that they have temporal space to do it in. University space is now a more congested, a more compressed space: there are more entities in it, and there are more activities in it. University life is more intense than it was, even as it has expanded to allow for new kinds of activity and engagement.

What is more to the point is less the curtailment of old space – much of which was either imagined or was unused – and more the character of the new or the widening space in which the university now has its being. The university has more space opening up to itself in which to develop new activities, embrace new values, and form new partnerships. At the same time, that space is, as it were, slanted in dominant directions, of being a signed-up member of the knowledge economy, of aiding and abetting globalisation, and of 'marketisation' (even if the 'm' in 'marketisation' is definitely a small 'm', and the markets in question are quasi-markets). The space for 'the civic university' may be not what it was; or at least, the steers are in other directions. So, more and less space all at once: this has to be our interim conclusion.

Ideas of the Civic University

The space for the realisation of the idea of the civic university seems to be shrinking. But is it? It may be that old-style 'civic-ness' is no longer on the cards but perhaps a new model may be glimpsed. If the old style of the nineteenth century civic university (at least in the UK) was a university borne of civic pride, that may still be with us. Whereas once a town proclaimed its identify visually in its largest church (or even a cathedral, if it was fortunate), and then in its shopping mall, now it looks to have its own university. Civic pride in the university lives on. But perhaps the university-town relationships of the nineteenth century were rather distant; while some technical problems in the local economy – in brewing, in engineering, in agriculture – might have prompted the founding of the local university, the university was largely accorded space to develop in its own way. Now, institutions take on the title 'university' and are much acknowledged by their local communities but on the assumption that they 'deliver' – whether in the form of jobs, opportunities for local youth to obtain degrees or in 'knowledge transfer'. In short, civic acknowledgement is part of a compact wherein the university plays its part in and for its community in a variety of ways. So if the idea of civic is to do real work for us today, it has to be surely in the context of working out what a compact for the twenty-first century might be.

As discussed by Taylor in Chapter One, the idea of 'civic' relates both to a 'city' and to a 'citizen'. The citizen performs his or her civic duty by fulfilling the responsibilities of being a citizen (of a city). There are two separate sets of ideas in these elementary observations. Firstly, the idea of 'civic' works at two levels, that of the collectivity (the city, the city state) and of the individual (who gains rights but has responsibilities to fulfil). Secondly, the link between the individual and his/her identifying region (city/state) is an ethical link. The civic university, therefore, suggests a dual orientation of service: towards individuals as responsible persons, and towards the political region (the city and/or the state).

There are also, and it is implicit in these remarks, matters of identity and self-understanding wrapped up here, and again at the two levels of individual and of institution. We can ask of the university: is it enabling its members – staff and students – to see themselves as *contributing* members of its wider community? To what extent do they, by way of an example, see themselves as citizens of a multicultural world? *And* we can also ask of our university: does it itself have a sense of itself as having that kind of identity? Does the idea of civic service – howsoever interpreted – have a place in its mission, in the way it understands itself, projects itself and conducts its activities?

In these preliminary remarks, we have already moved – I believe – some way. We have glimpsed something of the potential complexity of the idea of the civic university. Distinctions, and therefore practical possibilities, have opened up as between a university on the one hand and its individual members on the other; and between that university being oriented towards individuals in society or the wider society in a more general way. The dimension of the ethical has also opened up and, thereto, have emerged matters of the responsibilities of the university – at the internal and external levels that we have just identified. In turn, the dimensions of identity and self-understanding also emerge here, and those concepts, too, could be explored again at both the levels of the individual and of the university itself.

So the idea of the civic university is opening a large canvas on which we might do work. But, in a globalised world, the canvas that presents itself is still larger yet. In the mediaeval world, and its predecessors, the immediate city provided the individual's collective calling and identity. Now, that calling and identity has transcended even 'society' to embrace the world. Universities, in particular, will often see themselves as operating on a global basis, both physically and virtually, via the Internet and its derivatives (Robins and Webster 2002). And so our second axis as to the focus of identity (with its poles of individual/ society) now has to be pulled out even further, such that 'society' is understood to include, potentially at any rate, the world. Putting it simply, does the university understand itself as a 'global citizen' and is the university concerned to enhance global citizenship, even on a global basis? For the university, both internal identity and external reach can have global dimensions.

Universities for Citizens

In his book, *Challenging Knowledge: The University in the Knowledge Society*, Gerard Delanty distinguishes between 'cultural citizenship' and 'technological citizenship':

cultural in so far as it has led to the preservation and dissemination of cultural traditions among the society as a whole, and technological as a contributor to professional society, the demands of the occupational system and the extension of the equality of opportunity. (Delanty 2001, 50)

The distinction at once prompts the question as to whether the contemporary university is giving prominence to technological citizenship at the expense of cultural citizenship. That is to say, it may be that the contemporary university, rather than living in the past, is being enjoined to live in the future. As a result, it would rather emphasise its credentials in the reshaping of society than it would continue to endorse past traditions of thought and being. Seen in this way, the idea of 'technological citizenship' points to patterns of identity formation that are system oriented. The citizens of the twenty-first century are those – it might be thought – who can make their way comfortably through global systems of information exchange and networking. Here, 'culture' is understood to be old hat, a concept of a past age; and with it, the idea of 'cultural citizenship'. If it has resonance in the modern age, it is in the remaking of culture rather than its reproduction.

This line of thought is, I think, productive but it can be overdrawn. What can be said is that different ideas of citizenship open up in contemporary society – some relatively old-fashioned and some avant-garde; some around patterns of consumption and some around patterns of contribution (think of ecological movements) – and that the university can do some justice to many if not all of them. The university is a site of the formation of competing forms of citizenship.

The forms of knowing now found in the university are themselves reflective of competing definitions of citizenship; and even within particular knowledge forms. Think, for instance, of a field such as midwifery. In being educated in universities as midwives, students are exposed to technical, scientific, humanistic, empathic, managerial, social and psychological modes of understanding the world and of engaging with it. What are these if not competing ideas of citizenship, for each mode is a set of rights and responsibilities in the world: the scientist and the manager, not to mention the human being, claim rights of kinds and in turn have their responsibilities. And the midwife is all of these at once: multiple identities and multiple offerings in and to her professional environment. The midwife is several citizens in one. And her education, consequently, can be seen as a process of professional formation that enables the co-handling of these multiple identities of citizen in the one person.

But higher education works at even more subtle levels. It is clear from work around the world – quite apart from their heightened contribution to the economy – that graduates from higher education tend to be more healthy, make greater contributions to their communities and to the political sphere (and hold less extreme political views). The processes of higher education are themselves conducive to the formation of citizens, ordinarily conceived. Much less clear is how these processes of citizenry formation come about. My view is that, in significant part, it lies, to use a Heideggerian phrase, in 'the principle of reason'. In Western higher education, students are put on the spot to take responsibility for their thoughts and actions, that responsibility lying in reason as such. Graduates come to realise that they can say and do pretty well anything that they like provided that those utterances and actions have a backing in reason and that they can articulate those reasons. In turn, the principle of reason leads directly to processes of dialogue, of responsibility and of self-critique.

But, in a globalised world, a world in which there is little in the way of sure ground on which reason can operate, on what ground is citizenship to rest? Surely, we should turn the basis of citizenship away from epistemology and towards ethics and ontology? Knowledge, after all, is now contaminated or partial or both. (The science on which pharmaceutical companies rely is in the dock for being both contaminated *and* partial. The formulation of an energy policy amid global warming is fraught with just those two dimensions. And being clear about aid policies in the developing world in a context of corruption and civil wars poses equal difficulties.) And if knowledge is in difficulty, what is left? What is left, surely, are the challenges of identity and belonging in just such a world in which our knowledge of it is now so flimsy and contestable. Hence, my suggestion that a new basis for citizenship lies in ethics and ontology; in matters of how we are to go on in the world and how we understand ourselves in the world.

This is not the place for a detailed exposition of such a position; I can only give a few pointers here. Central among the resources for such a project would be authors such as Levinas and Paul Ricouer. In both authors, we find prominence given to 'the other', a sense of the other having claims upon us and through which we gain from seriously engaging with the other. Mutual understanding may not be completely possible but we can go on working at it. And such an understanding is not to be thought of as an inventory of knowledge items about the other, and still less the economic value that the other offers to me. And through the growth of such mutuality, I may come even to know myself better.

What is the connection here with citizenship? Simply this: that we might come to understand citizenship as a matter of *being* a citizen. A citizen is one not who knows a lot about the world but who lives towards the world in certain ways, of mutuality, of respect, and (to use some Heideggerian language) of *care* and *solicitude*. And – going back to a distinction that we made earlier in this chapter – this idea of being a citizen has application not just to individuals (to each student and each member of staff, say) but it also has application to institutions. So we can inquire into the being of a university: (to use another Heideggerian term) how does it *comport* itself in the world? To what extent does it understand itself, as a university, as a citizen of the world, with citizenly responsibilities towards the world?

A Will to Serve

Let us recap and draw some temporary conclusions. In effect, we are suggesting that, if it is to do work for us in the contemporary age, the idea of the civic university has to be recast. In a globalised world, it has to depict a certain set of relationships between the university and potentially the world itself (or at least, society read in a very generous way). The civic university is not one that just attends to its immediate municipality. Those relationships can be cast in terms of the idea of citizenship, but then that idea has here to be understood not so much in terms of formal rights and responsibilities but, rather, in terms of a university's mode of being in the world. Does it, in its stance towards the world, really see itself as having a public service role? Does the being of the university embody a citizenly aspect?

Such a citizenly aspect can work its way out both at the level of individuals and of the institution itself. Individual staff, say, may be accorded house room to engage in community activities or individual courses may look to place its students on 'study service' placements but the dominant value ethos of the university may be quite elsewhere. The being of this university turns out to stand more on the ground of world university rankings, say, or perhaps the financial return on its activities.

To put matters straightforwardly, we can ask of a university: does it live in the world? And if it does, with what stance? Is it largely in the university's own interests *or* does it have a *will to serve* the wider society? Is that how it sees itself and how it is seen by others?

Not uncommonly, these days, universities either feel themselves propelled towards missions that are *extractive* in character. That is to say, universities look out for the main chance, seeing how they can yield a return to themselves on their investment in activities, whether that return be in terms of money, reputation or position. In a competitive environment – or, at least, an environment that is felt to be competitive – institutions will seek to extract benefit to themselves out of situations. Such extractive orientations can come in softer or harder varieties – respectively, in the form of 'enterprise' and 'exploitation', as we may term it.

In contrast, what might more *beneficent* stances look like? Picking up our earlier distinction between an orientation towards persons as citizens and towards the wider society, we can distinguish between orientations respectively of 'care' and 'service', where 'care' is an orientation towards persons and 'service' is more an orientation towards society. Admittedly, these are not and cannot be tightly separated orientations.

If the line of thought I am extending here has face validity, at once, a host of questions arise: is the care-service axis such that universities could, in theory, be positioned along it, depending on the extent to which it has a concern for persons as such or is engaged in beneficent ways with the wider society? Are there tensions between these two orientations? Are these more civic stances on the part of a university necessarily in tension with the extractive orientations? Can the entrepreneurial university also be a civic university? Or are there here, implied by those ideas, mutually conflicting sets of values?

Significant though I believe such questions to be, we can sidestep them to a large extent here. Their importance for us here, though, is surely to underscore the general thesis that I have been advancing here. Being a civic university in the current age is to *be* in a certain way in the world. This is not to pretend that such a stance is straightforward; on the contrary. The questions imply both that the idea of the civic university is itself a fuzzy idea and that it has to eke out its realisation in a milieu of competing orientations to which the university to some degree or other will be following. The university is a site of fluidities, some merging and some in tension with each other. The civic 'mission' has to find its place in that liquid swirl of 'missions'.

Living Citizenship

What is also clear, I think, from these reflections, is that being a civic university is not a matter simply of drawing up the table of goals, actions, responsible officers, deadlines and performance indicators; still less producing the 'risk analysis'. For the being of the civic university is itself working on a different plane altogether from such a calculative and performative orientation. The civic university is precisely one in which it is understood that the idea of the civic requires:

- continual refreshment
- an abiding sense of its problematicity
- emotional effort
- a care for persons
- a vision of the almost impossible
- a sense of delicacy, as the university steers amid sensitivities (as to 'inclusiveness', 'social justice' and 'openness').

This is a university that has a civic character in its soul. That the 'soul' is not easily theorizable or even articulable in any straightforward way does not leave this university in an embarrassed state. On the contrary, this university lives its civicness in its being, exemplified in a myriad of ways each day. This will to serve shows itself, therefore, in all the main functions of the university and thoroughly so.

Teaching will take on citizenship in many ways. Not just service learning will be seen as a helpful adjunct, but the curriculum will be infused with the theme. This aim will be achieved subtlety: courses can be oriented towards citizenship without there being units or modules on citizenship itself. Courses will bring out value dilemmas and links with the wider society. Students will be encouraged to develop a heightened sense of the 'other' (other persons; other viewpoints; other practices) in group tasks and to enhance their capacities for collaborative learning. Assessments will be designed to stretch students' capacity for making connections between their studies and societal dimensions and will encourage the formation of communicative capabilities on the part of students.

The university's research strategy will be developed so as to encourage researchers and scholars to understand that they have responsibilities towards the wider community. This was well understood in the nineteenth century but that sense of societal obligation has diminished over the past hundred years. Giving public lectures still has its place but, in the twenty-first century, newer media may be used to enable scholars to reach out to the wider polity. In sharing their ideas with the wider world, researchers can help to advance citizenship. This is to understand academic life as a public good; but an implication of that consideration is that the academic life has to be made transparent and communicated to the wider public in ways that the public can comprehend. And with such considerations, go of course, further considerations as to reward systems in universities, national evaluation systems and the identity of academics in seeing the wider polity as having a claim on their academic being.

These are but examples of what it is to be a civic university; but they are merely that, and perhaps, in themselves, they cannot bear much weight. On the one hand, these examples are indications of how the main university functions might be rethought so as to incorporate a civic dimension. As such, these examples have an obviousness about them. Equally as telling would be the way in which the university's civic-ness might display itself in the interstices of university life, in the practices of the estates office, the library and information services, the catering services, the alumni office and so on and so on.

There are sharp questions to be addressed, not with easy answers. For example, if the university is really wanting to be open to the community, how accessible should its estate and premises be? Should the university have security gates at every egress and even 'security' cameras liberally sprinkled across the campus and inside its buildings? With what level of hospitality are visitors to be welcomed? How and where is the budget to be found?

On the other hand, much larger issues are not far away. For example, 'mission' – as in 'university mission' – betokens a wide set of ideas here. Is it part of the university's felt calling that it reach out and into the community? Is it part of its sense of itself that it should serve others? Does it have a sense of otherness to which it is responding – that there might be societal needs where the university might have resources that could be put to some purpose outside of itself and without obvious financial or positioning gain? Statements about service to society may even be present in the university's 'mission statement' – but to what extent are these claims about itself realised in practice? To what degree are those self-claims reflected in the tone and the vigour with which the university opens itself to and engages with the wider community? Do its academics feel responsibilities towards the wider society as part of their academic role? (Macfarlane 2006) Do the service and civic aspects of the university mission have a dedicated champion among the pro-vice chancellors, presidents or senior managers?

Outside In

Let us draw together the threads of this exploration and offer some further reflections. In order to realise a civic function for the university in the twenty-first century, the university has the challenge of living 'outside in'. That is to say, it should take its bearings from the wider society. But 'civicness' points to certain kinds of dimensions of the wider society, not to do with money per se, or competition or the economy as such, but more to dimensions of democracy, of the 'public sphere', of social justice and societal belonging. The civic university, accordingly, is conscious of its responsibilities towards society and fulfilling a 'public service' role is a way of acting out those responsibilities.

All of the key terms of that last paragraph are very large terms indeed, and deserve much more exploration, each in its own right. This is not the place for such explorations; instead, I shall just dogmatically press my argument a little more.

Firstly, 'civicness' has to be realised anew in the contemporary age. The contemporary age poses new challenges, as we have noted, on any such realisation.

Competition between institutions such that institutions compete with each other; 'academic capitalism', in which institutions came to understand the value of their intellectual capital in relation to the financial return it yields; and the transformation of academic identity such that academics have to be parsimonious about the use of their time, often again looking to an economic return: these elements are just part of the aetiology of universities in the contemporary age, that deflect from an agenda of public service. But the new positioning of universities in society is bringing the university into contact with diverse interest groups. At the same time, technologies open up new possibilities of outreach into the public realm. New challenges and new opportunities: both present themselves in the shaping of the university's new public service role.

This is, too, an age of complexity; even of supercomplexity. A condition of supercomplexity arises where there are multiplying and conflicting readings of a situation. This is the nature of the world today – as our newspapers and news bulletins testify. It is partly a world that the university has helped to usher in, for universities are characteristically places of argument (of 'dissensus' as Readings called it). Accordingly, a particular public service role falls upon the university to assist the world in its handling of argumentative difference and even of argumentative conflict. And the university can play such a role in extensions both of its teaching and its research functions. Teaching can become more a process by which students come to handle themselves in argument (where there can be no clear resolution of different points of view). Research, on the other hand, becomes more a process by which academics engage as public intellectuals, not just informing the public sphere but displaying in public the dispositions and qualities required in the handling of argumentative dispute. Again, nowadays, the 'public sphere' has to be understood as a virtual space, with its blogs, discussion lists and bulletin boards.

But talk of argumentative dispute is liable to underplay the potential of this new civic role of the university. For the phrase 'argumentative dispute' can, in an academic context, imply just the cerebral domain. Here, it may be tempting to point to the emotional side of argument: arguments may become heated, after all. And it is surely part of our contemporary malaise that the passions that may accompany argument become unbridled. Passion and emotion more broadly are important but they are aspects of a wider set of considerations as to *being*. How are we to *be* in a world that is ineradicably contested? It is here, surely, that a new idea of civicness awaits for the university, namely that of encouraging forward the dispositions and qualities, the mode of being, that are called for in a world of ontological difference.

Conclusion

We may, just, recover the idea of the civic university in the contemporary world but if we are to do so, we shall be alert to several ways in which this world is complex. It is complex as to the relationship of culture and the university, society and the university, the economy and the university, and discourse and the university. And all of these dimensions tumble over each other, and in a crazily speeded up fashion. The university is both an arch-user but also a supreme developer of the internet. We cannot seriously develop an idea of the civic university in the contemporary age outwith a sense of the university as a virtual university. The civic university moves at different levels that are inter-connected.

This means that we shall have to re-*cover* the civic university. We visit and recall earlier ideas of social justice, of community and of outreach and we refashion them in the modern age. Crucially, this is a supercomplex age, an age of multiplying and conflicting readings of any situation. The university – especially through modern technologies – can reach out to the wider world in new ways; can form new kinds of community; and it has barely begun on this enterprise. The university can assist the development of citizenship in the modern age; and one of the challenges here is that citizenship itself needs to be re-formulated in the contemporary age, irrespective of the role of the university. We cover the university in new formulations of older traditions. We re-cover the civic university.

But this idea will have to be worked at, both by individual universities and as national policy. Being a civic university is precisely that – developing the university's being in the world. Such an orientation can only be achieved steadily over time and it cannot ever be achieved in any complete sense. Identities, strategies and reward systems all require continual vigilance. Ultimately, though, being a civic university is a matter of the university's being, the extent to which it is open to the world, and the university's 'other'; to what extent it takes that 'other' into account. Accordingly, in becoming (again) a civic university, the university helps the wider society itself to understand what civicness itself might mean in the contemporary age.

References

Bjarnason, S. and Coldstream, P. (eds.) (2003), *The Idea of Engagement: Universities in Society* (London: Association of Commonwealth Universities).

Delanty, G (2001), *Challenging Knowledge: The University in the Knowledge Society* (Buckingham: Open University Press).

Gokulsing, K.M. and Da Costa, C. (eds.) (2000), *A Compact for Higher Education* (Aldershot: Ashgate).

Heidegger, M. (1996), *The Principle of Reason* (Indiana, IN: Indiana University Press).

Macfarlane, B. (2006), *The Academic Citizen: The Virtue of Service in University Life* (London: Routledge).

Readings, B. (1997), *The University in Ruins* (Cambridge, MA: Harvard University Press).

Robins, K. and Webster, F. (2002), *The Virtual University: Knowledge, Markets and Management* (Oxford: Oxford University Press).

Slaughter, S. and Leslie, L. (1997), *Academic Capitalism* (Baltimore: Johns Hopkins).

Chapter 4

The Case for Service Learning

Edward Zlotkowski

Higher Education and Contemporary Society

One of the most important questions of our time involves the role higher education should play in helping to sustain and strengthen the workings of democracy. While, on one hand, colleges and universities have themselves become more 'democratic' in their increasing openness to people from diverse backgrounds, on the other hand, their practices and the outcomes for which they are willing to assume formal responsibility have changed relatively little over the course of the last century. To be sure, new kinds of institutions have been developed to address new areas of expertise. Nevertheless, as William Sullivan has noted with regard to American higher education:

> In the absence of an updated version of its founding conception of itself as a participant in the life of civil society…much of higher education has come to operate on a sort of default programme of instrumental individualism. This is the familiar notion that the academy exists to research and disseminate knowledge and skills as tools for economic development and the upward mobility of individuals. (Sullivan 2000, 21)

In other words, higher education has come to function almost exclusively as a vehicle of private advantage. Insofar as it also serves the common good, it does so indirectly – by advancing the interests of individuals who perforce help constitute the 'common' good.

The failure of most colleges and universities to see themselves as *directly* responsible for contributions to the common good is hardly unique to the United States. Indeed, if in some ways this issue has surfaced more often there than elsewhere, that is only because the American system has long prided itself on advancing social well being through an active commitment to public responsibilities. In Europe and elsewhere, such a commitment has traditionally been far less explicit. Hence, the question of higher education's current social and civic responsibilities has been less visibly contentious. Nevertheless, according to the Executive Summary of the *Final Report of the Universities as Sites of Citizenship Project* – a project based on site reports from European as well as American universities:

> The challenge of advancing universities as sites of citizenship comes from the tension between the fundamental mission of developing expertise and human capital while attempting to devote the time and resources to the development of attitudes, dispositions, and functionality of democratic citizenship. The educational aims are often treated as

something mutually exclusive or conceived in zero-sum terms in decisions pertaining to the allocation of resources and in the reward structure of universities. (Final Report of the Universities as Sites of Citizenship Project 2000, 2)

In such a context whatever does not clearly contribute to expertise tends to be academically suspect and unworthy of professional attention.

However, it is not just with regard to citizenship and concern for the public good that contemporary higher education may be said to be less than fully adequate to the needs of modern democratic societies. Consider, for example, the following statement from the proceedings of the Santa Fe Institute:

> The method people naturally employ to acquire knowledge is largely unsupported by traditional classroom practice. The human mind is better equipped to gather information about the world by operating within it than by reading about it, hearing lectures on it, or studying abstract models of it. (as quoted in Abbott and Ryan 1999)

And yet, texts, lectures, and abstractions remain the mainstays of higher education just about everywhere. Even if the only public responsibility of colleges and universities were, in fact, to develop the expertise of individual students, one would have good reason to conclude that what higher education offers and what contemporary society needs remain far apart.

Nowhere have these cross purposes been better illustrated than in a 1993 article by Charles Schroeder. Based on a study in which Schroeder looked at the learning style preferences of both first-year American college students and American faculty members, the article notes that:

> ...approximately 60 percent of entering students prefer [a] sensing mode of perceiving compared to 40 percent who prefer [an] intuitive mode. The learning styles of those who prefer sensing are characterised by a preference for direct, concrete experiences; moderate to high degrees of structure; linear, sequential learning; and, often, a need to know why before doing something. In general students who prefer sensing learning patterns prefer the concrete, the practical, and the immediate. (Schroeder 1993, 22)

It then goes on to point out that (1) unlike the majority of students, most faculty members evince the learning style preferences characteristic of intuitive learners (that is, learning via abstractions and theory), and (2) 'approximately 75 percent of the general population [of the United States] has been estimated to prefer the sensing learning pattern' (Schroeder 1993, 24). Thus it would seem as if the traditional faculty approach to learning is not only at odds with that of many students, it is also at odds with that of a large majority of the general population.

Abbott and Ryan, in their article *Learning to Go with the Grain of the Brain* (1999), could not be more explicit when they articulate the implications of studies like Schroeder's: 'For those who have been able to succeed in abstract terms, there are many for whom schooling has been a disaster.' Indeed, Schroeder himself notes that, thanks to the disparity between faculty and student learning styles, '[w]hat suffers...is the learning process itself – an observation that pervades in numerous national reports' (Schroeder 1993, 25). Exacerbating this problem still further is a widespread faculty tendency to interpret 'natural differences in learning patterns' as 'deficiencies', in this way turning what is a perfectly legitimate way of developing interest and motivation into an alleged lack of intellectual ability.

Ironically, even as many faculty members assume the superiority of their own approach to learning, still other research suggests that even for those who flourish in a system dominated by abstract conceptualisation, there are significant disadvantages to neglecting the educational potential of concrete experiences. In a 1996 interview, the same Abbott who co-authored *Learning to Go with the Grain of the Brain* suggested that traditional pedagogies – by their very nature – cannot hope to prepare students adequately for the competencies the future will demand of them. Indeed, even the ability to solve problems with the help of abstraction requires more than abstraction itself:

> ...today, people worldwide need a whole series of new competencies – the ability to conceptualise and solve problems that entails *abstraction* (the manipulation of thoughts and patterns), *systems thinking* (interrelated thinking), *experimentation,* and *collaboration*... I doubt such abilities ca be taught solely in the classroom, or be developed solely by teachers. Higher order thinking and problem-solving skills grow out of direct experience, not simply teaching; they require more than a classroom activity. They develop through active involvement and real-life experiences in workplaces and the community. [original emphasis] (Abbott 1996, 3–4)

If Abbott is correct – and the thrust of his remarks is echoed in numerous other studies (for example, *Report of the AAHE, ACPA, and NASPA Joint Task Force on Student Learning*, 1998; Ewell, *What Research Says About Improving Undergraduate Education*, 1997) – attempts to better prepare students to become 'intentional' or lifelong learners (Francis, Mulder and Stark, 1995) will not succeed simply by rearranging the curriculum, introducing new classroom exercises, or even by expanding available technological resources. What is needed, above all, is that students literally get out of the classroom and begin learning to learn in unstructured, 'real-world' situations.

The Uses of Engagement

Given the above, it may not be an exaggeration to claim that higher education is failing contemporary society in a number of important ways. Despite its much celebrated ability to help a certain (relatively small) percentage of the population acquire the technical expertise needed for personal success, its willingness – and ability – to help society prepare the majority of today's learners for both personal success and civic responsibility is clearly limited. As Russell Edgerton, former director of the Education Programme of the Pew Charitable Trusts, notes in a 1997 *Higher Education White Paper*:

> Held to a standard in which quality is defined as the absence of obvious defects, there are a few trouble spots in higher education, but no deep or serious flaws. Held to a standard of making it through the pipeline, there are troubling issues of quality throughout higher education but especially at institutions with open admissions. Held to a standard of

learning for understanding and acquiring the literacies needed for our changing society, there are pervasive issues of quality throughout the entire system. (Edgerton 1997, 38)

Edgerton then goes on to say that the key to addressing this situation is the development of 'new pedagogies of engagement that will turn out the kinds of resourceful, engaged workers and citizens' democracies now need.

Clearly the key concept here is 'engagement,' and it is interesting that this term has come to be used in two very different, but not incompatible ways in contemporary debates about higher education. On the one hand, 'engagement' refers to a new partnership between the academy and civil society. It was to just such a partnership that Ernest Boyer referred in his influential call for a 'scholarship of engagement':

> I am convinced that...the academy must become a more vigorous partner in the search for answers to our most pressing social, civic, economic, and moral problems... At one level, the scholarship of engagement means connecting the rich resources of the university to our most pressing social, civic, and ethical problems, to our children, to our schools, to our teachers, and to our cities...But, at a deeper level, I have this growing conviction that what's needed is not just more programmes, but a larger purpose, a larger sense of mission, a larger clarity of direction...Increasingly, I'm convinced that ultimately, the scholarship of engagement also means creating a special climate in which the academic and civic cultures communicate more continuously and more creatively with each other... enriching the quality of life for all of us. (Boyer 1996, 19–20)

Boyer's call has not gone unheeded, and over the last ten years dozens of initiatives have been launched to support the programmes and the partnerships he saw as central to 'engaged' academic work.

On the other hand, 'engagement' is also the term used to signify a student's personal commitment to his/her studies. Perhaps the single best example of this use of the word occurs in the National Survey of Student Engagement (NSSE)[1], an assessment tool 'designed to obtain, on an annual basis, information from scores of colleges and universities nationwide about student participation in programmes and activities that institutions provide for their learning and personal development'. As such, NSSE draws upon 'empirically confirmed "good practices" in undergraduate education'. Many, though not all, of these good practices include active learning strategies and dovetail with the kinds of recommendations made by researchers like Abbott, Ryan, and Schroeder discussed above.

At first sight, these two understandings of 'engagement' would seem to point in very different directions. While Boyer uses it to emphasise the academy's need to work more closely with other social institutions, NSSE focuses its attention on the academy's ability to promote more or less traditional student learning more effectively. If engagement in the first sense almost necessarily implies increased engagement in the second sense, engagement in the second sense does not necessarily lead to academy-civil society collaborations.

---

1   Further information on the National Survey of Student Engagement (NSEE can be accessed at www.nsse.org

And yet, it should. For both in their origin and in their deeper implications, these two kinds of engagement have much in common. Just as it was Boyer who recognised the need for a 'scholarship of engagement,' so it was also Boyer whose unpacking of the concept of scholarship promoted the idea that teaching itself could be a form of scholarship (Boyer 1990). In both cases his position challenged the prevailing assumption that the academy achieves its ends simply by serving as a more or less self-contained repository of expertise.[2] In both cases his position stressed the importance of social interaction and context-relevant knowledge as fundamental to the academy's claim to public support. Only by shifting its internal practices as well as its external relationships in this direction could it demonstrate its relevance to the future of democracy.

Boyer's emphasis on the need for a change in internal as well as external practices finds a clear echo in the analysis with which this essay began. William Sullivan's contention that American higher education has largely ceased to be more than a 'private benefit' (Sullivan 2000, 21) links this development to an underlying epistemic turn. Our reduction of education to a 'programme of instrumental individualism'

> rests upon a conception of rationality variously denominated as technocratic or scientific. This conception in its several forms has assumed dominance within much of the academy. Its core tradition and values are those of positivistic empiricism...The conclusion positivists have drawn is that while factual knowledge can be objectively verified, all questions of ethics and meaning are merely matters of taste and subjective judgment. Hence the affinity of positivistic understandings of research for "applying" knowledge to the social world on the model of the way engineers "apply" expert understanding to the problems of structure. (Sullivan 2000, 29)

In other words, the academy's evolution into an institution largely unresponsive to society's most pressing needs ultimately involves its having accepted the premise that 'real' knowledge is independent of affect and value judgments. The fact that research from across the disciplines has shown exactly the opposite to be true; namely, that 'The learner is not a 'receptacle' of knowledge, but rather creates his or her own learning *actively and uniquely*' (emphasis added) and that 'Learning is about making meaning for each individual learner' (Ewell 1997, 4) has simply been ignored. Thus, engagement turns out to be as essential on the micro (classroom) level as it is on the macro (societal) level.

Indeed, the two levels would seem to be far more than just parallel. Are students who see knowledge as something an instructor imparts to them likely to see the community and the society in which they live as entities requiring their active participation? To what degree is a consumer approach to education the corollary of a consumer approach to government? Clearly, Paolo Freire, the influential Brazilian educator saw educational and civic passivity as going hand in hand. In his 1970 classic *Pedagogy of the Oppressed*, he suggests that:

---

2 See, for example Stanley Fish's *Why We Build the Ivory Tower* (2004) for a succinct defence of this view.

In a humanising pedagogy the method ceases to be an instrument by which the teachers… can manipulate the students…Teachers and students…co-intent on reality, are both Subjects, not only in the task of unveiling that reality, and thereby coming to know it critically, but in the task of recreating that knowledge. (Freire 1971, 55–6)

Similarly, Parker Palmer has pointed to the fact that 'every epistemology tends to become an ethic, and that every way of knowing tends to become a way of living' (Palmer 1997, 21). If this is true, then not only does a disengaged way of learning presage a disengaged way of living but 'the mode of knowing that dominates higher education,' what Palmer calls 'objectivism' cannot help but lead to a depersonalised view of society:

> Objective, analytic, experimental. Very quickly this seemingly abstract way of knowing, this seemingly bloodless epistemology, becomes an ethic. It is an ethic of competitive individualism, in the midst of a world fragmented and made exploitable by that very mode of knowing. The mode of knowing itself breeds intellectual habits, indeed spiritual instincts, that destroy community. We make objects of each other and the world to be manipulated for our own private ends. (Palmer 1997, 21)

Engagement, it would seem, must not only characterise both student effort and institutional posture, it must also – *in both its forms* – play a constituent part in the way in which students learn. If disengaged students can easily turn into disengaged citizens, even engaged students whose engagement is limited to their own academic achievement can wind up as citizens who have never learned to see either their fellow citizens or their society in general as more than factors in their own personal advancement. In neither case, has there developed any deep appreciation of the concept of a common good.

Service Learning

Service learning, or community based learning as it is often called, is the teaching dimension of the scholarship of engagement. Like participatory action research and professional service, two other dimensions of that scholarship, it can be seen as a set of practices organised around both the substitution of problem-solving for self-contained analysis and the recognition of academic-civic partnerships as a central educational value. One of the more commonly cited definitions of service-learning is that of Bringle and Hatcher:

> We view service learning as a credit-bearing educational experience in which students participate in an organised service activity that meets identified community needs and reflect on the service activity in such a way as to gain further understanding of the course content, a broader appreciation of the discipline, and an enhanced sense of civic responsibility. Unlike extracurricular voluntary service, service learning is a course-based service experience that produces the best outcomes when meaningful service activities are related to course material through reflection activities such as directed writings, small group discussions, and class presentations. Unlike practica and internships, the experiential activity in a service learning course is not necessarily skill-based within the context of professional education. (Bringle and Hatcher 1996, 222)

Informing this definition are four key considerations. For an activity to be considered service-learning in the full sense of the term, it must evidence:

- explicit, assessable learning objectives,
- community-sponsored activities that promote civic responsibility,
- structured, multi-layered reflection opportunities, and
- reciprocity between the academic and community partners with regard to the resources, needs, objectives, and priorities that define the partnership.

Also important to an understanding of this approach is the distinction Bringle and Hatcher make between, on the one hand, service-learning and community service and, on the other, service-learning and traditional experiential education. The following diagram may help clarify both the overlaps and the distinctions at issue here.

Service-Learning Spectrum

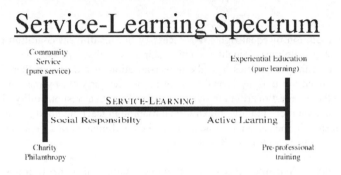

Figure 4.1   **Service-Learning Spectrum**

Service learning shares with traditional community service many of the same work sites and problem-solving/community-supporting activities. With traditional experiential education it shares the same theoretical model of how learning takes place in a 'real world' setting (for example, the Kolb 1984 learning cycle). However, as a 'bridge' concept service learning has its own distinctive objectives.

Despite the fact that students in service-learning courses frequently make use of the traditional language of 'charity' or 'philanthropy' to describe their community experiences (for example, 'volunteering,' 'giving back'), service-learning is not in fact grounded in a voluntaristic model; that is, it does not regard community engagement as a form of personal generosity. Instead, it seeks to develop in students an ethos of civic and social responsibility – an understanding of the engaged role individuals *must* play if communities and democracies are to flourish.

One political scientist who has contributed significantly to our understanding of the conceptual sphere within which service-learning takes place is Benjamin Barber. Over the last two decades Barber has produced a series of books that address both the nature and the importance of what he calls 'civic space':

To envision a democratic civic entity that empowers citizens to rule themselves it is then necessary to move beyond the two-celled model of government versus private sector we have come to rely on....Civil society, or civic space, occupies the middle ground [between the two]. It is not where we vote and it is not where we buy and sell; it is where we talk with neighbors about a crossing guard...a benefit for our community school... (Barber 1996, 281)

Furthermore, Barber has been very clear in recognising the special role service-learning can play in creating 'civic space' and strengthening civil society. Especially important in this regard are the ways in which it can help students learn to respect social diversity – whether that diversity is based on race, language and culture, socio-economic status, or factors like religion, sexual orientation and ability/disability. Indeed, in most modern democracies, diversity is the context within which civic competencies are best developed. As the culture critic Christopher Lasch has pointed out,

The recognition of equal rights is a necessary but insufficient condition of democratic citizenship....Political equality – citizenship – equalises people who are otherwise unequal in their capacities, and the universalisation of citizenship therefore has to be accompanied not only by formal training in the civic arts but by measures designed to assure the broadest distribution of economic and political responsibility, the exercise of which is even more important than formal training in teaching good judgment, clear and cogent speech, the capacity for decision, and the willingness to accept the consequences of our actions. (Lasch 1995, 88-89)

Because service learning insists, first, that addressing public problems is an essential component of education in a democracy and, second, that public problem-solving requires the collaboration of all relevant stakeholders, it challenges students to move beyond a merely sentimental and/or *noblesse oblige* approach to social and civic engagement. Through activities intentionally designed to develop civic knowledge, civic skills, and civic values, it establishes a far more reliable base for building and maintaining healthy communities than does any regimen of personal appeals, however often repeated.

On the 'learning' side of the service learning spectrum, service learning makes an equally critical distinction between itself and other, more traditional forms of experiential education such as field studies, internships, and practicals. Whereas the educational value of the latter rests primarily on their usefulness in helping to prepare students for a specific career or field of advanced study, the primary value of service-learning rests on a more fundamental educational objective. That objective encompasses nothing less than the development in students of a habit of active learning – a felt appreciation of the necessity of their becoming, themselves, knowledge producers. In this regard service-learning cuts directly across the grain of one of contemporary culture's most ubiquitous phenomena: consumerism.

Robert Sternberg, former president of the American Psychological Association, sums up the situation succinctly:

The nub of the problem, I believe, is that our society encourages a consumer rather than a producer mentality. In school, for example, students spend much of their time reading and listening and taking notes. At all levels they are merely consuming what their teachers and their textbooks tell them, while the only products they learn to produce are usually in the form of tests that measure comprehension rather than intelligence. (Sternberg 1996, 259)

What teacher, however wedded to traditional teaching methods, has not at sometime thrown up his/her hands in despair at his/her students' failure to question, to think, to assert? And yet, those students' entire social experience, including their involvement in the educational system, pushes in a largely passive direction. Is it any wonder that the 'shelf life' of most things students learn is even shorter than that of what they buy?

Traditional experiential education could itself serve as a corrective to passive 'knowledge transfer' were it not for the fact that the cultural hegemony of the latter has largely confined the former to a pre-professional transition role – an opportunity for inductive learning and/or workplace experience before one has actually completed one's course of studies. This means at least three factors typically circumscribe the educational potential of this opportunity. First, as an experience outside the standard academic curriculum it tends to receive insufficient attention. Off-campus experiences are expected to be their own justification and receive little intellectual guidance. Rather than serving as a testing ground for theory, or even as a generator of new theory, they simple follow theory like a tail on a dog. Second, except in the health disciplines, traditional experiential education typically comes too late to have a decisive influence on the course of a student's studies: it neither shapes the main academic programme nor provides a timely opportunity for the student to reconsider his/her disciplinary interests. Third, because of its pre-professional orientation, traditional experiential education usually has no relevance to students not following a specific career path: accounting students do not do psychology internships, even if they are interested in psychology.

Service learning, however, unties the justification for experiential work from its pre-professional/advanced studies mooring. An accounting student taking an introductory psychology course will be involved in that course's community-based work in just the same way that a psychology major will. In both cases one logic prevails; namely, community-based work enriches the course as a whole by giving students an opportunity to become, in however limited a sense, knowledge producers, making for themselves and others discoveries of demonstrable value. Such experiences lay the foundation not only for lifelong learning – learning outside the classroom and beyond the direct supervision of the instructor – but also for democratic engagement. For despite the frequent coupling of democracy and a market economy, the two do not necessarily seek the same kind of graduate. To cite Barber again, 'On the level of the individual, capitalism seeks consumers susceptible to the shaping of their needs and the manipulation of their wants while democracy needs citizens autonomous in their thoughts and independent in their deliberative judgments' (Barber 1996, 15). Thus, in the end, the distinction between service-learning and community service, and that between service-learning and traditional experiential education converge in the service of what Barber elsewhere calls 'strong democracy' (Barber,1984).

Dynamic Tensions

In looking at the ways in which service-learning can help address the needs of a diverse democracy, we have thus far considered both key characteristics and key distinctions. Also worth considering are the two dynamic tensions that account for much of service-learning's power – and not a few of its challenges (Zlotkowski 1997).

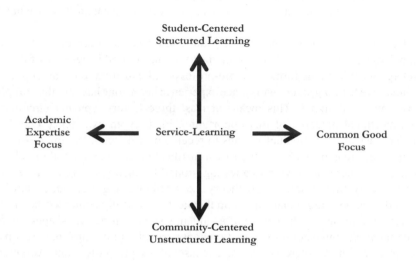

Figure 4.2   Service Learning

The tension indicated here on the horizontal access spans the traditional academic goal of helping students achieve mastery in a given area and the goal of helping them develop a rich appreciation of the social circumstances that affect – or should affect – utilisation of that mastery. To a considerable degree, these two goals coincide with a distinction Sullivan makes between 'technical' and 'civic' professionalism. While the former denotes the knowledge needed to demonstrate expertise in one's field, the latter 'means becoming more conscious of [the public] values' that define that field (Sullivan 1995, 149). Such a consciousness requires serious reflection on the ethical, social, and even historical factors that necessarily inform individual practice. What results from this dynamic tension is something Sullivan calls 'practical rationality':

> Civic democracy demands the ability to think in terms of complex balances rather than the maximisation of effectiveness as measured by a single objective…The critical step in this direction lies in the rehabilitation of nonformal modes of rationality which do not screen out the practical, the moral, and historical standpoint of both the subject and the object of knowledge. That means the rediscovery and expansion of the idea of practical rationality. (Sullivan 1995, 171)

The vertical axis of the above diagram suggests a related but nonetheless essentially different kind of tension – a tension based on the circumstances that define how knowledge, both technical and civic, is generated. At the upper end of this axis we have the classroom and the campus, those privileged environments whose very *raison d'etre* is student learning. Here not only are circumstantial variables designed to facilitate such learning, but students are also under the direct supervision of instructors and other mentors at least one of whose primary responsibilities is student intellectual development. However, as both instructors and students are fond of pointing out, neither the classroom nor the campus represents the 'real world,' and one could even argue that, in themselves, neither classroom nor campus provides an adequate preparation for that world. At the very least, 'real world' problems tend to be much messier and less tractable than the tasks students learn to perform in their coursework. As Sternberg notes in his book *Successful Intelligence: How Practical and Creative Intelligence Determine Success in Life*,

> An unfortunate feature of much education today, as well as the assessment of educational progress, is its overwhelming emphasis on well-structured problems. It is easier to teach the facts and only the facts, and then to test on these facts. Facts lend themselves to well-structured problems…with a clear, correct solution…The strategies that work in solving well-structured problems, however, often do not work particularly well, or at all, for ill-structured problems. (Sternberg 1996, 171–72)

Hence, the learning that takes place in the classroom and on campus in general may do little to help students succeed when confronted with real world problems even in their chosen field. Beyond the campus, problems are not only more difficult to address but are also more difficult to define. Furthermore, the environment within which one must work is often less than completely favourable, with other key stakeholders paying little or insufficient attention, distracting emergencies, and the absence of a mentor to show the way.

This is the learning environment indicated at the bottom of the vertical axis – a setting in which student learning must take place in a context primarily defined by other concerns and priorities. Here students must learn, first, to fit in if they are to learn anything at all. They must also learn to ask questions, live with ambiguity, improvise, and work with relatively little supervision. Fortunately for them, however, they still have a classroom and a campus to return to – a place that has many of the resources their community setting lacks, and a place where they can learn how best to take advantage of what their community setting does provide. By moving back and forth between the classroom and the real world, students can learn to deal with a level of complexity they will otherwise not have to face until most of their formal education is over. It is perhaps for this reason that John Abbott has suggested that the 'new competencies' people will find increasingly more important cannot:

> …be taught solely in the classroom, or be developed solely by teachers. Higher order thinking and problem-solving skills grow out of direct experience…they require more than a classroom activity. They develop through active involvement and real-life experiences in workplaces and the community. (Abbott 1996, 3–4)

Hence, the dynamic tension indicated by the vertical axis complements the tension indicated by the horizontal axis in an especially useful way: unless the learning process is itself structured to draw directly upon real world experiences, neither traditional (academic) nor civic (common good-related) goals can be reliably achieved.

Nor can they be achieved unless all four stakeholder groups involved in the service-learning enterprise are brought fully into the process. Instructors, student leaders, academic units and institutions, and community/neighbourhood organisations all have key roles to play. Faculty members need to develop a new set of skills, perhaps the most important of which is educational design – an understanding of when and where different kinds of activities should be utilised and how they can best complement each other. This means deliberately moving away from 'content transfer' as the faculty's primary concern. This, in turn, means re-visiting of the idea of 'coverage' and the tyranny it exercises over so many curricular programmes. Coverage may, indeed, be important, but so is engagement and deep understanding. Furthermore, coverage is not the same thing as a lecture: topics can be 'covered' through inductive as well as deductive pedagogical strategies.

Students also need to learn new roles. Despite their potential as knowledge producers, students will continue to play the far easier role of knowledge consumer just as long as they are allowed to. However important active learning may be to their futures and their ability to become lifelong learners, 'what's on the next test?' will dominate their thinking unless they have concrete incentives to change. This means not only new faculty expectations but also new peer models – fellow students whose temperament, maturity, and/or experience allow them to take a leadership role in projects with real world significance. Ideally, such students should be deliberately sought out and recognised as critical to the future of education for personal and civic empowerment – much as traditional education has long rewarded students with superior abstract analytical abilities.

Clearly, neither faculty members nor students will succeed in learning new roles unless the academic institutions with which they are affiliated are themselves willing to recognise the importance of and commit significant resources to this new approach. Faculty development funds, the revision of standards for promotion and retention, criteria for student financial assistance, and student leadership programmes all represent investments that go beyond simple verbal encouragement. Indeed, institutionalisation of service-learning and the scholarship of engagement in general constitute themselves a topic of considerable complexity that is now receiving increased attention. Whether the academic unit in question is a department, a division, a disciplinary association, or an entire higher education institution, more and more resources are becoming available to guide the institutionalisation process.

Finally, community partners – be they non-profit organisations, neighbourhood associations, or public institutions – must never be regarded merely as 'placement' sites. Their participation in the entire service-learning process, from project identification and design through all phases of implementation, reflection, and assessment, must be seen as equal in importance to that of all three academic stakeholders. One could, in fact, argue that 'the integrated involvement of the community' is an essential predictor of progress across all stages of institutionalisation (Holland 1999, 69). Ultimately, the potential of community-based work to promote the kinds of skills, values, and dispositions needed by a diverse democracy depends as much on recognition of the community's role as educator as it does on recognition of the university's role as a partner in public problem solving.

The Future of Service Learning

Over the past decade community based academic work has spread throughout colleges and universities in the United States. Whether one looks at conference programming, dissertation topics, institutional accreditation standards (undergraduate and professional schools), or surveys of faculty interest, there can be no doubt that such work has become a part of the American academic mainstream. At present, this interest shows little sign of abating though it is only to be expected that swings in academic 'taste' will eventually make service-learning less overtly fashionable.

At the same time, the service learning movement has begun to develop international momentum. While some countries, like Mexico, have long featured a version of service-learning as part of their higher education system, other countries, like South Africa, have made a deliberate effort to adopt this approach in universities nationwide. In still other countries, individual institutions have shown interest while the overall educational system has not been much affected. It remains an open question as to whether service-learning will develop any kind of traction in the countries of the European Union.

Several factors that have helped to facilitate the acceptance of this approach in the United States may show themselves to have few European equivalents. Perhaps the most important of these is the focus on public purpose that has been a prominent part of the American educational scene from the very start. In different but distinctive ways, the colonial colleges of the eighteenth century, the Land Grant universities of the nineteenth century, and the new, urban graduate schools launched at the turn of the twentieth century have all subscribed to this focus. So have America's community colleges, hundreds of faith-based institutions, Historically Black Colleges and Universities, and tribal colleges and universities. Indeed, in the mission statement of almost every American higher education institution one can find an explicit commitment to serving the common good and/or developing leaders with strong social values. Such statements make it relatively easy to claim institutional legitimacy for community-based work.

At the same time, America's marked distrust of government-administered programmes; its history of forming civic associations and alliances to deal with social needs; its self-identity as a nation built on initiative and innovation; the relative informality of its culture, even in the classroom – all these help make the kind of 'self-help' modelled in academy-community partnerships look, if not compelling, at least familiar. Indeed, the very variety of higher education institutions in the United States almost guaranteed that some constituency would step forward to champion this kind of work. With approximately 3,500 colleges and universities looking for ways to make themselves distinctive and attractive, it would have been surprising if some significant minority had not recognised in community-based work a potential institutional advantage.

However, even if higher education in the United States has had some unique incentives to embrace service-learning as an approach to teaching and learning, the fact remains that many of the specific social issues – those 'pressing social, civic, and ethical problems' Boyer (1996) refers to – are by no means uniquely American; indeed, even an issue like ethnic and racial tensions, once thought to be a particularly American concern, has in the last few years shown itself to be more or less ubiquitous throughout the Western democracies. Similarly, while the phenomenon of low voter turnout has been a part of the American scene for years, other developed democracies are now also beginning to show troubling signs of civic disengagement.

This 'globalisation' of many issues related to the health and strength of our communities and our democracies is hardly surprising, given the growing influence of market forces and market-based values worldwide. As the global market system promotes ever greater socioeconomic stratification both between and within countries, we find increasing opportunities for something former US Secretary of Labour, Robert Reich has labelled a 'form of secession':

> America's symbolic analysts [i.e., highly educated knowledge workers] have been seceding from the rest of the nation. The secession has taken many forms, but it is grounded in the same emerging economic reality. This group of Americans no longer depends, as it once did, on the economic performance of other Americans. Symbolic analysts are linked instead to global webs of enterprise, to which they add value directly. (Reich 1991, 252–53)

There is little uniquely American about this set of circumstances. Nor is the growth of what Robert Bellah and his associates have identified as 'lifestyle enclaves', residential patterns that replace communities with as pseudo-communities:

> Whereas a community attempts to be an inclusive whole, celebrating the interdependence of public and private life and of the different callings of all, lifestyle is fundamentally segmental and celebrates the narcissism of similarity. It usually explicitly involves a contrast with others who 'do not share one's lifestyle.' (Bellah 1986, 72)

Like the secession of the well educated, retreat into lifestyle enclaves seriously undermines any sense of a common good, and as such is ultimately subversive of democracy.

Community-based teaching and learning can be a powerful tool to mitigate the effects of phenomena like these. Not only does it create structures that lead to contact among groups divided by income, culture, even locale; it also gives students a chance to explore what community is, what it provides, and what it requires if it is to flourish. By complementing the general and the abstract with the specific and the concrete, it brakes the tendency of higher education institutions to contribute, however inadvertently, to their students developing a sense of being privileged and apart. In the end, this deliberate reconnecting, experienced as a form of personal enrichment, not as an exercise in self-sacrifice, may be one of the most important contributions contemporary higher education can make to our collective future.

References

Abbott, J. (1996), *The Search for Next-Century Learning AAHE Bulletin*, 48:7, 3–6.

Abbott, J. and Ryan, T. (1999), 'Learning To Go With the Grain of the Brain', 21st Century Learning Initiative [website] <http://www.21learn.org/publ/edcanada.html> accessed 24 November 2006.

Barber, B. R. (1984), *Strong Democracy: Participatory Politics for a New Age* (Berkeley, CA: University of California Press).

Barber, B. R. (1996), *Jihad vs. McWorld: How Globalism and Tribalism Are Reshaping the World* (New York, NY: Ballantine Books).

Bellah, R. N., Madsen, R., Sullivan, W. M., Swindler, A., and Tipton, S. M. (1986), *Habits of the Heart: Individualism and Commitment in American Life* (New York, NY: Perennial Library).

Boyer, E. L. (1990), *Scholarship Reconsidered: Priorities of the Professoriate* (Princeton: Carnegie Foundation for the Advancement of Teaching).

Boyer, E. L. (1996), 'The Scholarship of Engagement', *Journal of Public Service & Outreach* 1:1, 11–20.

Bringle, R. G., and Hatcher, J.A. (1996), 'Implementing Service Learning in Higher Education', *Journal of Higher Education* 67:2: 221–239.

Bringle, R. et al (eds.) (1999), *Universities as Citizens* (Needham Heights, MA: Allyn & Bacon).

Edgerton, R. (1997), *Higher Education White Paper,* Unpublished paper for the Pew Charitable Trusts.

Ewell, P. (1997), 'Organising for Learning', *AAHE Bulletin*, 9:4, 3–6.

'Final Report of the Universities as Sites of Citizenship Project' (2000) International Consortium for Higher Education, Civic Responsibility and Democracy [website] <*http://iche.sas.upenn.edu/reports/European%20Report%20Executive%20Summary.pdf*> accessed 24 November 2006

Fish, S. (2004). 'Why We Build the Ivory Tower', <http://www.nytimes.com/2004/05/21/opinion/21FISH.html>

Francis, M. C., Mulder, T. C. and Stark, J.S. (1995), *Intentional Learning: A Process for Learning to Learn in the Accounting Curriculum*, (Sarasota, FL: American Accounting Association).

Freire, P. (1971), *Pedagogy of the Oppressed* (New York, NY: Herder & Herder).

Holland, B.A. (1999), 'From Murky to Meaningful: The Role of Mission in Institutional Change', in *Universities as Citizens*, ed. Bringle et al. (Needham Heights, MA: Allyn & Bacon).

Kolb, D. (1984), *Experiential Learning: Experience as a Source of Learning and Development*, (Englewood Cliffs, NJ: Prentice Hall).

Lasch, C. (1995), *The Revolt of the Elites and the Betrayal of Democracy,* (New York, NY: W.W. Norton & Co.).

National Survey of Student Engagement (2006), Annual NSSE 1999–2006 [website] http://nsse.iub.edu/html/quick_facts.cfm

Palmer, P.J. (1997), 'Community, Conflict, and Ways of Knowing', *Change,* 29:5, 20–25.

Reich, R.B. (1991), *The Work of Nations: Preparing Ourselves for 21st-Century Capitalism.* (New York, NY: Knopf).

Report of the AAHE, ACPA, and NASPA Joint Task Force on Student Learning. (1998). (Washington DC).

Schroeder, C.C. (1993), 'New Students – New Learning Styles', *Change*, 25:5, 21– 26.

Sternberg, R.J. (1996), *Successful Intelligence: How Practical and Creative Intelligence Determine Success in Life.* (New York, NY: Simon & Schuster).

Sullivan, W.M. (2000), 'Institutional Identity and Social Responsibility in Higher Education', in *Civic Responsibility and Higher Education.* Ehrlich, T. (ed.) (Phoenix, AZ: Oryx Press).

Sullivan, W.M. (1995), *Work and Integrity: The Crisis and Promise of Professionalism in America.* (New York, NY: HarperBusiness).

Zlotkowski, E. (1999), 'Pedagogy and Engagement', in Bringle et al. (Needham Heights, MA: Allyn & Bacon).

PART 2
Institutional Considerations

Chapter 5

Rethinking the Place of Community-Based Engagement at Universities

Ahmed C. Bawa

Introduction

University mandates throughout the world have statements that relate to community-based engagement in some form or other. It is important to understand why it is that this has happened, what forms these take, what effects they have on universities, what effects they have on the communities with which they are involved, what effects these have on the students who are involved, how they relate to teaching, learning and research and how they are organised internally in terms of the structures and governance of universities. Much has been written about these issues, but there are other important questions which relate to issues of context. For instance, how do external forces such as globalisation or the changes in national political, social and economic configurations alter the evolution of the nature of engagement and the way it is perceived within the institutions in which they are embedded? In this paper, we look briefly at the case of South Africa as a way of posing a set of questions that relate to community-based engagement more globally.

In a previous paper an aspect of the impact of the rapid globalisation on community-based engagement was discussed (Bawa 2003). It was argued that one of the challenges for community-based engagement, especially in developing contexts, is to systematically incorporate capacity-building of community participants and communities to become more integrated into the networked society (Castells 1996) so as to lay the seeds for their fuller and more active participation in knowledge and information processes. This would be taking into account the perceived separation of first and second economies in such developing contexts and to ensure that the engagement of universities with communities would provide for interesting pilot studies to address deeply structural challenges in developing contexts.

In this paper we approach the issue of community-based engagement from a different but complementary viewpoint which attempts to provide a knowledge-based conceptual framework for it. There are various reasons for this, the most important of which is that it partly addresses, in a more systemic fashion, the structural asymmetries that are built into university-community relationships. Much of the argument is drawn from South African experiences.

General Background

There are at least four driving imperatives for the experimentation with community-based learning by institutions of higher education. The primary one is to provide students with the opportunity to 'engage', to link their learning with 'the needs of society', to allow them to build positive kinds of social consciousness, and so forth. This is an important reason for community-based engagement. Such experiential learning takes many forms and there has been much written about the advantages and disadvantages of these. It is an attempt by universities to enhance/enrich the nature of curricula as a means to answer the need for higher education to generate cohorts of socially-engaged citizens (see Rhoads 1998).

While this response by universities is driven partly by internal institutional needs for improving the quality of learning and teaching and to address the issues of institutional social consciousness, it is also in response to valid and powerful critiques of higher education as being ivory-towerish brought to bear mainly from government and forces of social activism. These are structural charges that higher education as a sector is socially elitist and that it is responsible for the building and maintenance of elites, exclusivity, social and economic detachment, social and economic inequalities, and so on. The response is diverse and often complex but most activities take the form of community development projects in which staff and students are encouraged to perform some sort of service delivery either through acts of service, volunteerism or research and development.[1]

A third driving force arises from activist (students and/or academic) layers within the institutions who conceive of various forms engagement which arise from ideological imperatives to engage, to broaden the base of the university, to force the 'elitist' institution to address the needs of local development, etc. Often these academics would see their engagement as a way of building some forms of internal contestation over the way in which the university conceives of itself and the ways in which resources are distributed.[2] In more recent parlance, these forms of engagement would be seen to be counter-hegemonic, driven by the need to counter-balance the forces of globalisation or the Washington Consensus. As such there is often an ideological edge to the forms of engagement – to build the validity of community-based engagement as a legitimate and equal form of learning and research. This would then have implications for the ways in which institutions conceive of themselves and therefore adjust policies, procedures and protocols to resource and measure the activities of staff and students in such activities.

The fourth category represents the kinds of projects that emerge through the intervention of local governments and local communities who challenge the university to respond to specific development issues facing the relevant community. Depending on the urgency of the project it is often the case that these are a response to particular crises that have arisen in the communities or where some academic (or group of academics) decide to launch an intervention of some kind or the other as a form of service delivery.

---

1   For a South African case study see Hattingh 2003.
2   For an example see Harkavy 1998.

Needless to say these four elements feed into each other but there is also much institutional contestation related to these kinds of activities, presidential/vice-chancellor/dean statements about the community-based activities of their institutions notwithstanding. Most institutions experience points of discord or disjuncture and these stem from contestations that are largely systemic in nature and which are not easily solved. Mostly these contestations arise out of the way that core institutional resources are distributed. The result of this is that most community-based engagement projects are built on external (soft) grant funding usually on the basis that this would help to mobilise institutional core funding. Institutional policies and processes also militate against the proper and substantive embedding of community-based engagement. An example of this is what is often seen as a disparity in terms of the policies and processes for the securing of tenure and for promotions for individuals who are heavily involved in community-based engagement.

The Example of the University of KwaZulu-Natal

For these reasons it is often the case that community-based engagement initiatives are located at the edges of institutions. In the 1980s, during the Apartheid period, the University of KwaZulu-Natal (UKZN) (at that time the University of Natal) became home to eighty six non-governmental organisations and community-based organisations that sought some protection within the University from Apartheid South Africa's security forces. This provided the basis for an important infusion of interfaces that had the potential to impact on a significant diversification and radicalisation of knowledge processes at UKZN in terms of the relationship between university and society. These organisations were described by Richard Bawden as a 'dynamic interface' between the university and communities with which these organisations worked (Bawden 1992). His analysis indicated that the location of these interfaces on the edge of the institution provided the organisations with some level of freedom from the rigidity of a publicly subsidised institution – freedom to work flexibly with communities and to intersect with the University partly on their own terms. It is probably accepted now that while these organisations played an important role in shaping the ethos of the institution, their capacity and the institutional space for them to impact on the nature of the learning/teaching and research was very limited. Their location at the edge of the institution was both an advantage in terms of their effectiveness and a disadvantage in terms of the restricted spaces for them to impact on the core activities of the University.

As a fiscal crisis began to set in during the early 1990s and with the dismantling of the Apartheid regime, the University began to shed these organisations, so much so that by the late 1990s no more than twenty of them remained at the University. Their presence at the edge of the University was seen to be disadvantageous in the long run (both to themselves and to the institution) and it was argued and decided that their continued viability as university-based centres/units/organisations depended on the availability of internal funds and therefore on some form of integration with the 'core business' of the University which was seen to be research and teaching. This of course implies that the work done by these units were not seen as being at the core of the institution. They were seen to be nice to have but not necessary. The result of this integration was fully predicted by the Bawden study. As the units became integrated into the schools and faculties their mandates were altered by diffusion and by design.

The Ford Foundation funded a series of exciting experiments in the area of service learning which involved five or six South African universities. The overall experiment was referred to as CHESP (the Community Higher Education Service Partnership).[3] It created the opportunity for a new experiment that began with an important set of founding principles. The first of these was that participating institutions would commit to the proper institutionalisation of service learning into the core curriculum. That is, the service learning activities would be faculty-based and would lead to credits towards degrees that the participating students were enrolled for. The second condition was that this was to be done on the basis of Senate-approved policy. The third condition was that the CHESP activities were to be jointly conceived of and managed by the participating community, the service provider (a local government or a non-governmental organisation, for example) and the university. The fourth was that the university partner would make some form of resource allocation to the endeavour.

CHESP is an ongoing project and has tried to operate systemically. This has been successful in a particular way. It allowed a group of institutions to launch substantial and substantive experiments with the development of service learning modules. It permitted the evolution of some successful partnerships between the three sectors and forced institutions to institutionalise service learning. Perhaps most importantly, it resulted in the emergence of a national policy on service learning driven by the National Department of Education and the conceptualisation of a quality assurance framework for service learning by the Higher Education Quality Committee (HEQC 2006), the national body responsible for the quality assurance of higher education. The plan is that these developments will allow the Department of Education to fund service learning at an appropriate level.

Several years after the initiation of the CHESP project however, its impact on UKZN is very small. The key problem of course was that the institution did not adjust or transform key operational elements to facilitate service learning. So for instance, academics were reluctant to take on the challenges of institutionalising service learning because they were extraordinarily time intensive and because these activities did not contribute to the usual metrics for promotion and tenure purposes. The Senates of universities found it rather difficult to approve these experimental service-learning modules that were new in concept, shaped by university-community-service partnerships and hopelessly expensive to run. The communities were not really sure who was benefiting from all of this because it was rarely clear how service learning would improve the quality of the lives of their members. Service partners saw this mainly as an irritation.

Two examples of interventions are given here, one internal to the University of KwaZulu-Natal as it gave refuge to a host of organisations that were intricately linked with communities and the other external, driven through a large national project,

---

3   For further information access http://www.chesp.org.za.

CHESP. Neither has worked well in terms of institutionalisation of community-based engagement. One possible reason for this, and this will be explored further below, is that the basis on which community-based engagement is conceptualised places it firmly outside of 'core activities' of UKZN and of other universities.

Community-Based Engagement and Knowledge Production

An important challenge therefore is to understand how to shape programmes of community-based engagement so that they are philosophically and conceptually located within the core functions of the university. This would be different from transporting them from the edge to the centre. The one way of doing this is by placing community-based engagement firmly within a knowledge production framework so that the kinds of knowledge production and knowledge dissemination in community-based engagement activities are in competition with 'high' knowledge – knowledge that forms the basis of the traditional university. Partly this is due to a contestation over the idea of the 'university'. Partly it is due to the notion that the dominant knowledge tradition is the only one that is capable, capacitated to produce knowledge of any consequence. Partly it has to do with the way in which national higher education systems and science systems legitimise knowledge processes and knowledge.

For universities in the global South there is an additional issue. There is the additional complication that universities are colonial in their genesis and through their knowledge processes continue to seek their legitimisation in the colonial metropole. This has resulted to some extent, at least in the South African case, in the prevention of the emergence of research traditions which have as their locus local knowledge and local knowledge traditions.

This does not contradict those needs of universities discussed above to engage in visible community-based engagement. While the possibility of change at the national level (in terms of special funding mechanisms and the quality assurance steps) might play an important role in increasing the legitimacy of service learning, it is more important to understand that unless the epistemology of community-based engagement in all its forms is underpinned in terms of the processes of knowledge production, it is highly unlikely that it will expand beyond pilot experimentation. And for universities locked in the global South, it is just as important to conceptualise this underpinning in terms of a postcolonial project (see Hountondji 2002).

In more general terms we might begin to say that unless *community-based engagement* is seen as a legitimate and serious way to unlock knowledges which require deep community participation, it is unlikely that it will be seen as a 'core' activity of the university.

What are the implications of this for universities? Firstly, experiments with various forms of community-based learning at universities have been exciting, innovative and challenging.[4] Their dependence on 'soft' funding continues largely because they have found it extremely difficult to find a home within the core of

---

4   For early experiences in South Africa, see Perold 1998.

these institutions. This simply means that faculties do not yet see service learning as part of the knowledge enterprise in a way that contributes to the strengthening of their research and teaching/learning activities – notwithstanding the perseverance, commitment and innovation of activist scholars.

The second is that there are a significant number of knowledge frameworks operating in all societies but particularly in one such as South Africa. In the case of South Africa, there are knowledge traditions that are locked away within communities – traditions which do not receive any serious attention from the universities. In recent times however, the need for these marginalised knowledge frameworks to be brought into national research frameworks is being articulated through various kinds of policies and through the voice of new emergent political and intellectual elites (Odora Hoppers 2002). This is being increasingly seen as a mechanism that alters the nature of the relationship between the universities and society.

The third is the role of universities in the face of the rapid growth of the knowledge economy and the emergence of dual economy models (one formal and rich and the other informal and poor) in many developing nations. There are many characteristics of these dual economies but one of them is that the demographically small formal economies of these nations are globally connected. They function through the fundamentals of the knowledge economy. In this context it may be assumed that one of the roles expected of universities is to work with whole communities to find ways to broaden the notion of a knowledge economy into the notion of a more broadly conceived knowledge society. And this implies the need for communities in the second economy to become more effective as producers, users, commissioners of research and knowledge production.

Going Back to Some South African Experiences – Changing Contexts

The imperative to push the limits on this project in South Africa is driven by the changes in this society which are vast and rapid on the one hand, and complex on the other hand. They are apparent in all social sectors and higher education is constantly under pressure to re-vision itself. More importantly political change has opened the way for a new discourse on what have been called 'indigenous knowledge systems' (Odora Hoppers 2002), and this in turn has opened the way for a substantial discussion about power relations within the academy and within the world of science. How is this represented in everyday South Africa? Let's look at the two examples.

South Africa's Truth and Reconciliation Commission is a significant symbol of the nation's transition to democracy. It was central in an attempt to allow the people of this new democracy to understand the complex process of nation building in the face of deeply divided pasts. As the victims and perpetrators of oppression and torture began to face each other with constructions of that past it became clear that the production of knowledge about that past would be a complex process with multiple layers. It would have to take into account the existence of multiple truths with different cultural processes having been in play in the construction of those truths. In other words, this indicates the need for a more complex understanding of the way in which knowledge is constructed in deeply fragmented, parallel societal processes.

These will be overlaid by hierarchies that are related to these different processes of knowledge production. Much of the knowledge of that era resides in communities and it is the kind of knowledge that would escape traditional historical studies since so much of it is constructed in paradigms that lay outside of the dominant ones.

What this means is that the social construction of a history of this painful period of deep and systemic racism will require the establishment of interfaces that provide for different forms of knowledge construction to engage with each other in ways which address the hierarchies amongst diverse processes of knowledge construction.

There is yet another South African experience that forces us to consider different ways of dealing coherently with processes of the social construction of knowledge and different kinds of knowledges. One of the most powerful outcomes of the absolute devastation of the HIV/AIDS pandemic has been a serious debate related to the way in which decisions are made with regard to the roll out of an antiretroviral treatment programme. This debate spans a range of areas that are riddled with deep questions about the politics of the social construction of knowledge. Some of these are listed here.

- The relationship between medical science and its institutions and the needs of a developing society are highlighted because of a deep distrust of that system by certain politicians in terms of its orientation as being very first world, 'scientific' and therefore dismissive of indigenous health systems, and so forth.
- The relationship between medical science and the pharmaceutical industry has been identified as a driver of the dominant paradigm.
- The statement by the current Minister of Health that she cannot allow the findings of a few scientists to determine how the Ministry responds to the crisis, even where the findings have been fully validated is a hint that the there are deep concerns about the role of experts in the production and dissemination of knowledge.
- Recent work by Adam Ashforth indicates the complexity of deeply embedded views and beliefs about witchcraft affects the way in which people respond to the pandemic (Ashforth 2005).

This tells us that the social production of knowledge about the pandemic is affected by a large array of issues. It is a complex weave of all of these elements and others. The investment of hundreds of millions of rand in education programmes to combat HIV infections seems to have had little if any impact on the rate of infections. Perhaps the reason for this is that these ignore the complexity of the knowledge terrain.

While I have used the Truth and Reconciliation Commission and the HIV/AIDS pandemic as a way to enter this discussion these are not isolated cases. These kinds of issues are prevalent in all policy discussions.

Community-Based Engagement and Building a Knowledge Society

So there are two questions that this paper hopes to address. The first is to understand how best universities should address the integration of large parts of the developing societies into the *knowledge society*. The second is for these institutions to understand how to deal with the contestation between different forms of knowledge or indeed different *knowledges* about the world and society and the hierarchies that define them. In the South African context both sets of challenges speak directly to the legitimacy of higher education.

So can community-based engagement address these two challenges? In this paper we explore the role that might be played by university-based community-based learning as a strategy to develop some level of coherence between what we refer to as the 'core activities' and these challenges. On the one hand it addresses the challenge of addressing the questions set out above. On the other it begins to address the question of how we might begin to find a systemic approach to integrating community-based engagement (with all its advantages) into higher education so that it resides in the centre of these institutions rather than at the edge.

The CHESP programme in South Africa attempted to address the issue of power imbalances by *requiring* that certain conditions be met. This failed because the playing fields were by no means equal and so while community partners in these service learning activities did work with university counterparts on issues of curriculum and modes of delivery, they were hopelessly decontextualised and thereby marginalised. The fundamental reason for this is that the CHESP programme operated in the dominant university knowledge tradition.

So if community-based engagement is important in developing the capacity of communities to become fuller participants in a knowledge society, then it would have to be on terms which make the communities fuller participants. One way of doing this would be to accept that there are forms of knowledge in communities which require the full participation of members of the community to surface, to codify and to disseminate. The involvement of academics and students in such community-based engagement projects would be as much to impart knowledge and techniques as to learn. This may help to address questions in the academy that relate to the drift towards scientism and other hierarchies.

Why does this have to be done in communities? It is mainly in communities that we can begin to perceive alternative knowledge paradigms. The social construction of knowledge must take into account these paradigms. community-based engagement may therefore provide the basis for an exciting approach to allow these different paradigms to intersect with each other and to provide the space for intellectual intersections between them.

How would this be achieved? The answer is simple. Only through a process of structured negotiations that allow for the construction of an overall philosophy, taking into account the variety of diversities involved, can relationships emerge which may be built on trust and equity of status. This philosophy will then play itself out in terms of the processes of community-based learning including the tools for the measurement of processes and outcomes. Michael Gibbons and his co-authors explore this in detail in their discussions of New Modes of Knowledge Production (Gibbons 1994), in particular with regard to university-industry partnerships and later in terms of university-community partnerships. The key challenge here is to construct negotiations that lead to the joint shaping of research questions. These are all very complex issues. For instance, neither the academy nor the community speaks with a single voice. It would appear to be important to allow a proliferation of different approaches to take root as a way to develop sets of exciting experiments.

Of paramount importance is the joint development of an ethical framework within which to anchor community-based engagement activities. Such a framework will ensure that suitable processes of consultation, capacity-building and negotiation occur within the devised philosophical framework, that the nature of the programmes of activity and their expected outcomes are clearly defined and that mutually agreed quality systems, both formative and summative, are in place and that the programme of activities are constructed as learning activities for all the participating sectors.

The outcome of this kind of engagement would be that communities would no longer be simply sites of learning, or sites of research for the academy, or sites for the delivery of services. These would be bona fide knowledge producing activities within which learning occurs by all participants. And most importantly, communities in such engagements see themselves as contributing to the generation of new knowledge (or even new *knowledges*) and thereby contribute to global knowledge systems.

References

Ashforth, A. (2005), *Witchcraft, Violence, and Democracy in South Africa* (Chicago, IL: The University of Chicago Press).

Bawa, A. (2003), 'Rethinking Community-Based Learning in the Context of Globalisation', *Service Enquiry* – Service in the 21st Century 1:1, 46–59.

Bawden, R. (1992), *From Extensions to Transactions: A University in Development for Development* (Ottawa: The International Development Research Centre).

Castells, M. (1996), *The Rise of the Network Society* (Oxford and Malden, MA: Blackwell).

Gibbons, M. et al. (1994), *The New Production of Knowledge: The Dynamics of Science and Research in Contemporary Societies* (California: SAGE Publications).

Harkavy, I. and Benson, L. (1998), *De-Platonising and Democratising Education as the Bases of Service Learning* in Rhoads et al (eds).

Hattingh, A. and Killen, R. (2003), 'Beyond the ivory tower: service-learning for sustainable community development', *South African Journal of Higher Education* 17:1.

HEQC (Higher Education Quality Committee, CHE) (2006), *A Good Practice Guide and Self Evaluation Instruments for Managing the Quality of Service Learning.*

Hountondji, P. (2002), 'Knowledge Appropriation in a Post-colonial Context', in Odora Hoppers (ed.).

Odora Hoppers C.A. (ed) (2002), *Indigenous Knowledge and the Integration of Knowledge Systems* (Cape Town: New Africa Books).

Perold, H. (1998), *Community Service in Higher Education* (Johannesburg: Joint Education Trust).

Rhoads, R.A. and Howard, J.P.F. (eds.) (1998), 'Academic Service Learning: A Pedagogy of Learning and Reflection', *New Directions for Teaching and Learning*, No. 73. (San Francisco, CA: Jossey-Bass).

Chapter 6

Institutionalising Service-Learning in Higher Education[1]

Andrew Furco

Abstract

The institutionalisation of service-learning in higher education is a complex process that is shaped by the confluence of a variety of factors. Based on current discussions in the literature and findings from a three-year exploratory study, this article discusses the central issues and critical leverage points for institutionalising service-learning in higher education. A conceptual framework that identifies five key dimensions of service-learning institutionalisation is presented.

Background

At the centre of what has become known as the engaged campus movement is service-learning, a pedagogy that links academic study to authentic public-service activities. Today, service-learning activities operate across the spectrum of academic disciplines and can be found at all types of higher education institutions, including two-year community and technical colleges, four-year liberal arts colleges, and four-year public and private universities. As Barbara Holland (2000) notes, service-learning has become a leading post-secondary educational reform that has reinvigorated higher education's engagement in the concerns of the local community.

However, despite the recent rise of service-learning in higher education, service-learning remains far from being institutionalised into the academic fabric of most colleges and universities. Even on campuses that have had a substantial history of service-learning implementation, service-learning continues to struggle to gain full academic legitimacy and institutional permanence (Zlotkowski 1999; Gray et al. 1998). In broad terms, the institutionalisation of service-learning requires moving service-learning from the 'margins to the mainstream' (Pickeral and Peters 1996, 2). To accomplish this, service-learning must become part of an institution's academic fabric so it can be legitimised by the faculty and supported by the administration.

In his report on service-learning institutionalisation, Michael Kramer suggest that for an educational reform to be considered 'institutionalised,' it must become

---

1 Funding for the study was provided by the Corporation for National Service. The author wishes to acknowledge the contributions of Rebecca A. Bell, Mary Sue Ammon, Valerie Sorgen, and Parisa Muller.

'routine, widespread, legitimised, expected, supported, permanent, and resilient' (Kramer 2000, 6). But beyond this conceptualisation, little is understood about the factors that impact and promote the institutionalisation of service-learning in post-secondary education. Indeed, leading experts on higher education service-learning conclude that the current process of service-learning institutionalisation is not fully understood (Holland 2000). According to Holland, the current research on service-learning needs to extend beyond studying 'service-learning's role in institutional change, impact, response, and adaptation' and more fully investigate the 'institutional issues related to the exploration, implementation, expansion, and sustainability of service-learning as a programmatic endeavour' (Holland 2000, 53). She and others suggest that a clearer understanding of the specific academic and institutional factors that are most influential in advancing and institutionalising service-learning in higher education need to be more fully explored in order for engaged campus efforts to advance (Holland 2000; Zlotkowski 2000). With a full understanding of the factors that drive the institutionalisation process, colleges and universities can design service-learning initiatives in ways that can ensure the development of an academically legitimate effort that has the greatest potential for becoming a widespread and expected part of the academy.

Conceptual Framework

This article explores some of the critical leverage points for institutionalising service-learning in higher education. The analysis applies the findings from a three-year exploratory study on service-learning institutionalisation to the existing literature on this topic. The exploratory study is based on forty-three colleges and universities that implemented a set of service-learning institutionalisation strategies over a three-year period. The goal of the study was to gain a better understanding of the service-learning institutionalisation process by identifying and investigating key institutionalisation factors. The sample of the study included two-year community colleges (n=12), four-year public institutions (n=18), and four-year private institutions (n=13) from four states participating in a service-learning institutionalisation grants programme.

This programme sought to advance the institutionalisation of service-learning by providing each institution with a small grant to conduct an annual self-assessment of the present level of service-learning institutionalisation and, from that annual assessment, initiate a set of action steps that would further institutionalise service-learning on the campus. In this regard, all of the activities proposed and subsequent actions taken by the institutions were intended specifically to advance the institutionalisation of service-learning on their campuses. This emphasis provided an opportunity to analyse the kinds of activities that the participating institutions saw as essential for service-learning institutionalisation.

Each campus's annual self-assessment reports were based on a set of coordinated assessment and planning activities, which included

- an annual self-assessment of the level of service-learning institutionalisation (using a *Benchmark Worksheet* assessment tool);

- the development and implementation of action plans for the advancement of service-learning institutionalisation (detailed in *Activity Worksheets);* and
- the submission of annual mid-year and year-end progress reports that detailed the challenges faced and progress made by the campus.

These processes were completed annually for three years by a small team of faculty, administrators, and community members at each institution.

The institutionalisation self-assessment process was outlined by a conceptual framework developed by Kecskes and Muyllaert (1997), which identifies three institutionalisation levels: Level 1 – Critical Mass Building, Level 2, – Quality Building, and Level 3 – Sustained Institutionalisation. The *Benchmark Worksheet* self-assessment tool is a simple eighteen-item, three-level rubric designed to assist institutions in pinpointing their level of institutionalisation. Using the *Benchmark Worksheet*, each participating campus identified its level of service-learning institutionalisation annually, developed and implemented action steps to advance the institutionalisation level, and reported on the progress of its service-learning institutionalisation effort every six months.

The eighteen items of the *Benchmark Worksheet* provided brief operational characterisations of four broad areas of institutionalisation: *Faculty* acceptance and support for service-learning, *Student* acceptance and support for service-learning, *Institutional* acceptance and support for service-learning, and the presence of *Evaluation* processes that help assess the advancement of service-learning on campus. Consequently, the institutionalisation activities proposed and implemented by the participating campuses primarily targeted these four areas.

After the start of the three-year programme, researchers from UC Berkeley were asked to analyse the reports and self-assessments completed by the campuses and identify cross-site themes, successful strategies, and best practices for institutionalising service-learning.

Specifically, the exploratory analyses focused on three research questions:

- What are the defining characteristics of how institutions move along a continuum of service-learning institutionalisation over time?
- Are there differences between types of institutions in the activities, challenges, successes, and patterns of movement across the continuum of service-learning institutionalisation?
- How do institutions at different levels of service-learning institutionalisation approach the advancement of service-learning?

Quantitative analyses were conducted by deriving Institutionalisation of Service-learning (ISL) scores, which were based on the mean of scores (weighted by the tree levels of institutionalisation) for each of the eighteen items of the *Benchmark Worksheet*. The ISL scores were used to quantify and track each institution's progression across three stages of service-learning institutionalisation over the three year period. Data from the grantees' reports regarding short-term objectives, accomplishments, and barriers were analysed qualitatively using Miles and Huberman's (1984) meta-matrix approach, which allowed for the organisation of multilayered data and the identification and coding of emerging and recurring themes across sites an institutionalisation levels. The findings from these analyses were used to expand on previous discussions on service-learning institutionalisation found in the literature.[2]

Elements of Institutionalisation

For the most part, the literature on service-learning institutionalisation can be classified into the following four areas:

1) the relationship between institutional mission and the purposes and goals of service-learning;
2) community participation and partnerships;
3) academic issues pertaining to faculty, departments, and students; and
4) structural and programmatic issues necessary to advance and sustain service-learning.

Each of these areas includes a broad range of issues that are believed to influence the institutionalisation of service-learning in higher education. Overall, these areas reveal that the institutionalisation of service-learning in higher education is a complex process that is shaped by the confluence of a variety of factors. The process of institutionalising service-learning involves not only the full development of the elements within each area, but it also requires the strategic coordination of all the elements across the four areas so that they operate synergistically to advance service-learning toward institutionalisation.

Although the full development of each area appears to be essential for institutionalising service-learning, findings from the three-year UC Berkeley study reveal that campuses emphasise some areas over others. While this emphasis might suggest that some institutionalisation elements are perhaps more essential than others, it might actually suggest that campuses are not fully considering *all* of the important issues in their service-learning institutionalisation efforts. A more complete understanding of these four institutionalisation areas can help shed additional light on the extent to which each plays an important role in institutionalising service-learning in higher education.

---

2   In interpreting the findings of this exploratory study, a number of limitations were considered. The primary limitations of the study involved issues of sampling (self-selected biases, small sample size), the validity of the *Benchmark Worksheet* (a pilot instrument), and the reliability of the self-reported data (the different standards and processes individual campuses used for their self-assessments). Overall, the goal of the analysis was not to make definitive determinations, but rather to identify patterns and issues that might warrant further investigation in an experimental study.

Institutional Mission and Service-learning

Although service-learning has been adopted across a broad range of institutions, it has not been adopted uniformly. With more than 200 published definitions of service-learning, there is no consensus as to what service-learning is or what purposes it should serve on college and university campuses. The three-year national evaluation of service-learning in higher education, done by Maryann Gray and her colleagues, found that a wide range of educational, institutional, and social purposes are served, including addressing important and vexing social problems, preparing students to meet the responsibilities of living in a democratic society, providing opportunities for students to explore career options, and promoting educational improvement initiatives such as collaborative learning and interdisciplinary education (Gray et al. 2000).

This broad array of purposes was mirrored in the various service-learning goals and objectives stated by the forty-three institutions participating in the UC Berkeley study. These campuses sought to institutionalise service-learning for a variety of reasons including improving undergraduate instruction, strengthening campus-community relationships, enhancing the civic mission of education, building learning communities, promoting interdisciplinary teaching and learning, strengthening departmental collaborations, and enhancing the institution's service role in the community (Bell et al. 2000). Just as the purposes of each campus varied, so did the approaches by which service-learning was advanced and institutionalised. On some campuses, institutionalisation activities were implemented in specific departments, while on other campuses institutionalisation activities centred on particular student programmes (for example, freshman seminars or senior capstones). On some campuses, institutionalisation activities were guided by the prevailing social issues in the community or by a particular community partnership that had been established or funded. Still, on other campuses, service-learning institutionalisation activities were primarily based on and driven by the particular interests and concerns of individual faculty members or administrators.

But, is the process of institutionalising service-learning absolutely unique to each campus? The service-learning literature reveals that there are some approaches to service-learning implementation and institutionalisation that may be essential for certain types of institutions. For example, O'Byrne (2001) claims that for service-learning to advance at teaching institutions, a working definition of service-learning must be established; high academic standard for service-learning need to be set; long-term visions need to be clarified; service-learning must be used to achieve other academic goals; and service-learning must be viewed as an effective approach to improve faculty teaching and student learning. In his assessment of advancing service-learning at research universities, Furco (2001) suggests that service-learning needs to be connected to faculty's research and scholarly agendas, be tied to university's research mission, and be integrated into the discipline-based, academic work of departments.

Robinson (2000), Pickeral and Peters (1996), and Edington and Duffy (1996) believe that *community colleges* have distinct needs and therefore require specific approaches for implementing and advancing service-learning. While they acknowledge that there is no one best way to implement service-learning, Edington and Duffy (1996) suggest that the centrepiece for advancing service-learning at community colleges is civic collaboration; this entails collaboration with faculty, collaboration within the institution, and collaboration outside the institution that is focused on advancing the civic mission of the college. But to what extent does institutional type influence the manner in which service-learning is institutionalised? Is it easier to institutionalise service-learning at certain types of institutions? Does the institutionalisation of service-learning occur at different rates at different types of institutions?

Questions related to these were explored in the UC Berkeley study. For example, an analysis of variance, also called ANOVA, was conducted on the *Benchmark Worksheet* scores provided in the three-year institutionalisation programme, to ascertain between-group differences by institutional type on the degree of movement across the service-learning institutionalisation continuum. This analysis tested for statistically significant differences between community colleges, four-year public institutions, and four-year private institutions on the mean differences in Institutionalisation of Service-learning (ISL) scores across the project period (See Table 6.1). The goal was to determine if there was any difference between institutional type in the degree to which the institutions progressed along the three-level institutionalisation continuum.

Table 6.1   Analysis of variance of the mean differences in institutionalisation of service learning scores from year one to year three by institutional type

Institutional Type	Mean Difference in ISL Score	F	Significance (2-tailed)
Community Colleges	+4.05	.994	.556
Public Institutions	+4.33	2.539	.124
Private Institutions	+4.39	1.245	.423

Note: Results are considered significantly different at the .01 alpha level

Differences between other institutional characteristics (for example, research, teaching, technical, and so forth) were not possible due to sample size limitations.

The ANOVA revealed no statistically significant differences ($p = .01$) between community colleges, four-year public institutions, and four-year private institutions in their advancement along the service-learning institutionalisation continuum.

The qualitative analyses of what the participating institutions considered to be critical elements (activities, barriers, and strategies for overcoming barriers) for institutionalising service-learning on their campuses also revealed no discernable differences in the ways two-year community colleges, four-year public institutions, and four-year private institutions approach the institutionalisation of service-learning. In fact, many of the critical elements for institutionalisation identified by different types of institutions were quite similar and could be grouped into comparable categories (See Table 6.2)

For example, the most frequently reported critical elements in the *Faculty* cluster focus on supporting faculty members in their service-learning work, building faculty awareness of service-learning opportunities, providing faculty development opportunities, and providing incentives for faculty to participate in service-learning. These elements transcend institutional type as well as institutionalisation level. Similar cross-cutting commonalities were found in the other three cluster areas. This finding suggests that perhaps there are some common, universal elements or activities that are important for all institutions to consider as they work to institutionalise service-learning, although each institution might apply these elements and activities in different ways to achieve their distinct and varied purposes.

One identifiable factor that appears to have influenced the focus of all the campuses' service-learning institutionalisation efforts is institutional context. For each campus participating in the study, there was a connection between the identified goals and objectives for service-learning institutionalisation and specific campus-wide goals and initiatives underway at the institution (Muller and Furco 1998). These broader, campus-wide initiatives and priorities provided "hooks" on which service-learning was secured; the importance of these broader campus initiatives (for example, advancement of outreach programmes, improvement of undergraduate teaching, interdisciplinary teaching programmes, and so on) provided a venue for service-learning to gain visibility and legitimacy. Thus one of the important factors for service-learning institutionalisation that emerges is the importance of tying service-learning to important educational goals and initiatives on the campus. In a way, theirs is a strategy for bringing service-learning from the margins to the mainstream.

Academic Issues and Service-learning

A second area the literature on service-learning institutionalisation has explored focuses on the relationship between service-learning and academic issues relating to faculty, students, and departments. Most of the literature has centred on the powerful role of the faculty in securing the academic legitimacy of service-learning. However, more recently, discussions on both the influence of departmental acceptance and the importance of student voice for institutionalising service-learning have started to emerge.

The Role of the Faculty

As a pedagogy, service-learning rests predominantly in the domain of faculty work, and therefore, its success is dependent on the acceptance and support from faculty. But, as the engaged campus movement has advanced, service-learning has extended beyond teaching functions of the institution and has become more formally connected to the broader research and service missions of the institution. Inevitably, this broader visibility of service-learning has raised the stakes and, in

Table 6.2   Comparison of the most critical activities for institutionalisation by institute type and institutionalisation level

		Critical Mass Building Level I (n=12 institutions) (3 community colleges; 6 public; 3 private)	Quality Building Level II (n=25 institutions) (8 community colleges; 10 public; 7 private)	Sustained Institutionalisation Level III (n=6 institutions) (1 community college; 2 public; 3 private)
Faculty	**Community Colleges**	* Support faculty's s-l work (12) * Educate faculty about s-l (7)	* Recruit key faculty for leadership roles (16) * Involve new faculty (9)	* Provide incentive grants to faculty (3) * Provide faculty release time for s-l course development (2)
	4-year Public	* Foster faculty awareness of s-l (17) * Provide incentives for faculty participation (8)	* Secure faculty acceptance through scholarly incentives (21) * Provide development and training opportunities for key influential faculty members (9)	* Encourage faculty to engage in strategic planning of s-l (3) * Maintain ongoing personal contact with faculty (1)
	4-year Private	* Foster faculty awareness of s-l (14) * Provide incentives for faculty participation (4)	* Foster involvement of leading faculty members in s-l (9) * Provide logistical support for faculty to carry out s-l activities (7)	* Assist faculty with course development (3) * Tie s-l to faculty scholarly work (3)
Students	**Community Colleges**	*None reported*	*None reported*	*None reported*
	4-year Public	* Keep students informed of s-l opportunities on campus (5) * Use students' voices and experiences in s-l to recruit faculty (3)	* Establish a student fellows/ scholarship programme for s-l (5) * Ensure that s-l students' voices are heard by administrators and budget allocators (2)	* Legitimise the role of student leaders in s-l (2) * Involve students in s-l committees (2)
	4-year Private	* Use students' voices and experiences in s-l to garner administrative support (3) * Maximise students' involvement in promoting s-l (1)	* Maximise opportunities for student participation in s-l activities (6) * Develop a student fellows/ scholarship programme (2)	* Provide opportunities for student leadership development (2) * Keep students informed and updated of all s-l opportunities on campus (1)

Institutions	**Community Colleges**	* Fund campus faculty grants for s-l (8) * Involve administrators in connecting s-l to campus priorities and mission (6)	* Secure administrative support for s-l (17) * Ensure there is adequate staffing and office personnel for s-l (6)	* Maintain a consistent administrative staff for s-l (3) * Secure funding for technical assistance and equipment needed to carry out s-l (2) * Secure administrative support for s-l (11) * Have academic affairs area of campus sponsor s-l (9)
	4-year Public	* Strengthen top-level administrative support for s-l by connecting s-l to campus mission (14) * Ensure there is adequate staff to recruit and train faculty (7)	* Formalise s-l advisory committee (5) * Maintain a consistent administrative staff for s-l (3) * Secure administrative support for s-l (10) * Include s-l in core courses (7)	* Develop a campus-wide functional definition of s-l that is tied to campus mission (18) * Secure adequate staff and office (7)
	4-year Private	* Formalise s-l advisory committee (4) * Maintain a consistent administrative staff for s-l (2)	* Maximise opportunities for student participation in s-l activities (6) * Develop a student fellows/ scholarship programme (2)	* Provide opportunities for student leadership development (2) * Keep students informed and updated of all s-l opportunities on campus (1)
Evaluation	**Community Colleges**	*None reported*	* Disseminate information and publications on s-l (2)	*None reported*
	4-year Public	*None reported*	* Conduct a campus-wide self-assessment of all s-l activities (3) * Formalised a long-range strategic plan for s-l (3)	* Clarify outcomes and assessment processes for s-l courses (4) * Develop course review and approval criteria (2)
	4-year Private	* Utilise both qualitative and quantitative Indicators of success (2)	* Promote and publicise the s-l programme (2) * Assess s-l periodically (2)	* Maintain the integrity of service as the academic and scholarly aspects of s-l, such as research, teaching, and publication are promoted. (2)

turn, has made the participation and a support from faculty even more important. As service-learning has crept closer to the academic mainstream, the importance of gaining broad faculty approval for service-learning has been heightened. As Holland states, 'The perception of the role of public service as a legitimate component of the institution's purposes is critically important to those faculty who do not have personal or disciplinary motivations for engagement.' (Holland 1999, 38). To move service-learning from the margins to the mainstream, a critical mass of broad faculty support for service-learning is necessary. However, this faculty support is likely to be influenced by broader educational initiatives to which service-learning is aligned and adhered. In this regard, institutional acceptance and support and faculty acceptance and support for service-learning go hand in hand.

An investigation of the strongest and most consistent predictor of movement across the institutionalisation of service-learning continuum, based on the four clusters of the *Benchmark Worksheet,* found that the *Faculty* cluster (focusing on faculty support and acceptance for service-learning) and the *Institutional* cluster (focusing on institutional structures and programmatic features) worked in some combination to facilitate campuses' forward movement on the continuum (See Table 6.3). In the first and second years of the programme, the Institutionalisation of Service-Learning (ISL) scores for years one and two were best explained by the items in the *Faculty* and *Institutional* clusters from the previous year. In the second year of the grant, it appears as if over two-thirds (67%) of the variance in ISL scores is accounted for by the *Faculty* cluster. While in the third year of the grant, over two-thirds (78%) of the variance in ISL scores was accounted for by the *Institutional* cluster of items.

Interestingly, when the first and second-year predictors were run together in the multiple regression analysis to predict the final (year three) ISL score, the *Faculty* cluster items turned out to be the strongest and most consistent predictor of movement across the institutionalisation of service-learning continuum. The *Faculty* cluster accounted for the largest portion of the difference in final ISL scores.

Table 6.3   **Percent variance explained by predictors across all 43 institutions**

Year of Study	Strongest Predictor	Second Strongest Predictor
Year One (1997–98)	Faculty Cluster (67%*)	Institutional Cluster (65%*)
Year Two (1998–99)	Faculty Cluster (67%*)	Institutional Cluster (10%)
Year Three (1999–2000)	Institutional Cluster (78%*)	
Overall (1997–2000)	Faculty Cluster (40%)	

Note: Percent variance not unique due to non-stepwise regression.

This finding suggests that while institutional supports remain an important dimension in the institutionalisation of service-learning, faculty involvement, acceptance, and participation become more important as service-learning advances on a campus over time. Future studies on service-learning institutionalisation should investigate this issue and its relationship to institutional factors for service-learning institutionalisation. As discussed later, most of the critical elements for institutionalisation that were cited by the forty-three institutions participating in the study were focused on faculty and institutional issues.

The Role of Students and Departments

While the role of students and departments in the advancement and institutionalisation of service-learning in higher education remains unclear, there is an emerging literature to suggest that they might play an influential role. For example, Gray et al. (2000) suggests that student awareness of service-learning opportunities can affect the extent to which students involve themselves in service-learning. Providing incentives and rewards for students to participate in service-learning (for example, tying service-learning to students' academic degrees or graduation requirements) has the potential to substantially increase the student demand for service-learning courses (Gray et al. 2000). In addition, there is some evidence to suggest that having students share their personal stories about their service-learning experiences can be an effective way to affirm the educational value of service-learning and garner additional faculty and administrative support for service-learning (Bell et al. 2000). While these claims require additional investigation and exploration, especially in regard to their effect on service-learning institutionalisation, they do shed light on the potentially influential role students might play in advancing service-learning on college campuses.

Similarly, increased attention is being paid to the role of departments and the discipline-based work of faculty in influencing service-learning's move from the margins to the mainstream. Furco states that as service-learning is featured more prominently in the disciplinary, academic work of departments, 'faculty members will begin to perceive it as something that their peers value and consequently something of which they should be cognizant' (Furco 2001, 76).

According to Holland (1999), when service-learning is genuinely valued within a discipline, faculty members within that discipline begin to view service-learning as a legitimate scholarly pursuit. Thus, given that the predominant association faculty members have is with their discipline, the departmental and discipline-based support for service-learning has the potential to raise the academic legitimacy of service-learning. As the issues of service-learning institutionalisation are studied further, the role of the department should be more fully explored.

Community Participation and Partnerships

The third area of institutionalisation focuses on the role of the community. A campus cannot institutionalise service-learning without strong campus-community partnerships (Zlotkowski 1999). Most of the issues regarding the institutionalisation of service-learning in post-secondary education are viewed from the campus perspective. Therefore, it is not surprising that most of the recommended strategies for implementing, and institutionalising service-learning are campus-focused rather than community-focused. While it is primarily the campus's responsibility to establish structures and implement activities that will ultimately institutionalise service-learning, the community plays a central role in ensuring the sustainability of a campus's service-learning effort.

Holland and Gelmon (1998), Seifer (1998), Saltmarch (1998), and others reveal that strong campus-community partnerships are based on mutual respect, genuine community voice, partnership status, and mutual agreement and understanding. According to John Saltmarsh, 'Community is both a place and a set of relationships' (Saltmarsh 1998, 6). The campus-community relationship is based on mutual respect in which the campus views the community as equal partners in the service-learning initiative (Holland and Gelmon 1998). In high-quality service-learning partnerships, the campus and community members have equal status, whereby the community voice is as influential as all other voices (Seifer 1998). This respect for the community is what distinguishes service-learning from other forms of campus-community engagement. Zlotkowski states, 'It is only through full service-learning partnerships that the academy and community come together as equals for the purpose of better fulfilling their core missions' (Zlotkowski 1999, 112). The advancement and ultimate institutionalisation of service-learning, therefore, must account for the role of the community and its needs. The community needs to be an active partner in the development and planning of the campus service-learning initiative. Incentives and rewards need to be made available to ensure that the community receives the collateral benefits service-learning is intended to deliver (Zlotkowski 1999).

Despite its important role in service-learning, the community has not been a central figure in service-learning research, and consequently, little is known about the impact of the community and community partnerships on the institutionalisation of service-learning in higher education. Since the self-assessment process used in the service-learning institutionalisation programme studied by UC Berkeley did not include dimensions of community and community partnership issues, no data are available to report from the study. This limitation in the study's instruments speaks to the inadequate attention community issues tend to receive. Given the central role partnerships play in service-learning, it is imperative that the field gains a better understanding of how these partnerships affect and influence the institutionalisation of service-learning in higher education.

Structural and Programmatic Issues

The fourth area on which the service-learning institutionalisation literature has focused has to do with the various institutional structures and programmatic elements that need to be put in place on campuses in order for service-learning to advance. Unlike the scant research on community issues, there has been much work done in this area. While additional study is needed to understand more fully the optimal combination of programmatic features that produce high-quality service-learning experiences, there is some agreement around particular structural and programmatic features that are known to be essential elements for advancing and sustaining service-learning.

One of these features is the presence of a campus-wide coordinating entity for service-learning. In their national study of service-learning programmes (Gray et al. 1998), it was found that the campuses that had a coordinating centre for service-learning activities were able to advance their service-learning initiative more substantially over a three-year period than campuses that did not have a coordinating entity. While the existence of such centres for advancing service-learning has been generally accepted, the location of these centres has been a subject of debate. Much of the debate has focused on whether the centre should be housed in academic or student affairs. There is no published study that has investigated the strengths and weaknesses of housing a service-learning centre in a particular unit; however, a perusal of campus service-learning centre web sites reveals that a growing number of centres are being established in academic affairs. Presumably this is occurring to help further embed service-learning into the academic fabric of the institution.

Another issue that has emerged as being especially important for service-learning institutionalisation is the campus's establishment of faculty review, tenure, and promotion policies that support faculty members' participation in service-learning. According to Ward (1998), Driscoll (2000), and others, faculty involvement in service-learning hinges upon being rewarded and supported for their efforts. Because they set the expectations and standards for faculty scholarship, promotion, and tenure policies that do not reward faculty for their work in service-learning, this will discourage faculty participation and long-term involvement (Ward 1998). Indeed, campuses that have embraced service-learning, such as Portland State University and California State University, Monterey Bay, have established promotion and tenure guidelines that acknowledge faculty's scholarship of engagement. In her analysis of institutional commitment to service-learning, Holland (1999) considers an institution's support for faculty scholarship in service-learning as a key factor for the success and advancement of service-learning. This important issue exemplifies the way in which the faculty and institutional factors of service-learning institutionalisation are intertwined and mutually influential.

Other institutional structural issues that have been considered important for the advancement of service-learning include the establishment of a policy-making entity responsible for setting the academic and service standards for service-learning; the development and implementation of long-term strategic plans for service-learning; the establishment of formal course-review policies and procedures that ensure the academic and service integrity of service-learning are met; the importance of not having service-learning support be reliant solely on external funding; and the importance of establishing programme evaluation and accounting systems for service-learning. Although each of these factors has been described as being important for advancing high quality service-learning in higher education, the extent to which each of these factors affects the institutionalisation of service-learning has yet to be explored.

Some of the institutional programmatic features regarding service-learning institutionalisation have focused on the following: establishment of course review and approval procedures that ensure the academic rigour and service integrity of service-learning courses; the establishment of service-learning requirements for graduation; the development of official recognition of student service-learning participation in student transcripts; and the incorporation of service-learning identifiers and insignia in the schedules of classes and course catalogues. These institutional efforts are helpful in further securing service-learning is role in the mainstream activities of the academy. However, little is known about how these factors ultimately affect the institutionalisation of service-learning.

Issues to Consider

The implementation of the critical elements across the four previously mentioned areas takes much time, coordination, and effort. This begs the question: How long does it take to institutionalise service-learning on a college campus? The recent wave of service-learning funding initiative has, for the most part, imposed a de facto, three-year time line for institutionalisation. Most of the federal and foundation-supported grants for service-learning are based on three-year funding cycle. Campuses are usually expected to be able to sustain and ultimately institutionalise their service-learning activities beyond the grant. But does and can the institutionalisation of service-learning occur within this time frame, given the broad range of factors that must be considered and the many elements that must be carefully put in place?

The UC Berkeley study explored this issue for each of the three types of institutions. To determine significance of change in institutionalisation level (based on each institution's ISL score) over a three-year period, t-tests for significant differences within institutional type were conducted using the data from the *Benchmark Worksheet*. Despite the campuses' formal implementation of a broad set of service-learning institutionalisation activities, including the critical elements described in Table 6.2, the analysis found that none of the institutional types showed a significant advancement in its level of service-learning institutionalisation during this programme (see Table 6.4[3]). The implications of this finding are that perhaps, in actuality, it takes several years for institutions to move from one level of service-learning institutionalisation (for example, Level 1 – Critical Mass Building) to the next (for example, Level 2 – Quality Building) and that the full institutionalisation of service-learning requires a comprehensive, sustained effort that lasts for many years.

This finding should not be surprising given the slowness with which change occurs in higher education, especially when it comes to curricular reform. In his comprehensive review of American higher education, Lucas (1994) details how throughout its history, American higher education has not done well to welcome new reforms, even when those reforms were in alliance with the prevailing academic norms and goals. In this regard, there should be no expectation that the

---

3   Only twenty-nine institutions are represented in this analysis due to unreported data in either year one or year three. Only matched samples were used, which lowered the number of institutions represented in this analysis.

Table 6.4   Mean institutionalisation of service learning scores by institutional type and programme year

n=29³			
Year of Study	**Community Colleges (n=8)**	**Public Institutions (n=10)**	**Private Institutions (n=11)**
Year One ISL mean	31.06	34.81	31.40
Year Three ISL mean	35.11	39.14	35.79
Difference	+4.05	+4.33	+4.39
Probability	.04	.10	.16

Note: Results are considered significant at the .01 probability level.

institutionalisation of an effort like service-learning, which still has not gained full academic legitimacy, is likely to occur forthwith.

In addition, there is likely to be no universal road for institutionalising service-learning in higher education. Aside from prevailing contextual differences between institutions and their goals for service-learning, the institutionalisation of service-learning appears to be a multi-dimensional and some what amorphous process. Judit Ramaley suggests that service-learning is a complex endeavour that involves 'traversing swampy grounds' (Ramaley 2000, 92). Thus, the institutionalisation of service-learning may not be a linear process, as is suggested by the structure of the three levels of the *Benchmark Worksheet*, but rather, more likely involves the complex interplay of a broad set of multi-faceted dimensions that converge with an ever-evolving set of institutional, academic, and social factors.

There is some indication that the process for institutionalising service-learning is more spiral-like than linear. As was reported in a final report of the UC Berkeley study, institutions at the most advanced stage on institutionalisation (Level 3 – Sustained Institutionalisation) often found themselves periodically revisiting old concerns and issues regarding service-learning implementation and institutionalisation, suggesting that specific challenges in institutionalising service-learning often re-emerge even though they have been previously addressed (Bell et al. 2000). Consequently, the process for institutionalising service-learning is not finite, nor does it ever appear to reach completion. As the institution changes and evolves, the service-learning initiative, too, must change and evolve in order to stay in the mainstream of the academy.

Conclusion

Collectively, the issues presented uncover some of the important factors that are key to institutionalising service-learning in higher education. A deeper exploration of these and other factors can help us gain a better understanding of the essential elements that affect service-learning institutionalisation and provide insights into the ways institutions of higher education can move service-learning from the 'margins to the mainstream' (Pickeral and Peters 1996, 2).

The role of the faculty and the support of the institution's administration play major roles in the ways and extend to which service-learning is institutionalised on campuses. Despite some commonalities across campuses and various types of institutions, there is no one way to institutionalise service-learning in higher education. The unique and individual culture of a campus shapes the nature and tenor of service-learning and determines the hooks on which service-learning is secured. While some institutions adopt service-learning as a pedagogy to make learning more meaningful and relevant to students, other institutions adopt service-learning as a philosophy for enhancing their institution's public or civic mission. Regardless of the purpose for adopting service-learning, service-learning needs to be tied to the institution's mission.

Table 6.5   Dimensions of service learning institutionalisation

Dimensions	Components
Mission and Philosophy	Definitions of service learning
Faculty Support for and Involvement in Service Learning	Faculty involvement Faculty support Faculty leadership Faculty incentive and rewards
Institutional Support for Service Learning	Coordinating agent Policy-making entity Staffing Reporting lines Funding Administrative support Evaluation
Student Support for and Involvement in Service Learning	Student awareness Student incentives and rewards Student voice Student opportunities
Community Participation and Partnerships	Community awareness Community incentives and rewards Community agency voice Partnership status Mutual understanding

For all campuses, the institutionalisation of service-learning does not happen overnight. Even after three years of working toward institutionalisation, there was no significant advancement in the institutionalisation of service-learning on the forty-three campuses that participated in the UC Berkeley study. Therefore, the establishment of a long-term vision and strategic goals for service-learning becomes essential for providing a strong grounding and clear direction for service-learning.

Overall, more comprehensive study is needed to gain a deeper understanding of the dimensions that contribute most to the institutionalisation of service-learning in higher education. Although faculty and institutional issues appear to be primary in institutionalising service-learning in higher education, the full range of factors must be considered. At the very least, new investigations should consider at least five interdependent dimensions that appear to be part of all campuses' service-learning institutionalisation efforts (See Table 6.5).

Although not an exhaustive list, these dimensions form a conceptual framework that touches upon the key elements of service-learning institutionalisation. Understanding the ways in which each of these dimensions and their components are advanced on campuses, and how each dimension influences and interacts with the other dimensions, can hold the key to understanding how to best secure the long-term survival and success of service-learning in higher education.

References

Bell, R. et al. (2000), *Institutionalizing Service-Learning in Higher Education: Findings from a Study of the Western Region Campus Compact Consortium* (Western Region Campus Compact Consortium, Bellingham, WA: Western Washington University).

Bringle, R. et al (eds.) (1999), *Universities as Citizens* (Needham Heights, MA: Allyn & Bacon).

Canada, M. and Speck, B. (2001), *Developing and Implementing Service-Learning Programs* (San Francisco, CA, Jossey-Bass).

Driscoll, A (2000), 'Studying Faculty and Service-Learning: Directions for Inquiry and Development', *Michigan Journal of Community Service-learning* (Special Issues), 35–41.

Edington, P and Duffy D.K. (1996), 'Collaboration is Action: Service-Learning at Middlesex Community College' in Pickeral and Peters.

Furco, A. (2001), 'Advancing Service-Learning in Research Universities', in Canada and Speck (eds.)

Gray, M. et al. (1998), *Coupling Service and Learning in Higher Education: The Final Report of the Evaluation of the Learn and Serve American, Higher Education Programme* (Santa Monica: The RAND Corporation)

Holland, B. (1999), 'Factors and Strategies That Influence Faculty Involvement in Public Service', *The Journal of Public Service and Outreach* 4, 37–43.

Holland, B. (2000), 'Institutional Impacts and Organizational Issues Related to Service-Learning', *Michigan Journal of Community Service-learning* (Special Issue) Fall, 54–60.

Holland, B. et al. (1998), 'The State of the Engaged Campus: What Have We Learned about Building and Sustaining University and Community Partnerships', *AAHE Bulletin, American Association for Higher Education*, 51:1, 3–6.

Kecskes, K and Muyllaert, J. (1997), *Benchmark Worksheet for the Western Region Campus Compact Consortium Grants Programme* (Bellingham, WA: Western Washington University).

Kramer, M. (2000), *Make it Last Forever: The Institutionalization of Service-learning in America* (Washington DC: Corporation for National Service).

Lucas, C. J. (1994), *American Higher Education: A History* (New York: St. Martin's Griffin).

Miles, M. B. and Huberman, M.A. (1984), *Qualitative Data Analysis: A Sourcebook of New Methods* (Beverly Hills: Sage Publications).

Muller, P and Furco, A. (1998), *Evaluation of the Western Region Campus Compact Consortium (1997–1998)* (Berkeley: University of California, Berkeley).

O'Byrne, K. (2001), 'How Professors Can Promote Service-Learning in a Teaching Institution', in Canada and Speck.

Pickeral, T. and Peters, K. (1996), *From the Margins to the Mainstream: The Faculty Role for Advancing Service-Learning in Community Colleges* (Mesa, AZ: Campus Compact National Centre for Community Colleges).

Ramaley, J.A. (2000), 'Strategic Directions for Service-Learning Research: A Presidential Perspective', *Michigan Journal of Community Service-learning*, (Special Issues) Fall, 97–97

Rhoads, R.A. and Howard, J. (eds.) (1998), *Academic Service-learning: A Pedagogy of Action and Reflection* (San Francisco, CA: Jossey-Bass).

Robinson, G. (2000), 'Service-Learning at Community Colleges', *Horizons*, (Washington DC: America Association of Community Colleges).

Saltmarsh, J. (1998), 'Exploring the Meanings of Community/University Partnerships', *NSEE Quarterly* 23:4, 21–2.

Seifer, S. (1998), 'Service-Learning: Community-Campus Partnerships for Health Professions Education', *Academic Medicine* 73, 273–277.

Ward, K. (1998), 'Addressing Academic Culture: Service-Learning Organisations, and Faculty Work,' in Rhoads and Howard (eds.).

Zlotkowski, E. (1999), 'Pedagogy and Engagement', in Bringle et al.

Zlotkowski, E. (2000), 'Service-Learning Research in the Disciplines', *Michigan Journal of Community Service-learning*, (Special Issue) Fall, 61–67.

Chapter 7

The Process of Localising Pedagogies for Civic Engagement in Ireland: The Significance of Conceptions, Culture and Context

Josephine A. Boland and Lorraine McIlrath

Introduction

As the civic role of higher education attracts renewed critical attention internationally, a range of strategies have emerged which are designed – implicitly or explicitly – to foster greater civic engagement. Amongst these, certain credit bearing curriculum initiatives have been developed, variously called *community based learning* or *service learning*, primarily as pedagogic strategies to promote civic engagement, enhance student learning and serve community needs – principles, practices and examples of which are detailed in other chapters in this publication. This chapter is primarily concerned with how the 'localisation' process is enacted, that is the processes whereby the philosophy, principles and practices of a particular curriculum innovation are adapted (or even subverted) to reflect and serve local culture, context and conceptions. We have borrowed the term 'localisation' from industry, where it refers to the way in which products are adapted to non-native environments – often involving translation – to reflect local language and other practices. We argue that any attempt to embed a civic dimension or achieve what Furco (2003a) describes as the institutionalisation of service learning, requires a greater appreciation of and sensitivity to the significance of such factors. These mediating conditions pertain at national, institutional and disciplinary level and within those individual sites of practice inhabited by unique and autonomous academics.

An essential aspect of any localisation process is the development of a discourse – including terminology and labels – to signify the key characteristics, core principles and values inherent in the practices. To date, a number of terms exist to denote an array of closely related activities – for example internships, volunteering, service learning, community-based learning, community-university partnerships. Dialogue about their meaning and purpose is often hindered by the way some of these terms are used interchangeably, when in fact the practices they signify have quite different intentions. This becomes most evident as we research policy and academic practice in this field. The term 'service learning', which originated in the USA, has been adopted in Ireland as a catch-all for quite diverse practices. However, as evident from contributions to the first 'Service Learning Academy' held in Ireland in 2006, many academics were professionally uncomfortable with the concept of 'service'

(McIlrath 2006). While the term may resonate positively in the US, the various associations which the term 'service' has for many in Irish academic and public life renders it inappropriate and unhelpful. We also question the appropriateness of the term 'community based learning' especially, since, at this developmental stage the meaning of and place for 'community' remains largely unresolved. Moreover, community can be a highly contested space. For these reasons, we advocate the suspension of any attempt at definition or labelling. For the purpose of this discussion, we have provisionally adopted the term *pedagogies for civic engagement (PfCE)*, as a more apt, if rather unwieldy, label for the practices with which we are concerned.

Our discussion is informed by relevant literature, our research (individual and collaborative) and our reflections on experience gained in this field as teachers, researchers, educational developers and as participant observers in this fledgling arena, within Irish higher education and beyond. Our empirical research is ongoing and some initial findings have been presented elsewhere (Boland 2006; Boland et al. 2004; Boland and McIlrath 2005b). A number of case studies are in progress within a range of higher education institutions in Ireland, based on a multi-site case study methodology rooted in the interpretative paradigm, using interviews, documents, questionnaires and observation as sources of data (Boland forthcoming). Insights gleaned from key actors and individual academics in one particular institution (Boland and McIlrath 2005b) provide valuable perspectives into motivation and purpose. Opinions gathered in the two jurisdictions of Northern Ireland and the Republic of Ireland regarding citizenship education, by Niens and McIlrath (2006), have also informed our developing conceptual framework. While this paper is exploratory rather then evaluative in its intent, our initial research findings suggest some enabling conditions that support the development and sustainability of pedagogies for civic engagement within higher education. They also highlight some of the inherent tensions and inevitably raise some fundamental questions about the purpose of higher education.

The Term – Pedagogies for Civic Engagement (PfCE)

The concept of 'engagement' is a core value permeating any education project. Within higher education this concept comprehends engaging students in academic life, approaches to the design of an engaged curriculum and the realisation of an engaged campus – one that engages actively with the economy and civic society. The idea of engagement in higher education has been the subject of an unfolding debate, on both sides of the Atlantic and in both hemispheres – such concerns are shared, if articulated in diverse ways (Bjarnason and Coldstream 2003). The concept is multifaceted and challenging, and Coldstream (2003), Rooke (2003) and Barnett (2003) identify some key characteristics. Engagement infers mutual listening, reciprocity and dialogue which is focussed on something beyond the self. It comprehends both a promise of action and the outcome of action. Usually, it infers a permanent rather than a temporary condition and in certain contexts, rules of engagement exist. Engagement is full of potential, promise, risk and uncertainty, often because it entails a willingness to change. It entails accommodating the other and preparedness to be transformed in the process. It is concerned with strenuous, thoughtful, argumentative interaction with the wider world.

Clearly, engagement is a complex condition, but for the purpose of this chapter our focus is on curriculum strategies which are designed with engagement in mind. We characterise pedagogies for civic engagement as strategies designed to actively engage students in the learning process in a reflective and critical manner, through interaction and engagement with others. We use the term in its plurality to denote the multiplicity of potential academic practices which fulfil these characteristics. We include all aspects of strategic intent and curriculum design, including pedagogy and associated assessment methodologies. Coldstream (2003) suggests that civic engagement involves, not merely links to the outside world, but a genuine response to the needs of a myriad of constituencies. PfCE are designed to promote students' interaction with a range of constituencies, including the community (itself a contested term) and the non-profit sector (which is increasingly difficult to delineate in recent times). The role of the academic is to incorporate activities and learning experiences which afford students the opportunity to attain academic credit for reflection on experiential learning gained while engaged. Academic credit is gained on the basis of demonstrated application of theory (from the academic discipline/programme) to practice and for reflection on the experience.

Our conception of pedagogies for civic engagement draws upon the Barnett and Coate's (2005) model of the engaged curriculum, namely one which encompasses an appropriate balance of three domains of knowing, acting and being. PfCE provide an opportunity to promote the 'being' domain, in a manner which ensures integration with other aspects of the curriculum. These complementary dimensions are also reflected in Barnett's (2003) earlier elaboration of modes of engagement; *viz.* knowing (intellectual/disciplinary engagement); doing (work and practical engagement); and communicating (engaging with others). Pedagogies *for* civic engagement aim to achieve the integration of these dimensions, by requiring interrogation of the experience gained with a view to developing a sense of the civic self and a confidence in the potential for individual and collective civic engagement. This explicit focus on this affective and civic domain is also evident in the new European Qualifications Framework which identifies three strands of competences; *viz.* knowing and understanding; knowing how to act; knowing how to *be*. Clearly, this renewed interest in engagement, evident in both theory and policy, is suggestive of important conjunctures which will be revisited later in the discussion of the Irish policy context.

Philosophy, Principles and Practice – A Fundamental Question of Purpose

There is a substantial and growing literature in the field of service and community based learning. We share the view of Billig and Waterman (2003), however, that much of the research to date in this field has been largely descriptive and has failed to problematise the philosophy, principles and practice of service learning. The challenges which such pedagogies pose to traditional practices within academe, not least from an epistemological standpoint, have received some attention

(Howard 1998; Richman 1996). While philosophical defences have been offered by Liu (1995), Kezar and Rhoads (2001) and Scheman (2006), consideration of epistemological matters remain at the margins of educational discourse. Liu (1995) posits that the lack of a robust philosophical rationale for service learning partly accounts for its failure to challenge what he refers to as 'the dominant paradigm' and for its limited penetration into the mainstream of higher education. Barber (1984) traces the malaise of modern liberal politics to an epistemological stance that reifies a quest for certainty – a quest which proves so futile as to result in a generation of hesitant political sceptics, too unsure of right action to be active citizens in public life. A rather unfair dismissal of an entire generation, perhaps? Given their inherent (if seldom articulated) epistemology, pedagogies for civic engagement aim to tap into the desire of many young people to be informed and actively engaged citizens.

Of more fundamental importance, however, is ontological purpose, raising challenging questions which go to the heart of the purpose of higher education (Ehrlich 1998; Gutmann 1987). Transactional models of pedagogies of engagement are characterised by an exchange process; with the community as recipient of a service while students gain academic credit for experiential learning. Such exchanges leave conditions unchanged at best or worse, in the wake of withdrawal of a needed service to the community. Transformative models, on the other hand, seek to question and change the circumstances, conditions, values or beliefs which are at the root of community's or society's need. Conceptual models (Welch 2006) and academic practices (Avila 2006) have been developed which attempt to challenge existing models of civic engagement and transform academic and civic culture, thereby reflecting principles of emancipatory education as espoused by Habermas (1971) and Freire (1970). While some of the essential characteristics of transactional, transformative or even transcendental learning can be identified, the challenge of realising 'deeper' learning is compounded by what Barnett (1990) refers to as the absence of epistemological egalitarianism within higher education. The hegemony of traditional approaches to assessment is an even greater potential barrier to innovation in pedagogic practice at programme level. At a strategic level, the competing imperatives which prevail within contemporary higher education (for example, research excellence, the modernisation agenda, marketisation and globalisation) often serve to relegate civic/social goals to the margins (Boland 2004).

Contextual factors, other than that of discipline, rarely feature in the literature which highlights an array of 'toolkits' identifying opportunities for service learning in particular academic disciplines (for example Battistoni 2002; Bringle et al. 1998, Brubaker and Ostroff 2000). While conceptions of community, citizenship and civil society are contested and problematic (Edwards 2004; Mc Clave 2005) they remain, with some exceptions, largely unexplored within the literature on service learning. We have already identified what we believe to be the most intractable challenge; ensuring reciprocity within the learning triad of student, academic and community partners (Boland and McIlrath 2005b). The nature and dynamics of these relationships are both complex and contextual. We argue that to achieve reciprocity within the 'localisation' process we need to appreciate the conceptions which key actors (including academics and strategic managers) bring to the partnership and the values that underpin them. Moreover, failure to respond to issues of local conception, culture and context may further marginalise pedagogies for civic engagement. We will return to this point, with some examples below.

The Context of the Irish Higher Education System: Policy and Practice

Irish higher education is a binary system made up of seven universities and an extra-university sector comprising thirteen institutes of technology, a number of colleges of education and other specialist colleges. In Ireland, the level of participation in higher education (with over 55% of the school leaving cohort) is one of the highest in Europe (O'Connell et al. 2006). Despite a degree of 'mission drift' in recent years, higher education institutions on either side of the binary divide have clearly defined remits which have been enshrined in legislation. Both the legislative and funding frameworks provide powerful drivers for the development of institutional strategic priorities. Universities are governed by the Universities Act 1997, a piece of legislation which affords them an unrivalled degree of autonomy. The act places an onus on universities to develop a mission statement and the 'objects of a university' provide ample scope for the inclusion of strategic priorities which relate to civic and social goals. The institute of technology sector (other than the Dublin Institute of Technology, with its own legislation) is subject to the Regional Technical Colleges Act 1992 and more recently the Institutes of Technology Act 2006. While this legislation is less explicit regarding a civic orientation, it does not preclude one. The influence of legislation on the nature of the institutional strategic mission has been highlighted by O'Byrne (2004), who suggests that universities and institutes of technology may be distinguished from each other in the extent to which a civic role features as an explicit part of their strategic mission. Arising from her analysis of institutional mission statements, she maintains that the development of 'active citizenship' rarely features explicitly among the institutional priorities of institutes of technology. The existence or otherwise of statements relating to 'active citizenship' however, may prove a rather limited basis upon which to seek evidence of a civic role. Mission statements often belie the range of ways in which institutions engage with the local community and the region in the pursuit of economic, social and civic goals. Indeed, distinctions made between activity which is more vocationally oriented and that which is more civically orientated deserve further examination – such dualities rarely capture the complexity that is higher education.

Ireland's unequivocal commitment to the creation of a European Higher Education Area, as enunciated by the Conference of Ministers responsible for Higher Education (2003) and to the Bologna process has a significant bearing on domestic higher education policy making. The new European Qualifications Framework, referred to earlier, identifies 'preparation for active citizenship' as one of four purpose of higher education (Ministry of Science Technology and Innovation 2005) and in Ireland this sense of social or civic responsibility finds expression in certain provisions of the Qualifications (Education and Training) Act 1999. This act represents one of the most significant developments in Irish education in recent years and has led to the development of a new national framework of qualifications – designed *inter alia* to promote the maintenance of standards of awards made by further and higher education bodies, other than the universities.[1]

One development of potential significance at national policy level is the way in which social/civic objectives have been articulated within the National Framework of Qualifications[2] by the inclusion of *Insight* as one dimension of all awards. The competence of 'Insight' has been described as:

> ...the ability to engage in increasingly complex understanding and consciousness, both internally and externally, through the process of reflection on experience. Insight involves the integration of the other strands of knowledge, skill and competence with the learner's attitudes, motivation, values, beliefs, cognitive style and personality. This integration is made clear in the learner's mode of interaction with social and cultural structures of his/her community and society, while also being an individual cognitive phenomenon (National Qualifications Authority of Ireland 2003).

In making provision for the development of Insight as an explicit element of all academic awards, the National Qualifications Authority of Ireland has attempted to address that oft-neglected dimension of the higher education curriculum, referred to by Barnett and Coate (2005) as the 'being' dimension. It also encourages higher education institutions to research and teach what Edwards (2005) refers to as 'the social science of love', which include, a set of theories, models and empirical cases that show how politics, economics, social and international relations could be transformed by a radically different form of rationality. The provision of opportunities for learners to develop Insight could equally comprehend the concept of 'care' – caring *about* and caring *for* – which McClave (2005) contends is missing from classical liberal notions of citizenship education. Pedagogies for civic engagement provide a potentially powerful medium for realising these objectives of the framework and for paying attention to the being, caring, loving and reasoning dimension of human and societal development.

While the 'Insight' dimension has been identified by (Maguire 2005) as a potential driver which could prompt a re-shaping of higher education curricula, its impact has been difficult to discern. Like many constructs of its kind, the meaning and significance of 'Insight' is far from clear to many users of the framework – this is clearly evident from case studies carried out to date (Boland forthcoming). Curriculum responses vary widely and academic staff are generally unaware of the existence of this dimension of the framework. It has proved possible to satisfy validation requirements of awarding bodies with notional, aspirational statements regarding Insight in programme documents, often written by programme directors

---

1   While the NQAI has no authority over the university sector, the act requires the existing seven universities to cooperate and give all reasonable assistance to the university.

2   The National Framework of Qualifications was launched in Ireland October 2003 by the National Qualification Authority of Ireland. The framework sets out explicitly, for the first time a set of descriptors, based on learning outcomes, for national awards over 10 levels, up to and including doctoral level. The eights dimensions of qualifications within the framework, including 'Insight', are described in detail on the Framework website at http://www.nfq.ie/nfq/en/.

rather than individual academics. The limited impact of this pioneering dimension of the framework could be regarded as indicative of a 'light touch' approach to policy implementation. Granville (2003) portrays the framework as consultative rather than directive, in marked contrast to more regulatory approaches to policy implementation in other jurisdictions (Philips 2003). A consultative, non-directive, enabling approach is characteristic of policy making within Irish education. It has served as an effective means of negotiating powerful conflicting interests in a cultural milieu characterised by an antipathy to regulation and control. Thus, the enabling framework provides further evidence of the significance of contextual, cultural and ideological factors which Walshe (1999), Sugrue (2004) and O'Sullivan (2006) identify as pervasive in consensual Irish education policy making. Such factors account for the individualised way in which policy is mediated in different settings and circumstances within Irish higher education. In particular, it helps account for the way in which embedding Insight will remain a highly individualised and contextualised process. Thus, while the concept of Insight represents a powerful and pioneering statement of intent in relation to the higher education curriculum, we contend that enabling legislation is an insufficient condition for the realisation of civic goals or for the effective 'localisation' of innovative and challenging dimensions of the framework.

Quite apart from legislative provisions and public policy considerations, funding, of course, provides a powerful incentive for action. The Higher Education Authority (HEA) is the statutory body responsible for planning and development of higher education and research in Ireland and, critically, for funding throughout the sector. Through its new funding models and targeted initiatives, the HEA has become a powerful instrument of public policy in the arena of higher education (Higher Education Authority 2006). HEA policy has proved an influential driver in support of organisational change, in particular the 'modernisation' agenda and the development of Irish higher education as a centre for world class research. While initiatives to support the achievement of broader social policy goals, access, widening participation, equity and diversity, feature prominently, support for initiatives specifically focussed on civic engagement have been less in evidence. Significantly, the most recent funding call for proposals, under the Strategic Innovation Fund (SIF), lists '…the development of the individual student to attain their full capacity both in careers and as citizens in a democratic society facing profound change' (Higher Education Authority 2006, 2). The explicit inclusion of education for citizenship as a strategic priority for higher education is important, especially since it did not feature in the recommendations arising from the OECD (2004) review of higher education. The priority afforded to transdisciplinary, collaborative projects, across institutions on either side of the binary divide augurs well for the further development of pedagogies for civic engagement across the sector. In addition to enabling legislation and strategic funding, however other conditions need to be in place to promote the 'localisation' process, not least of which is a sufficiently motivating rationale.

The Rationale for Pedagogies for Civic Engagement within Ireland

National Level

Our analysis of the rationale for and values inherent in PfCE reveals further evidence, if such were needed, of the competing imperatives within the discourse of higher education policy and practice. Many of these tensions have been explored on both sides of the Atlantic (Barnett 2000; Giroux 2002; Newman et al. 2004) and by Kelly (2002) and Lynch (2006) in the specific context of Irish higher education. These forces are acutely experienced by all higher education institutions as they adjust to the forces of managerialism, neo-liberalism and globalisation (Boland 2004; Deem 2001). Shumar (2002) claims that the pressures upon higher education institutions which arise from the inherent contradictions of global capitalism have produced two types of legitimacy crisis in higher education. The first is a crisis about the meaning and purpose of education. The second is a deeper challenge concerning the production of new knowledge; how to pay for it and who will control its production. He expresses some concern that, if service learning represents one way to address the legitimacy crisis and serve as part of the solution to the pressures of commodification, then implementation on a large scale might result in their adaptation to the needs of a more market-driven university. In recognition of *realpolitik*, we submit, however, that social/civic goals *need* to be aligned to, and supportive of, other institutional strategic objectives – such as the pursuit of excellence in teaching and research – and thereby contribute to the realisation of that pressing imperative, namely maintaining competitive advantage in an increasingly global marketplace. We argue that failure to do so inevitably relegates what Howard (1998) has termed a 'counternormative pedagogy' to the margins of academe.

The rationale proffered for PfCE is multifaceted and complex. In principle, many such initiatives have been adopted by institutions, or by individual academics, to enhance academic learning, promote institutional civic responsibility and the skills of citizenship while enhancing community capacity through service. In practice, the rationale reflects aspects of the prevailing policy discourse, which varies in different jurisdictions and from time to time, such as widening participation, promoting lifelong learning, facilitating knowledge transfer, strengthening civil society, supporting democratic practice or addressing social cohesion. This is an important element of the process of validation of practice within a given policy context. Lifelong learning policy in the UK, for example, features explicitly in the rationale for many university/community partnerships, where the widening participation agenda provides the strategic imperative and often the source of funding (Annette 2006). In England, many university/community engagement projects there can be seen to be closely aligned with knowledge transfer, or more recently 'knowledge exchange' policy, which provides the means for funding projects aligned with the Higher Education Funding Council for England (HEFCE) policy on 'third stream' activities (Whittmore 2006). Addressing social exclusion features prominently in initiatives aiming to support community projects (Banks and MacDonald 2003). The impact of the prevailing policy framework is also evidenced in the reorientation of projects so as to align with new priorities in public policy, for example from widening participation to diversity (Nursaw 2006).

The concept of social capital, and concerns regarding its perceived decline, features prominently in political discourse in post-Celtic Tiger[3] Ireland (Healy 2001). The need to foster the growth of social capital features in the rationale for civic engagement strategies within higher education and in other parts of the education system. While such concerns may exercise the hearts and minds of political leaders, public funding for such initiatives within higher education has been, until recently, unavailable. Prominent Irish examples of pedagogies for civic engagement in recent years have largely thrived on the strength of philanthropic funding matched by institutional commitment, both strategic and fiscal. Other sources of support include funding from national bodies, such the Department of Community, Rural and Gaeltacht Affairs and the Higher Education Authority..

A number of recent national policy initiatives aim to address these growing concerns regarding civil society and social capital. One such is the establishment of the 'Taskforce on Active Citizenship'.[4] The taskforce aims to consider the extent to which people in Ireland play an active role as members of their communities and society, identify factors affecting the level and nature of active citizenship in different areas of Irish life and suggest ways in which people can be encouraged and supported to play an active role (Taskforce on Active Citizenship 2006). In its submission to the 'Taskforce', the Higher Education Authority (HEA) affirms the role of higher education in advancing social and civic goals, highlighting the range of ways in which it has supported initiatives which address these goals, including their support for the 'Service Learning Academy'. This academy, comprising academics and policy makers, is the beginning of a movement to reassert the civic mission of higher education through the development and dissemination of values and practices which support pedagogies for civic engagement.

When it comes to recognition of the role which higher education has to play in advancing civic and social goals, clearly the rhetoric is not lacking. In her address to the Irish Universities Association, the Minister for Education and Science affirmed the particular value of the humanities and social sciences:

> ... the challenges that we face are also grounded in the older and more fundamental responsibilities of institutions of higher learning in any civilised society. These relate to the development of individuals as independent and creative thinkers, the promotion of active citizenship and support for ethical values. They relate to the protection and enhancement of vital tenets of our history and culture, to the search for social justice nationally and globally, to the questioning of authority, to the deepening of our understanding of ourselves and the world around us and to the enrichment of our lives through a deepened recognition and appreciation of the values that matter in society (Minister for Education and Science 2006, 1).

---

3   The *Celtic Tiger* is the term used for the Republic of Ireland during its period of rapid economic growth between the 1990s and the early 2000s.

4   For additional information on the establishment and work of the 'Taskforce on Active Citizenship', access http://www.activecitizen.ie

The task of realising this inclusive vision of higher education within individual institutions is more challenging. The range of curriculum initiatives reflects the diversity of the sector as institutions develop their own responses, which are situated within the prevailing national policy context and reflect local conditions and strengths.

Institutional Level

Within an institutional setting, the motivations of senior management and key actors supporting the embedding of pedagogies for civic engagement are diverse. Enhancing student learning, creating an engaged campus, countering the drift from the public to the private domain, getting the edge over competitors in the higher education market, all feature. Particular local contextual factors also prove significant.

> ...the markets sort of control the universities in very many ways and it's a bit concerning. And I think probably here .... We may be more of a left-leaning institution than somewhere else, so there's always been that concern for the community being left out, as it were. So there's been that attempt at least to balance that – we've always prided ourselves as having good links with the city and having good community knowledge, and remembering where we've come from. So there's that sense of obligation there. (Interview: key actor, university administration)

Different conceptions of citizenship, social capital and civil society have been explored in the literature (Demaine 1996; Edwards 2004; Kilpatrick et al. 2003). These conceptions are interrelated, contested and while their relevance for higher education is far from clear, they provide valuable theoretical lenses with which to explore ideological perspectives. Edwards (2004), for example, identifies three theoretical positions in relation to civil society (*viz.* Associational Life, The Good Society and The Public Sphere) and while each is acknowledged as legitimate and incomplete, they provide a valuable framework for analysing the rationale for pedagogies for civic engagement proffered by key actors at institutional level.

Civil society as *Associational Life* is concerned with the creation of a healthy associational ecosystem and sees civil society as that part of society formed for the purpose of facilitating collective action, which is the 'third sector' within a three sector model of society comprising the state, the market and non-profit groups. This conception of civil society is clearly evident in those who see volunteering and civic engagement as a means to prepare students to play their part as active citizens.

> That was our big goal when all this was set out... that with the despair that many people express with the collapse of community life, that we were saying 'how can we get students to equip themselves for a life of service, rather than just a few hours while they're here? (Interview: key actor in a PfCE project)

The prevalence of this conception of civil society is evident from the discourse of many key actors and academics currently engaged in pedagogies for civic engagement. This may reflect current concerns about declining social capital, referred to earlier. It may also derive from a deep rooted sense of community and the value which was traditionally placed on associational life in Irish society, pre-Celtic Tiger. This conception of civil society is also evident in much of the political discourse, as revealed in the words of the Taoiseach (prime minister of Ireland) Bertie Ahern T.D when launching the 'Taskforce on Active Citizenship':

> To me, an active citizen is one who is aware of what is happening around them and strives towards the common good. It is about accepting a responsibility to help others and being happy to contribute to improve the quality of life of those less fortunate than ourselves. I feel that active citizenship should be seen as a privilege – where we can make a difference to the lives of others by actively participating in the life of the society around us. …At the heart of active citizenship is that sense of shared values, of belonging in the community and of pride in our place and our country. (Ahern 2006, 1)

More normative models of civil society find expression in the *Good Society* conception – as the realm of service rather than self interest – with an emphasis on a desirable social order with high levels of trust, tolerance and cooperation and institutional arrangements across sectors of society (Edwards 2004). As such, the role of higher education in addressing systematic issues of equity and social exclusion is closely related to this conception, as evident in the rationale for PfCE proffered by one university senior manager.

> Where once school represented a postponement of maturity, university now does…. Students are going around in packs, attending lectures where they have no individual responsibility…. This retreat from the public domain is typified by the dominance of private entertainment devices which provide private self-gratification… While we have mass participation, only a particular 50% of society progress to higher education – we have a responsibility to do more than just serve the needs of the privileged. (Interview: senior manager in an institution with PfCE projects)

Civil society as *Public Sphere* is concerned with the creations of a polity that cares about the common good and has a capacity to deliberate about it democratically as active rather than passive players. This conception infers a capacity for dialogic politics as a means to reach a legitimate normative consensus around a plurality of interest – highly relevant to the needs of contemporary Irish society.

> Our graduates are key players in the process of change whether in the field of medicine, economics, law etc. Equipping people to *cope* with change puts the accent on the passive. I would propose that the equipping of our graduates to be active players in the process of change in our society (and beyond) should be one of our core aims. (Interview: key actor in the initiation of a PfCE project)

Edwards (2004) submits that these conceptions of civil society are complementary rather contradictory and that they can be combined into a mutually supporting framework. Within higher education, however, these different conceptions of civil society have implications for critical issues of pedagogic practice. The *Associational Life* and *Good Society* conceptions infer a pedagogy of engagement which can be located closer to the volunteering end of Furco's (2003b) taxonomy of service learning models. The *Public Sphere* conception infers a model of education shaped by principles and practices of academic democracy advocated by Apple and Beane, (1995) Roland (2003) and Dryzek (2000). Indeed, the co-existence of volunteering projects alongside pedagogies for civic engagement with a transformative purpose within the microcosm of individual higher education institutions, is testament to the complementarity of conceptions of civil society.

Academic Practice

The significance of prior experience, disciplinary field, orientations to practice and personal values is apparent in the discourse of academics who have used PfCE as a methodology in their courses. A survey of academic staff in one higher education institution reveals a range of motivations of academic staff for adopting this pedagogy (Boland and McIlrath, 2005a). The opportunity to enhance the student learning experience features prominently, as does the opportunity to develop civic responsibility and to give something back to the community. For some academics, the principles of PfCE resonate with their personal political standpoints and represent a welcome vehicle for advocating social justice. Within an institution that places value on, which is often referred to as, 'service to university and wider community' in the career promotional process, involvement in PfCE can also contribute positively to their professional portfolio. The availability of seed-funding for PfCE projects cannot be discounted as an inducement – but does not feature as a significant motivation.

The significance of academics' prior experience in volunteering, service learning or pro-bono work is a recurring factor in all institutional settings.

> …because I did it myself, my own personal background is when I went to college, I did three years with the Simon Community in Cork… part of it is my own personal beliefs of trying to give something back to the greater community. So that's a little bit of the propelling force (Interview: academic involved in a Pf CE project).

The significance of academic discipline is evident in how academics use discipline-specific theoretical constructs when determining learning outcomes for a PfCE project, providing guidelines to students and identifying criteria for assessment. Discipline specific constructs can also provide justification for PfCE – to students, other academic staff and senior management – within an institution where the practice might be deemed unorthodox and in need of legitimacy.

> I was doing the theory anyway as part of the learning outcomes of my course. So I decided to build in a practical component and I asked them to go out and find,…an organisation that had to have an altruistic bent to it. … [a discipline specific theory] became the name of the project – that was how I could link it in… I have to link that in otherwise how can I get away with justifying such a practical component unless there is a theoretical basis, because there is an exam as well …. (Interview: academic involved in a PfCE project)

Endorsement for PfCE features as an important enabling factor and the quest for legitimacy manifests itself in many ways. By developing intra and inter-institutional support networks, such as the Service Learning Academy, academics gain support and endorsement from their colleagues on a communities of practice model.

Strategies used within the host department include involving colleagues in evaluation of projects and mounting exhibitions of student work in public spaces. Where academics perceive an absence of institutional support, these counternormative practices generally survive by virtue of remaining 'below the radar' until they gain legitimacy – often on the strength of student endorsement.

Conclusions

The term *pedagogies for civic engagement* has been chosen to denote a range of academic initiatives which have civic engagement as a core value. This discussion has focussed on the process of localising the principles and practices of such pedagogies in the particular context of Irish higher education, where they are at an early stage of development. We assert that the process is mediated by a range of factors – including culture and context – at national and institutional level.

Despite being supportive of a civic dimension, the legislative framework – notably the new national framework of qualifications – to date has proved less than effective in bringing about a shift in that direction within higher education, largely through a combination of lack of awareness and the 'light touch' approach to implementation. The particular social, economic and cultural context of post-Celtic Tiger Ireland has a significant bearing – as highlighted by contrasting policy-led approaches in neighbouring jurisdictions. Conceptions of citizenship and civil society, including those held by our political leaders, have significant impact on the discourse of higher education policy, with translation into strategic funding priorities less in evidence. We argue that, despite repeated claims regarding the unrelenting effects of globalisation on higher education policy and practice, the process of adopting, adapting and subverting the concept of 'service learning' is a highly localised one.

References

Ahern, B. (2006), 'Speech by Taoiseach, Mr Bertie Ahern T.D. at the first regional seminar of the Taskforce', *Taskforce on Active Citizenship* [website] <http://www.activecitizen.ie/index.asp?locID=12&docID=52>, accessed 16 October 2006.

Annette, J. (2006), 'Birkbeck: linking London Lifelong Learning Network and civic/community engagement', *Conference on Higher Education and Civic/Community Engagement*, 7 July 2006 (London: Birkbeck College, University of London).

Apple, W. and Beane, J. (1995), *Democratic Schools* (Alexandria, Vermont: Association for Supervision and Curriculum Development).

Avila, M. (2006), 'Community Organising Techniques as a Model to Transform Academic and Civic Culture: Building a Relationship of Culture', *Service Learning Academy,* 31 April 2006 (Athlone: Service Learning Academy).

Banks, L. and MacDonald, D. (2003), *Refugees into Education: A Report from the Health and Social Policy Research Centre at the University of Brighton for the Community University Partnership Programme* (Brighton: University of Brighton).

Barber, B. (1984), *Strong Democracy* (Berkeley, CA: University of California Press).

Barnett, R. (1990), *The Idea of a University* (Buckingham: Society for Research into Higher Education).

Barnett, R. (2000), 'University Knowledge in an Age of Supercomplexity', *Higher Education* 40:4, 409–422.

Barnett, R. (2003), 'Engaging Students', in: S. Bjarnason and P. Coldstream (eds.).

Barnett, R. and Coate, K. (2005), *Engaging the Curriculum in Higher Education* (Buckingham: SRHE and Open University Press).

Battistoni, R. M. (2002), *Civic Engagement across the Curriculum: A Resource Book for Service-learning Faculty in all Disciplines* (Providence, RI: Campus Compact).

Billig, S. and Waterman, A. (eds.) (2003), *Studying Service Learning: Innovations in Educational Research Methodology* (New Jersey, NJ: Lawrence Erlbaum Associates).

Bjarnason, S. and Coldstream, P. (eds.) (2003), *The Idea of Engagement: Universities in Society* (London: Association of Commonwealth Universities).

Boland, J. (2004), 'A civic role for higher education? Some implications for policy and practice', *Globalisation and Inclusion Joint Conference of Development Cooperation Ireland (DCI) and University College Cork (UCC)*, 31 May 2006 (Cork: University College Cork).

Boland, J. (2006), 'Conceptions of engagement within the Irish higher education curriculum', *Education Studies Association of Ireland 2006 Annual Conference*, 1 April 2006 (Dublin: National College of Art and Design (NCAD)).

Boland, J. (forthcoming), *The Policy, Process and Practice of Embedding a Civic Dimension into the Irish Higher Education Curriculum* (Edinburgh: University of Edinburgh).

Boland, J., Mac Labhrainn, I. and McIlrath, L. (2004), 'Universities, Students and Community: Promoting Civic Engagement through Service Learning', *Annual Conference of the Society for Research into Higher Education*, 15 December 2004 (Bristol: University of Bristol).

Boland, J. and McIlrath L. (2005a), 'Culture and Context: the Process of Localising Service Learning in Ireland', *International Conference on Civic Engagement and Service Learning*, 23 June 2005 (Galway: National University of Ireland, Galway).

Boland, J. and McIlrath, L. (2005b), 'Developing New Learning Communities through Teaching, Research and Service – A Case Study', *All Ireland Society for Higher Education (AISHE) and Staff and Educational Development Association (SEDA) Annual Conference*, 13 May 2005 (Belfast: SEDA and AISHE).

Bringle, R. G. and Duffy, D. K. (1998), *With Service in Mind: Concepts and Models for Service-learning in Psychology* (Washington DC: American Association for Higher Education and American Psychological Association).

Brubaker, D. C. and Ostroff, J. H. (2000), *Life, Learning, and Community: Concepts and Models for Service-learning in Biology* (Washington, DC: American Association for Higher Education).

Campus Compact (2003) *Introduction to Service Learning Toolkit*, 2nd Edition. (Providence, RI: Campus Compact).

Coldstream, P. (2003), 'Engagement – an unfolding debate', in Bjarnason S. and Coldstream P. (eds.).

Conference of Ministers Responsible for Higher Education (2003), *Realising the European Higher Education Area: A communiqué of the Conference of ministers responsible for higher education* (Berlin: European Commission).

Deem, R. (2001), 'Globalisation, New Managerialism, Academic Capitalism and Entrepreneurialism in Universities: Is the Local Dimension Still Important?', *Comparative Education*, 37:1, 7–20.

Demaine, J. (1996), 'Beyond Communitarianism: Citizenship, Politics and Education', in: J. Demaine and H. Entwistle (eds.)

Demaine J. and Entwistle H. (eds.) (1996), *Beyond Communitarianism: Citizenship, Politics and Education* (London: Macmillan).

Dryzek, J.S. (2000), *Deliberative Democracy and Beyond* (Oxford: Oxford University Press).

Edwards, M. (2004), *Civil Society* (Cambridge: Polity Press).

Edwards, M. (2005), 'Love, Reason and the Future of Civil Society', *International Conference on Civic Engagement and Service Learning: Universities, Students and Community, 24 June 2005* (Galway: National University of Ireland, Galway).

Ehrlich, T. (1998), 'Reinventing John Dewey's 'Pedagogy as a University Discipline', *Elementary School Journal*, 98:5, 489–509.

Freire, P. (1970), *Pedagogy of the Oppressed* (New York: Continuum Publishing Corporation).

Furco, A. (2003a), *Self-Assessment Rubric for the Institutionalization of Service Learning in Higher Education* (Berkeley, CA: Service-Learning Research and Development Centre, University of California).

Furco, A. (2003b), 'Service-learning: A balanced approach to experiential learning', in Campus Compact.

Giroux, H. A. (2002), 'Neoliberalism, Corporate Culture, and the Promise of Higher Education: The University as a Democratic Public Sphere', *Harvard Educational Review* 72:4, 425–463.

Granville, G. (2003), '"Stop making sense": chaos and coherence in the formulation of the Irish qualifications framework', *Journal of Education and Work*, 16:3, 259–270.

Gutmann, A. (1987), *Democratic Education* (Princeton: Princeton University Press).

Habermas, J. (1971), *Knowledge and Human Interests* (Boston: Beacon Press).

Healy, T. (2001) 'Networks and social norms can be good for business: the role of social capital in organisations'. *Social Capital: Interdisciplinary Perspectives* (University of Exeter, Higher Education Authority (2006), Strategic Innovation Fund: Call for Proposals [website] <http://www.hea.ie/index.cfm/page/sub/id/1122>, accessed 2 October 2006.

Howard, J. P. F. (1998), 'Academic service learning: A counternormative pedagogy', in Rhoads R. and Howard J. (eds.).

Kelly, A. V. (2002), 'The Idea of a University Revisited', *Irish Educational Studies*, 22:2, 101–116.

Kezar, A. and Rhoads, R. A. (2001), 'The Dynamic Tensions of Service Learning in Higher Education – A Philosophical Perspective', *Journal of Higher Education*, 72:2, 148–171.

Kilpatrick, S., Field, J. and Falk, I. (2003), 'Social Capital: an Analytical Tool for Exploring Lifelong Learning and Community Development', *British Educational Research Journal*, 29:3, 417–433.

Liu, G. (1995), 'Knowledge, Foundations and Discourse: Philosophical support for service-learning', *Michigan Journal of Community Service Learning*, Volume 2, Fall:1996, 5–18.

Lynch, K. (2006), 'Neo-liberalism and Marketisation: The Implications for Higher Education', *European Educational Research Journal* 5:1, 1–17.

Maguire, B. (2005), 'Civic Engagement in the Irish National Framework of Qualifications', *International Conference on Civic Engagement and Service Learning*, 24 June 2005 (Galway: National University of Ireland, Galway).

McClave, H. (2005), '"Ourselves with others": exploring the boundaries of citizenship education', *Sixth Annual Citizenship Education Conference in England, Ireland, Northern Ireland, Scotland and Wales* (Killiney: Dublin)

Service Learning Academy (2006), Service Learning Academy Open Space Technology Report, *Service Learning Academy: A collaborative project between the National University of Ireland, Galway, National University of Ireland Maynooth, Dublin City University (DCU) and Dublin Institute of Technology (DIT)*. (Hodson Bay Hotel: Athlone)

Hanafin, M. (2006), 'Society values graduates from the humanities and social sciences', Mary Hanafin T.D., Minister for Education and Science, Humanities and Social Sciences in the 21st Century Ireland, 24 October, 2006 (Dublin: Irish Universities Association)

Newman, F., Couturier, L. and Scurry, J. (2004), *The Future of Higher Education: Rhetoric, Reality, and the Risks of the Market* (San Francisco, CA: Jossey-Bass).

Niens, U. and McIlrath, L. (2006), 'Understandings of citizenship education: Northern Ireland and Republic of Ireland', (Dublin: European Year of Citizenship through Education 2005, Curriculum Development Unit, NUI Galway and University of Ulster).

Nursaw, C. (2006), 'University and community partnerships', Conference on Higher Education and Civic/Community Engagement, 7 July 2006 (London: Birkbeck College, University of London).

O' Byrne, C. (2004), 'Higher Education in Ireland – should it, can it, and does it promote active citizenship?', International Conference on Civic Engagement and Service Learning, 23 June 2005 (Galway: National University of Ireland, Galway).

O'Connell, P. Clancy, D. and McCoy, S. (2006), Who went to college in 2004: A national survey of new entrants to higher education' (Dublin: Higher Education Authority).

O'Sullivan, D. (2006), *Cultural Politics and Irish Education since the 1950s: Policy, Paradigms and Power* (Dublin: Institute of Public Administration).

Organisation for Economic Co-operation and Development (2004), Review of national policies for education: Review of higher education in Ireland (Strasbourg: OECD).

Philips, D. (2003), 'Lessons from New Zealand's National Qualifications Framework', *Journal of Education and Work*, 16:3, 289–304.

Richman, R. (1996), 'Epistemology, communities and experts: A response to Goodwin Liu', *Michigan Journal of Community Service-learning*, Volume 3, Fall: 1996, 5–12.

Rhoads, R and Howard J. (eds.) (1998), *Academic Service Learning: A Pedagogy of Action and Reflection. New Directions for Teaching and Learning* (San Francisco, CA: Jossey- Bass).

Roland, S. (2003), 'Teaching for democracy in higher education', *Teaching in Higher Education*, 8:1, 90–101.

Scheman, N. (2006), 'A post-modern epistemology for 21st century universities', The University and Civil Society: Autonomy and Responsibility, 19 May 2006 (Bologna: University of Bologna and University of Denver).

Shumar, W. (2001), 'Service learning and internet-based learning: two movements in the effort to de-commodify higher education', Higher Education Close Up Conference 2, 16 July 2001 (Lancaster: Lancaster University).

Sugrue, C. (2004), *Ideology and Curriculum: Irish Experiences, International Perspectives* (Dublin: Liffey Press).

Taskforce on Active Citizenship (2006), Public Consultation Paper 'Together, We're Better' (Dublin: Taskforce on Active Citizenship).

Walshe, J. (1999), *A New Partnership in Education. From Consultation to Legislation in the Nineties* (Dublin: Institute of Public Administration).

Welch, M. (2006), 'Service learning as Deeper Education', Service Learning Academy, 31 April 2006 (Athlone: Service Learning Academy).

Whittmore, S. (2006), 'Higher Education-Community engagement in the developing policy and funding framework', Community-university partnerships for community-university benefits CUPP Conference, 7 April 2006 (Brighton: University of Brighton).

PART 3
Embedding Process and Practice

Chapter 8

Identifying and Teaching Civic Engagement Skills through Service Learning

Marshall Welch

Introduction

Service learning as been viewed as a form of civically engaged scholarship (Billig and Welch 2004) and as such, has the potential to help students develop as good citizens in a just and democratic society (Harkavy 2004). Similarly, there is increasing discussion and demand for infusing civic engagement into the academic experience of students, especially within higher education (Colby et al. 2003). Kahne, and colleagues maintained that higher education has a critical role in promoting civic engagement. They also proposed that research on civic engagement should focus on 'strategies for supporting the development of informed, thoughtful, and active citizens' (Kahne et al. 2000, 49). This moves us 'away from questions of whether service learning works and toward richer conceptualisations of service, of learning, of citizenship, and of the relationship between them' (Kahne et al. 2000, 49). Specifically, these authors proposed that higher education has a role of preparing participatory citizens.

A new type of civic engagement known as 'service-politics' has emerged as part of this discussion. The term was defined in *The New Student Politics*: *Wingspread Statement on Student Civic Engagement* as:

> The bridge between community service and conventional politics...participation in community service is a form of unconventional political activity that can lead to social change, in which participants primarily work outside of governmental institutions; service politics becomes the means through which students can move from community service to political engagement. Those who develop connections to larger systemic issues building on their roots in community service adopt a framework through which service politics lead to greater social change (Long 2002, 18).

The challenge, then, is to explore how to create and assess learning opportunities that combine service and citizenship. Integrating service-politics into service learning classes appears to be one viable approach that warrants exploration and critical analysis. This is in keeping with calls within the professional literature for continued assessment of what constitutes effective service learning courses (Eyler and Giles 1999; Eyler 2000). Gelmon and colleagues argued that we must demonstrate the impact of service learning and in the context of the engaged campus. They suggested that 'assessment serves a useful purpose as a mechanism to tell the story of what one has learned from one's work – articulating that learning for oneself as well as for others' (Gelmon et al. 2001, 4).[1]

This chapter describes a response to that charge by describing an innovative service learning course that incorporated service-politics to help students develop skills that promote civically engaged citizens. A review of civic engagement skills is provided. The enumeration of skills includes a brief description and overview of a method known as reciprocal validity (Welch Miller and Davies, 2005) used to validate and cross-reference skills found in the professional literature with perspectives of multiple constituencies. The chapter continues with a description of class activities and outcome measures to assess course impact on the community as well as students' cognitive and civic development.

Civic Engagement Skills

Saltmarsh (2002) suggested that preparing students to be civically engaged requires generating and teaching new knowledge and skills such as how to problem solve and think critically to initiate social action in community settings. Colby and colleagues (2003) identified and described principles of best practice that constitute a pedagogy of engagement. These include: active learning, learning as a social process, knowledge shaped by contexts, reflective practice, and capacity to represent an idea in more than one modality. Battistoni (2002) enumerated eight specific skills students need to be engaged citizens. These include:

1) Political knowledge and critical thinking skills.
2) Communication skills.
3) Public problem solving.
4) Civic judgment.
5) Civic imagination and creativity.
6) Collective action.
7) Community/coalition building; and
8) Organisational analysis.

To validate these theoretically based skills, a cadre of five undergraduate student research fellows conceptualised and implemented a series of focus group dialogues with four distinct constituencies. The process employed a process characterised as reciprocal validity. (See Welch et al. 2005). The investigation was designed to identify critical components of civic engagement, necessary skills for students to become civically engaged citizens, and the role of an urban research institution to promote civic engagement. A total of twenty seven discrete skills were identified and then cross-referenced with skills enumerated in the professional literature (See Table 8.1). The initial results indicate a general consensus of skills identified by focus group participants and those listed in the literature. More importantly, an authentic

---

1   Note assessment here means research and/or evaluation.

audience of directors from non profit agencies and religious leaders, who would be expected to value and practice civic engagement, validated thirteen (48%) of the skills enumerated in the professional literature. Students also reported thirteen skills (48%) found in the literature, although there was some difference from those identified by the non profit agency directors and religious leaders. It was somewhat surprising that faculty only identified eight skills (29%) found in the literature. The results were useful in conceptualising the course in an attempt to include and teach as many of these skills as possible. While it is generally not feasible to incorporate all twenty seven skills into a single course, those consistently identified were addressed in the course described below.

Course Description

The course was part of an honours programme at the junior level (third year) entitled *Service-Politics and Civic Engagement*. The honours programme promotes an enriched academic environment for talented and highly motivated students in an effort to foster values of social responsibility, inclusiveness and academic quality. Students must apply and be admitted to the programme in which class enrolment is typically limited to fifteen students. The course met once a week for three hours per session over fifteen weeks during the fall semester of the 2003/2004 and 2004/2005 academic years. The course texts included *The New Student Politics*: *Wingspread Statement on Student Civic Engagement* (Long 2002), *The New Citizenship: Unconventional Politics, Activism, and Service* (Rimmerman 2001), assorted readings and a supplementary curriculum. The instructor created an informal 'handbook' on service-politics and civic engagement that students accessed online during the second year the course was taught (Welch 2004). As described later in detail, the service learning component was somewhat unique from traditional applications of the pedagogy. Typically, service learning projects provide direct service to individuals or clients such as serving meals at a shelter, tutoring children at a school, or doing restorative work at environmental sites. Instead, the concept of service-politics as defined above was incorporated by having students provide indirect service working directly with an organisation to create, implement, and assess activities that promoted systemic change or addressed policy issues.

Topics and Skills

The topical areas for readings and class discussions were taken primarily from the texts and discussions included an exploration of typology of service, ranging from occasional/once-off volunteer service projects to service-politics. The American Civil Rights movement was featured in the text by Rimmerman (2001) as a model for other forms of social change. To supplement this, the instructor more or less impulsively assigned students to conduct a 'scavenger hunt' of social change agents. A list of names ranging from Saul Alinski to Lech Walesa was cut up into small pieces of paper that were randomly drawn by students. Students were instructed to 'research' these individuals and be prepared to give a ten minute report the following

Table 8.1   Twenty-seven skills identified in the literature

Skills in Current Literature	Source	Students	Faculty/Staff	Business/Political	Nonprofit/Religious
1. Communication	Battistoni 2002; Colby et al. 2003; Morse 1992; Ramaley 2000	■			■
2. Political knowledge	Battistoni 2002	■	■	■	■
3. Collaboration	Carnegie Corporation and CIRCLE 2003; Colby et al. 2003;	■	■	■	■
4. Wholeness and inclusiveness	Peng 2000; Ramaley 2000	■		■	■
5. Listening	Peng 2000	■	■		■
6. Public discussion of problems	Peng 2000; Rimmerman 2001	■	■		■
7. Self-understanding	Colby et al. 2003	■	■		■
8. Community/coalition building	Battistoni 2002			■	■
9. Understanding of relationship between self and community	Colby et al. 2003; Ramaley 2000			■	■
10. Collective action	Battistoni 2002	■			■
11. Compromise	Colby et al. 2003	■			■
12. Cultural awareness	Colby et al. 2003	■			■
13. Problem solving	Battistoni 2002; Carnegie Corporation and CIRCLE 2003; Colby et al. 2003; Coplin 1997; Peng 2000	■			■
14. Organising	Colby et al. 2003	■			

No.	Competency	Reference							
15.	Public speaking	Carnegie Corporation and CIRCLE 2003					■		
16.	Civic judgment	Battistoni 2002; Carnegie Corporation and CIRCLE 2003; Peng 2000; Tormey-Purta and Vermeer 2003		■					
17.	Critical thinking	Battistoni 2002; Colby et al. 2003; Rimmerman 2001			■				
18.	Gathering information	Coplin 1997				■			
19.	Willingness to experiment	Ramaley 2000			■				
20.	Caring, trust, teamwork		■						
21.	Appreciation of global dimensions of issues	Colby et al. 2003							
22.	Assessment								
23.	Base of shared values	Ramaley 2000							
24.	Civic imagination and creativity	Battistoni 2002; Ramaley 2000							
25.	Confidence in importance of community	Ramaley 2000							
26.	Organisational analysis	Battistoni 2002							
27.	Self-responsibility	Ehrlich 2000							

week. Other topical areas included; civic indifference, legislative change process, advocacy, and understanding the administrative structure of the university to bring about change on campus.

Skills included learning how to create measurable goal statements and action plans. Students learned how to articulate goals with a degree of specificity by including components such as behaviour/action, condition, criteria, and duration (Welch 2002; Welch and Sheridan 1995). Action plans included a matrix specifying roles of specific individuals, a list of necessary steps and resources, timelines, locations, and a product or outcome for each step. The course also presented collaborative skills such as running meetings, decision-making and problem-solving, working with others, conflict management, and communication skills. Students also learned basic principles of public relations and how to make press releases, which was an actual assignment for their individual projects. Skills related to community-based research were also examined as a service-politics tactic. All of these skills were applied in the students' project as well as the compilation of the answer key to the final exam and the student handbook that served as the culminating cognitive assignment, which are described below.

Guest Speakers

A number of guest speakers were invited to the class sessions, the majority of whom participated in the first year the course was taught. However, these same guest speakers unexpectedly were unable to participate in the second year because of demands associated with the 2004 USA national elections. The guest speakers included directors of non-profit agencies and/or advocacy organisations to talk about their work, approach to problem solving and civic engagement. A state senator discussed the legislative change process and a former student leader at the 'Bennion Centre for Community Service' at the University of Utah[2] and recipient of the Swearer Award from Campus Compact[3] came to discuss her role as a campaign manager for a congressional representative and focused on the use of action plans. As previously mentioned, a representative from the university public relations office discussed public relations and press releases and similarly, a reporter on political issues from a local television station talked about working with the media.

Activities and Assignments

The course consisted of six major activities and assignments:

1) Complete five reflection entries.
2) Create the answer key to the post-test cognitive measure.

---

2   Additional information on the Bennion Centre for Community Service based at the University of Utah can be accessed at http://www.sa.utah.edu/bennion/

3   As referred to in the Foreword of this publication and subsequent chapters, Campus Compact is a coalition of more than 1,000 institutions of higher education across the USA and further information on the organisation can be accessed at http://www.compact.org.

3) Make one oral presentation.
4) Compose a press release.
5) Publish a class handbook.
6) Create an action plan to complete the service learning project.

Reflection entries   Students were required to submit five reflections incorporating the ABCs of reflection (Welch 1999) in which responses had to address affect, behaviour, and cognition, by integrating class topics with their service learning experience. Students had the option of submitting written reflection journals, oral journals on audio cassette tapes, or video journals. (Both the students who employed the audio or video journals and the instructor enjoyed the 'conversational' style of the entry). During the first year of the course, the instructor generated the reflection topic, however, after one particular guest speaker, the students asked if they could reflect on a specific topic that had been presented during the discussion. The instructor acquiesced and ultimately found these reflection entries from topics generated by the student group to be much richer and deeper, assuming this was due to the personal interest and investment on the part of the students. Subsequent reflection topics were collectively generated by the students while still following the ABCs format for the rest of that year and practiced that way throughout the second year.

Answer key   Students were assigned to collectively create the answer key to fifty terms or strategies that were compiled from the various reading assignments to be used as the 'final exam'. The instrument was used as a pre and post measure in which the initial responses were used as baseline data. The intent of the collective creation of the answer key reflects constructivist concepts and allowed students a sense of ownership in the learning and assessment process. Collectively creating the answer key to the post-test measure that served as the course's final exam proved to be an interesting process during the first year of the course. Initially, the students laboured over the semantics of definitions, often expending thirty minutes or more on the minutia for a single definition. Later, students realised the value of verbal economy and collaboration and gradually became more proficient at the process. Students also began to delegate specific terms to each other who would then report back the 'correct' answers to the class. Through class reflection, students related this experience to other collaborative tasks they had conducted in the past and recognised the importance of balancing efficiency with accuracy. The class collectively reviewed the definitions and revised them if necessary. In the second year of the course, there was a 'dinner study session' at the home of one of the students to finalise their definitions. The instructor was invited to attend and participate. This also proved to be an important activity for three reasons. First and unexpectedly, the event provided an important and meaningful social gathering toward the end of the course that seemed to provide emotional bonding and a sense of closure to the course. Second, the discussion on the topics was rich as students were empowered to relate the concepts back to the course and service learning experience. The process explicitly employed important civic engagement skills of collaboration, decision-making, and articulating ideas as enumerated in the literature. Finally, students taught each other mnemonic devices to help them recall the information.

Oral presentation   Students were given the opportunity to collectively determine the salient features of an effective oral presentation following the guest speaker who discussed public relations and public speaking. The class was given a set number of points the assignment was worth and then discussed what elements the presentation should include (for example introduction, body, conclusion, visual aids, interactivity) as well as criteria and point value for each. Students then critiqued each other's oral presentation using that set of criteria to be used in calculating a final grade. The exercise was a mock presentation to groups such as an advisory or governing board of a non-profit organisation, legislative subcommittee, a group of potential donors/ funders, or some other type of administrative body.

Press release   Using essential features described by the university public relations specialist during her guest presentation, the students once again were allowed to collectively determine what the press release should include as well as evaluation criteria and points. Students created and submitted a press release for their respective projects. Three of the final press releases were actually disseminated by the university public relations office resulting in media coverage during the first year of the course. Again, this reflects authentic assessment of students' application of skills.

Class handbook   Students created their own handbook for service-politics and civic engagement and class time was allocated for them to compile a table of contents and then assign topical areas to each other. The content generally reflected topical areas and skills discussed in class. Students collectively identified a number of 'tactics' such as weekend education/experiential retreats, blogging, dialogues/forums, fact sheets, investigative journalism, letter-writing campaigns, petitions, phone trees, rallies, and student led courses to be included in the handbook. Each student was responsible for teaching the class about a tactic they selected to research. That student also composed a 'mini-chapter' on the tactic for the handbook. The information was compiled into a spiral bound booklet and reproduced for each student at the end of the course. Students created guidelines and evaluation criteria for the written passages describing the tactics.

Service learning partners   A total of five cooperating agencies were identified as service learning partners in the first year of the course. Of these, two students worked with an advocacy group on homelessness issues and a further student worked with another on poverty issues. A student requested permission to work with a state historical preservation agency that was not originally one of the five identified partners and two requested to work with campus based organisations. One of these students used the student leadership cabinet of the Lowell Bennion Community Service Centre to work in conjunction with an existing student-directed volunteer programme. Another student worked with the student union administration on recycling issues.

In the second year, the instructor attempted to use the same partners. However, many of the students expressed a desire to work with agencies they already knew or had worked with in the past. The instructor acquiesced and allowed students to do so, but in hindsight, only half of these arrangements proved to be totally satisfactory as the instructor had not had the opportunity to clearly articulate the objectives of the course or service-politics projects. Students who chose their own partner typically reported difficulty in maintaining contact and communication with the agency representative. During the final course debriefing, students recognised the difficulties associated with finding their own partners and agreed that the instructor should continue to find an array of partners and let students choose from that list. Likewise, students from the second year reported that the projects were quite challenging and recommended that students work in pairs or teams to help promote collaborative team-building skills and to facilitate the logistics of the projects.

Goal statements, action plans and service learning projects   Students created a goal statement with their community partner that included an observable behaviour as well as conditions, criteria, and duration of the behaviour. The goal statement essentially drove the project activities. Students then created an action plan that outlined specific tasks to meet the goal. The written plan articulated who would conduct what task, as well with what resources, where and when. The plan included tangible products or outcomes for each task.

This activity required students to collaborate with agency partners and to creatively problem solve and identify the steps necessary to complete the project. A list and brief descriptions of students' service learning projects from both academic years are presented in Table 8.2.

Assessment/Evaluation Procedures and Outcomes

Eyler has argued that we need 'convincing measures of important outcomes' for service learning courses (Eyler 2000). Specifically, she posed the following questions that are the basis for assessing this course:

How can we design measures of understanding and problem solving that allow students to demonstrate their competence rather than simply testify to it?

How can we embed authentic assessment measures into the service learning experience?

How can projects be designed to increase students' sense of engagement with community partners? (Eyler 2000, 15)

The assessment/evaluation procedures developed for this course were designed to address these questions. It is important to clearly understand that the outcomes reported here are the results of assessment procedures rather than the results of a carefully controlled experimental study. However, some of the measures employed quasi-experimental methodology and analyses. This assessment process was primarily designed to create authentic outcomes through application rather than self report surveys in what might otherwise be considered artificial conditions.

The course was assessed using five measures, two of which represent what Eyler characterised as 'authentic assessment' in which products or outcomes of student work are applied to meet a goal or need in an actual setting or context. The first

Table 8.2   Students' Service Learning projects in year one and year two

Year One

Student	Agency Partner	Service learning Project Description
1	University Student Union Building	Conduct a quantitative 'waste audit' of trash from the student union, to weigh and classify recyclable materials. A final report was generated with recommendations for creating a recycling programme.
2	Bennion Centre Volunteer Programme on Homelessness	Create an 'alternative weekend' experience in which university students worked with the homeless and staying at a shelter. Reflection activities included options for action and advocacy.
3	Poverty Advocacy Group	Conduct research on 'pay-day loan' businesses and their impact on poor and non-English speaking clients to be used in creating a bill to legislate interest rates and an information brochure in Spanish.
4	State Historical and Archeological Agency	Interview archeological site stewards and create a stewardship curriculum and training manual.
5	Health Advocacy Group	Conduct interviews with patients to identify issues related to service delivery to vulnerable populations. Results were used in creating policy statements.
6	Health Advocacy Group	Conduct research on a proposed marriage-bill for a health advocacy group to be used in policy and proposed legislation.
7 & 8	Poverty and Homeless Advocacy Group	Create an on-campus chapter of a national homelessness awareness and service organisation.

Year Two

Student	Agency Partner	Service Learning Project Description
1	Local Newspaper	Create/publish a 'legislators' report card' voting record on six popular bills that were not passed in previous legislative session.
2	On-campus animal rights group	Create a campus wide policy regarding student choice and options on dissection assignments.
3	On-campus student health services	Create and implement a student awareness/education programme to promote student insurance.
4	On-campus interfaith group	Create and conduct a series of religious dialogue to promote awareness and understanding between groups.
5	Poverty advocacy group	Conduct research on pay-day loan companies to be used for lobbying/legislation.
6	Poverty and homeless advocacy group	Continue campus chapter of a national homelessness awareness and service organisation.
7	Off-campus interfaith organisation	Create infrastructure for annual choral-fest fundraising event and coordinate first choral-fest.
8	Anti-pornography and Women's Advocacy Group	Create website and education materials on the topic of child-pornography and violence against women.
9	High School Student Leadership Programme	Create information brochure and educational materials to recruit high school student leaders to participate in summer programmes.
10	Environmental Education/ Advocacy Group	Create education programme on local environmental issues and bills, and present information at community meetings.
11	Community Youth Programme	Create and conduct a campus-visit programme for under represented youth to promote college education.

was a portfolio approach, by which students demonstrated their assimilation and understanding of key concepts from the course by creating a student handbook. Second, each cooperating agency received a tangible product or outcome that has sustainable and/or long-term impact through the students' service-politics assignment. Other assessment measures employed quasi-experimental designs to quantify students' development. A third method measuring students' cognitive growth was quantitatively assessed by a t-test of pre/post measures. A fourth procedure involved students' self-assessment of the citizenry skills which was assessed by a t-test pre/post measure. In the second year of the course, a comparison group was utilised to strengthen the quasi-experimental assessment. Fifth, course evaluations were designed to assess service learning courses based on criteria used to designate courses as service learning.

Portfolio Approach: Student Handbook

As previously mentioned the final product of the course was the creation of a student handbook for service-politics and civic engagement by the class. The creation of the student handbook explicitly addressed many of the theoretical constructs and skills of civic engagement articulated in the literature. Specifically, the handbook promoted active learning, learning as a social process, knowledge is shaped by contexts, reflective practice, and capacity to represent an idea in more than one modality (Colby et al. 2003).

Products and Outcomes for Cooperating Agencies

The service learning projects themselves provided tangible products to community partners that serve as authentic measures of the service learning experience. Likewise, the projects were designed to promote students' sense and level of engagement by working directly with community agencies (Eyler 2000). Students had to design and implement action plans to successfully complete the service learning projects. Likewise, as students worked with agencies, they had to utilise many of the skills presented in the class. It became clear that the authentic nature of this assignment was new and challenging to some of the students. The reality of 'coming through' with an actual product for a community partner transcended previous learning experiences of submitting papers or passing an exam. In the end, each project met most of its goal resulting in satisfaction from each participating agency. Many of the projects provided necessary infrastructure that allowed the community partner to continue the initial work of students' service learning projects after the course was completed. A final written report of each project was also submitted at the end of the course. Thus, the service learning component of the class appears to have addressed many of the issues and questions posed by Eyler (2000) and enumerated earlier in this chapter

Cognitive Growth

A t-test comparing pre and post-test scores on fifty key concepts, terms, and strategies derived from the text and readings assessed cognitive impact of the course in both years. The students were given the pre-test during the first class session. The format consisted of a short written response for each item and each were graded by the instructor using a dichotomous scoring procedure of one point for correct responses and zero for incorrect responses. The grading process for the pre-test was actually quite simple as the vast majority of the instruments were returned with no responses as the students clearly did not know the terms or concepts listed. The scores were recorded and the actual pre-test instruments were returned to the students who used them as a baseline to collectively create their own 'answer key' for the post-test. Time in each class session was devoted to student led discussion of correct responses. A consensus of accuracy was achieved with the instructor through class discussion and then used as the answer key for the post-test. For both years, students came into the course essentially only knowing approximately 10% of the terms or concepts on the cognitive measure. By the end of the semester, students were able to articulate an understanding of 90% of the items. Regardless of the small enrolment or sample size, these results strongly suggest a degree of growth over time. The use of a comparison group in the second year of the course supports this supposition by controlling for exposure to course content.

Year one results   Results of a t-test (t = - 44.2344, SD = 2.67) revealed highly significant gains in student scores. The post-test mean score of 45.87 was significantly higher than the pre-test mean score of 3.87 (p < .000).

Year two results   To strengthen the measure of cognitive growth, a comparison group was utilised during the second year of the course to create a quasi-experimental design. A pre/post measure was gathered from a third year junior level honours course on *African-American History* as a comparison group. There was no significant difference between the pre-test mean score of 2.60 (n= 10, SD = 1.17) and the post-test mean score of 3.20 (n=10, SD= 2.61) from the comparison group. However, there was a significant difference (t = -31.225, p < .000) between the pre-test mean score of 7.54 (n=11, SD 4.52) and post-test mean score of 45.54 (n=11, SD = 5.04) of the course. Despite relatively small sample sizes, the limited change in mean scores of the comparison group, when compared to the large difference between pre and post mean scores of the treatment group, suggest cognitive growth occurred.

Students' Perception of Citizenry Skills

Students' perception of citizenry skills was measured using a hybrid instrument based on a survey developed by Eyler and Giles (1999). Part I consisted of twenty six items assessing students' opinions regarding citizenship. Part II assessed students' skills and activities they engaged in and consisted of twenty one items. Students' behaviours were assessed by twenty five items in Part III. Student demographic information was collected in Part IV. A 6-point Likert-type response format was used to respond to items ranging from a low of one (strongly disagree or strongly unlike me) to a high of six (strongly agree or strongly like me). Items were positively worded so that higher response rates revealed positive gains in mean scores.

Year one results   Student attrition, due to three students dropping the course after the first session, resulted in a very small sample of only five matched pre and post instruments. It should be noted that three other students enrolled in the course but they were not included in the pre-test as they did not participate in the class discussions of the first class session. Therefore, the small sample size may have had an adverse impact on the statistical results. However, the results of a t-test revealed statistically significant gains were made on Part II of the measure assessing students' skills and activities (p < .02). General trends of improvement were noted in Parts I and III.

Year two results   As with the cognitive measure, a comparison group was used with the citizenry measure for the second year. There were no significant differences between the pre-test and post-test mean scores of comparison group on Parts I, II, or III of the citizenry survey. However, the results revealed significant differences between the pre-test and post-test scores of the students taking the course in the treatment group on Parts I, II, and III. Likewise, there was a significant difference between the post-test mean scores of the comparison group and the treatment group taking the class on Parts I and III. The class post-test mean of 5.5 (n=8, SD= .244) was significantly higher (p < .000) than the comparison post-test mean of 4.7 (n=9, SD = .234) on Part I assessing students' opinions on citizenry. Likewise, the class post-test mean of 4.7 (n=8, SD= .497) was significantly higher (p < .007) than the post-test mean of 3.7 (n=9, SD = .805) from the comparison group on Part III assessing students' citizenry behaviours. There was a slight difference between the post-test scores on Part II of skills and activities with the class mean score of 5.3 and the comparison groups mean score of 4.9 but not to a statistically significant degree.

Course Evaluations

The course was evaluated during both years using an instrument from the Lowell Bennion Community Service Centre. The service learning course evaluation form consisted of sixteen items employing a Likert-type response format with 1 = strongly disagree to 6 = strongly agree. Of these sixteen items, eight were directly correlated to the criteria used to designate courses as service learning.[4] The other six items assessed students' opinions on other salient features of service learning courses such as developing leadership skills. The last two items asked students to respond as to whether this was an effective course and effective instructor. The students' means responses on the entire course evaluation instrument for both years ranged from a low of 5.0 on 2 items ('I learned to be a better citizen' and 'I would recommend the

---

    4   These criteria can be found at the Lowell Bennion Community Service Centre website http://www.sa.utah.edu/bennion/.

community partner I worked with') to a high of 6.0 ('I reflected on what I learned in class') with an overall mean rating of 5.565.

Discussion

Based on the results of this assessment process, it would appear that this course and its products reflect and met the theoretical constructs and skills associated with civic engagement enumerated earlier. These principles can, should, and were used as benchmarks to assess the impact of this service learning course. The class activities and projects appear to have enabled students to become a social reformer (Kahne et al, 2000) to varying degrees. In the process, the eight civic engagement skills proposed by Battistoni (2002) were presented to and assimilated by students to a large extent. Perhaps most importantly, the course activities and outcomes reflect most of the tenets from the pedagogy of engagement described by Colby et al. Likewise, class activities addressed some of the skills identified in the focus groups that were not enumerated in the professional literature. Specifically, students were engaged in active learning and the learning experience was a social process. Students' knowledge was shaped by contexts and reflective practice. Students demonstrated an ability to represent an idea in more than one modality through written products such as the handbook, action plans leading to programmes that were implemented in authentic settings, and oral presentations.

This course also reflects Eyler's (2000) recommendation to design measures of understanding and problem solving that allow students to demonstrate their competence rather than simply testify to it in self report surveys by embedding authentic assessment and using service learning projects to increase students' sense of engagement with the community partners. Students' problem solving abilities were demonstrated through the creation and implementation of their action plans to complete their projects as well as through their collaborative efforts to produce a student handbook.

Additional anecdotal evidence also suggests assimilation and application of knowledge and skills. One humorous example is worth noting. A political reporter from a local television station was a guest speaker in class to discuss how to work with the press. During the course of the discussion, the reporter who has a reputation for being quite aggressive in his reporting style, stated his opinion that no major social change had ever emerged from the arts. Based on the change agent scavenger hunt briefly described above, a student confronted the reporter and asked him about the impact of playwright and poet, Vaclav Havel, who later led the 'Velvet Revolution' in the Czech Republic and became its President. The reporter responded with, 'I retract my statement' and the class burst into applause. Similarly, many of the press releases created as a learning exercise for the class were actually used, resulting in coverage by the local media. Nearly a third of the students continued to work with their cooperating agencies after completion of the course and some gained employment in non-profit agencies after graduation.

Limitations

This chapter describes a comprehensive evaluation of a course rather than a carefully controlled experiment and a comparison group was not utilised in the analysis of the first year. Likewise, the relatively small number of students enrolled in the class may have an impact on the results of the statistical analysis that was conducted as part of the assessment procedures. Similarly, the small number of students (and highly motivated honour students at that) was a luxury that larger, required courses cannot provide, thus making it less complicated to manage. As such, the quantitative results alone do not adequately demonstrate students' growth. However, coupled with authentic outcomes and unexpected anecdotal evidence, strong inferences can be drawn that the course had some kind of impact on not only on students' knowledge and understanding, but on student performance and behaviour as well. Small sample sizes from both years are acknowledged, however, both informal examination of the pre and post mean scores and formal statistical results of the p-value strongly suggest students' growth over time. Borg and Gall (1983) note the danger of confusing statistical significance with practical significance. Carefully controlled studies with large sample sizes can have relatively small differences between mean scores that are *statistically* significant and yet have little to no *practical* meaning in terms of actual practice or application. In this case, small sample sizes resulted in both statistically significant results and practical significance.

Results from the citizenry survey are based on students' self report. However, even with these self reports, the results of a comparison group in the second year revealed a significant difference between students' opinions, skills, and behaviours. Students who enrolled in the class may have been predisposed to participate in civic engagement and therefore the class activities may not have had a direct impact on their actual behaviours.[5] It is also not possible to tell if the service learning component alone made a difference on the cognitive and citizenry self report scores. It could be that a traditional course on the same topics and skill sets without the service learning assignment may have had the same results on the cognitive and attitudinal measures. However, the service learning experience did result in actual products or projects that were utilised by community partners. A traditional course on civic engagement would not have generated those outcomes. A regression analysis was not incorporated to determine if certain demographic factors may have influenced student responses and outcomes. Finally, the results of this class and the assessment procedures are limited to the students at this particular university and are not generalisable to other types of institutions in other settings.

Conclusion

The course appears to have had an impact on students' sense of civic engagement, thus addressing the issues and question posed by Eyler (2000). These measures represent

---

5   This was evident by the fact that the three students withdrew from the class in the first year after they discovered it was incorrectly listed in the course catalogue as a class on business strategies.

an array ranging from quantitative data to tangible products created by students and utilised by community partners. It also appears that incorporation of service-politics and a pedagogy of engagement within Service learning courses is a viable approach and alternative to traditional direct service projects to preparing students to be good citizens in a just and democratic society. Additionally, the information gleaned from teaching this course provides new and useful information that address Kahne and colleagues' call for exploring higher education's role in teaching civic engagement.

References

Battistoni, R. M. (2002), *Civic Engagement Across the Curriculum*. (Providence, RI: Campus Compact).

Billig, S. H. and Welch, M. (2004), 'Service learning as civically engaged scholarship: Challenges and strategies in higher education and K-12 settings', in Welch M. and Billig S. H. (eds).

Borg, W. R. and Gall, M. D. (1983), *Educational Research: An Introduction* (New York: Longman).

Colby, A. et al. (2003), *Educating Citizens: Preparing America's Undergraduates for Lives of Moral and Civic Responsibility* (San Francisco, CA: Jossey-Bass).

Eyler, J.S. (2000), 'What do we need to know about the impact of service learning on student learning?' *Michigan Journal of Community Service-learning*, (Special 2000 Fall Issue), 11–17.

Eyler, J. and Giles, D. (1999), *Where's the Learning in Service-Learning?* (San Francisco, CA: Jossey Bass).

Gallimore, R. and Tharp, R. (1990), 'Teaching mind in society: Teaching, schooling, and literate discourse', in Moll (ed.).

Gelmon, S. B., Holland, B., Driscoll, A., Spring, A., and Kerrigan, S. (2001), *Assessing Service Learning and Civic Engagement: Principles and Techniques*. (Providence, RI: Campus Compact).

Harkavy, I. (2004), 'Service learning and the development of democratic universities, democratic schools, and democratic good societies in the 21st century', in Welch and Billig (eds.).

Honnet, E. P. and Paulson, S. (1989), *Principles of Good Practice in Combining Service and Learning*, Wingspread Special Report. (Racine, WI: The Johnson Foundation).

Kahne, J. Westheimer, J. and Rogers, B. (2000), 'Service learning and citizenship: Directions for research', *Michigan Journal of Community Service-learning*, (Special 2000 Fall Issue), 42–51.

Long, S. E. (2002), *The New Student Politics: The Wingspread Statement on Student Civic Engagement* (Providence, RI: Campus Compact).

Moll L. C. (ed.) (1990), *Vygotsky and Education* (New York, NY: Cambridge University Press).

Rimmerman, C. A. (2001), *The New Citizenship: Unconventional Politics, Activism, and Service*, 2nd Edition. (Boulder, CO: Westview Press).

Root, S. et al. (eds.) (2005), *Improving Service-Learning Practice: Research on Models to Enhance Impact*. (Greenwich, CT: Information Age Publishing).

Stephensen, M. et al. (2002), *Service Learning in the Curriculum: A Faculty Guide*. (Salt Lake City, UT: Lowell Bennion Community Service Centre, University of Utah).

Strand, K. et al. (2003), *Community-based Research and Higher Education: Principles and Practices*. (San Francisco, CA: Jossey-Bass).

Vygotsky, L. S. (1976), *Mind in Society: The Development of Higher Mental Processes*. (Cambridge, MA: Harvard University Press).

Vygotsky, L. S. (1986), *Thought and Language*. (Cambridge, MA: MIT Press).

Welch M. and Billig S. H. (eds.) (2004), *New Perspectives in Service-learning: Research to advance the field*. (Greenwich, CT: Information Age Publishing).

Welch, M. (1999), 'The ABCs of Reflection: A template for students and instructors to implement written reflection in service-learning', *National Society of Experiential Education Quarterly*, 25:2, 1, 23–25.

Welch, M. (2004), *Handbook for Service-politics and Civic Engagement*. (Salt Lake City, UT: University of Utah).

Welch, M., Miller, P. and Davies, K. (2005), 'Reciprocal validity: Descriptions and outcomes of a hybrid approach of triangulated qualitative analysis in the research of civic engagement skills', in Root et al. (eds.).

Welch, M. and Sheridan, S. M. (1995), *Educational Partnerships: Serving Students at Risk* (Ft. Worth, TX: Harcourt-Brace).

Chapter 9

Towards Enhanced Citizenship: The Potential of Service Learning in Teacher Education – A National and International Perspective

Timothy R. Murphy

Introduction

In the autumn of 2004, the concept of service learning was introduced at the National University of Ireland, Galway (NUIG) as a pedagogical approach that had the potential to enhance the civic capacities of the students enrolled there. In my capacity as a foundations lecturer for the education department, I felt that this approach could significantly enrich the experience of pre-service teachers. These students enrol in the higher diploma in education course (H. Dip.), which is of one year duration, after successful completion of which, they are recognised as fully certified post-primary (high school/secondary) teachers.

Having responsibility for the *Education and Society* module on the H. Dip. course, I decided that the designated learning outcomes for this module could be potentially enhanced if the students had the opportunity to engage in service learning activities. Specifically, I was keen to explore the extent to which exposure to such activities could enhance the students' understanding of their own professional identity as educators and, also the extent to which such learning could enlarge their thinking and understanding with respect to some of the principal issues that are currently facing the Irish educational system. In that respect, then, I invited the students to consider how their engagement with service learning opportunities informed/deepened their understanding/ knowledge of any aspect(s) of the course content for 'Education and Society'.

As part of their requirements for the 'Education and Society' module the students were given the option of completing a reflective essay on service learning and teacher education, with a particular focus on the aforementioned aspects. I will return to some samples of the students work a little later, but, at this juncture, I would like to clarify for the reader the understanding of service learning that informed our work over the course of the academic year. The students were informed that service learning is a teaching/learning method that connects meaningful community service with academic learning, personal growth, and civic responsibility, so as to gain further understanding of course content, a broader appreciation of the discipline, and an enhanced sense of civic responsibility (National Service-Learning in Teacher Education Partnership 2002).

Need for Service Learning?

There is a need for such a pedagogical approach in the context of the current educational system in the Republic of Ireland. It is suggested, for example, that in certain respects the current system is performing admirably. This is clearly evident, for example, in a recent publication by Garret Fitzgerald where he claims, in a chapter entitled *The Productivity of Irish Education*, that in terms of what one might refer to as 'educational productivity' – output in qualitative and quantitative terms related to inputs of resources – Ireland seems to have been performing 'about fifty per cent better than the rest of the EU' (Fitzgerald 2003, 130). This productivity was further highlighted in the recent OECD study 'Programme for International Student Assessment' (PISA). The findings from this study indicated that students in Ireland achieved a mean score that was significantly higher than the OECD average score in reading literacy and science. In mathematics and cross-curricular problem solving, Ireland's mean scores were not significantly different from the corresponding OECD country average scores (Cosgrove et al. 2004).

In certain respects, then, it could be argued that there is no need at all to change the system of education in Ireland. There are voices, however, which suggest otherwise. One of those is Gearóid Ó Tuathaigh, who claims that what is missing in many communities on the island of Ireland today 'is a rooted and coherent sense of collective responsibility and capacity for building their own community' (Ó Tuathaigh 2001, 48). In a recent speech, the Irish Taoiseach (Prime Minister) also acknowledged the importance of collective engagement, stating that 'the quality of life in society, and the ultimate health of our communities, depends on the willingness of people to become involved and active' (Department of the Taoiseach 2005). In a manner similar to Ó Tuathaigh, however, he went on to state that there are many pressures today which militate against such engagement. Some of these, he contended, related to lifestyle, particularly the pressures of combining working life with home and family commitments (Ó Tuathaigh 2001, 48).

It is the author's firm conviction that engagement with service learning activities will help to underpin a broader appreciation of the importance of civic capacities for society. Indeed, some commentators would contend that such an appreciation is all the more necessary in the context of an education system that appears to be increasingly responsive to economic imperatives. When referring to the dramatic changes that occurred in educational policy in the Republic of Ireland in the 1960s, Patrick Clancy, states that in the wake of 'the adoption of a programme for economic development, with its commitment to economic growth and export oriented industrialisation, the educational system would henceforth be assessed by its capacity to facilitate the achievement of these new economic objectives' (Clancy 1995, 125).

Service Learning and its Pedagogical Underpinnings

In the context of an education system where economic considerations have an increasing centrality, it is even more important to create "a new inspiring language and social vision that goes beyond the valorisation of economic growth as an end in itself and as the hegemonic discourse of human endeavour and human achievement" (Ó Tuathaigh 2001, 49). For several years, I have had the very privileged opportunity of experiencing the rich social vision of Maxine Greene. She is a world-renowned educationalist who has lectured for a number of years at Teachers' College, Columbia University. She is principally concerned with espousing a conception of the educational project that allows for the flourishing of human freedom. In her view, education today must 'be conceived as a mode of opening the world to critical judgments by the young and to their imaginative projections and, in time, to their transformative actions' (Greene 1995, 56). As a native New Yorker, however, she is very conscious of the obstacles that challenge human beings, as they endeavour to grow and develop fully as persons, especially in the context of modern post-industrial societies. In her view, the nurturing of the capacity to see beyond the given, ought to be at the heart of what we do as educators.

The workings of the invisible hand in modern society, however, what Greene refers to as 'the impersonal or invisible forces', has seriously eclipsed the extent to which people today can 'conceive of a different state of affairs' (Greene 1995, 69). These same forces also have important implications for a person's understanding of what it means 'to be alive among others, to achieve freedom in dialogue with others for the sake of personal fulfilment and the emergence of a democracy dedicated to life and decency' (Greene 1988, xii). Such a recognition has very serious educational implications. In fact, Greene suggests that a concern for "the critical and the imaginative, for the opening of new ways of 'looking at things,' is wholly at odds with the technicist and behaviourist emphases we still find in American schools" (Greene 1998, 126). Such emphases are in line with what is often considered to be the taken for granted prime purpose of education as the preparation of people 'for a continually expanding (and, yes, an increasingly stratified) industrial and commercial system and that, at least for some, upward mobility would be ensured' (Greene 1987, 182).

There are many parallels between the aforementioned demarcation of the enormous challenges facing the project of education in the United States and the practice of education in Ireland. Accordingly, I invited the pre-service teachers to consider Greene's pedagogical approach, especially in its relation to a service learning approach.

Service Learning and Teacher Education at NUIG

As part of my role as lecturer, I introduced an optional reflective essay on service learning and teacher education for the pre-service teachers enrolled in the 'Education and Society' module, which is a core foundations course of the H.Dip. Those students who elected to do this reflective essay were invited to consider how engagement with service learning opportunities can potentially deepen their awareness/appreciation of their role as educators and also how their engagement with those same activities informed and/or, deepened their understanding or their knowledge about any aspect(s) of the course.

Approximately 15% of the cohort of students (that is thirty five students) elected to do the reflective essay on Service Learning and Teacher Education. Such interest from them, especially during the pilot phase, is certainly a positive development and it augurs well for future development. Some examples of the students work are presented below.

One student, for example, decided to complete her reflective essay on the experience that she had as a voluntary tutor with the Galway Adult Literacy Organisation. The student stated that her involvement with the organisation forced her to reassess her comfortable, middle class views on the current education system and that it also made her think more seriously about the processes involved in learning to read and write, something most of us take for granted. In her own words, she commented that:

> In order to become a successful tutor I had to put myself in the shoes of the student, and each student was unique. Did they prefer to process information visually or aurally or spatially? Was it possible to use their experience as a foundation for learning? I think this is why William Ayers' musings on teaching struck such a deep chord – "to reflect on the process of learning and teaching by consciously being in the role of one who doesn't know". What service learning did for me was to remove the scales from my eyes and see that education should be about individuals and ensuring that each individual maximises their potential as a human being.

It is clearly evident then that this pre-service teacher benefited greatly from her involvement with service learning. It is very much in evidence that such involvement helped this student to clarify her own role as an educator. The transformative potential inherent in the project of educating, for example, is clearly evident when she describes what service learning did for her, which she likened to removing the scales from her eyes. This vivid imagery, in my estimation, goes to the heart of the educational project. I am reminded of Greene's concept of 'wide awakeness'. Such a conception of the educational endeavour is extremely important, especially in the context of "an educational system that is increasingly expected to process the young (seen as 'human resources') to perform acceptably on some level of an increasingly systematised world" (Greene 1988, 12).

Furthermore, this student articulates very succinctly the necessity of integrating service learning into teacher education courses. This is clearly evident in the following extract:

> It is up to this generation of trainee teachers to work transformation on our creaking and unequal education system. In the words of Bernie Wade and Maggie Moore (Experiencing Special Education) "we need to make mainstream teaching more effective by matching what is taught to the needs of students". I believe that the first step in achieving this would be to make service learning for all educators a mandatory requirement. I have no doubt that this would meet resistance initially but having had the benefit of such learning

> I cannot stress enough the impact this service learning had on my personal views on the role of education. It certainly made me take a less biased view and taught me, as a teacher, not to judge anyone simply on the basis of his or her academic ability.

Another student reflected on her involvement with the 'The Outreach Society' programme while completing her studies at the University of Limerick. In a manner similar to the previous student, she clearly demonstrates how her involvement with the service learning initiative helped her to clarify her own role as an educator and that it also afforded her a privileged insight into the reality of educational disadvantage. One project that she participated in, for example, involved students from the university travelling out to a community school in South Hill, which is a disadvantaged area of Limerick city with considerable socio-economic problems, and taking students for one to one tuition in English. She reported that she benefited greatly from this, especially given that she is from a rural middle class background which did not bring her into significant contact with people from lower socio-economic backgrounds. She acknowledges that she initially possessed an element of the "cock-eyed" optimist when she became involved with the various outreach projects. The experience that she gained as an educator through her involvement with service learning allowed her to arrive at a richer understanding of education. In her own words, she came to realise that:

> the principal aim of these projects was not to radically improve the students academically but to change their attitudes to education and the usefulness of it to them in their futures, something I didn't appreciate at the time and perhaps to enable them, as Maxine Greene suggests "to see beyond the actual to a better order of things." On reflection the experience for me was a formative one and had a significant impact on my decision to enter the teaching profession. According to Greene, teachers should 'challenge that which is taken for granted, the given, the bound and the restricted.' Teachers should also be taught, 'to educate our children to take responsibility for our collective well being' aims I very much believe in and aspire to. To me teaching is about more than educating the child for our economy, which is of course important but it has become the central focus of our education system.

The third example also clearly illustrates the enormous potential that service learning offers to engage students in socially meaningful activities which have important learning outcomes attached to them as well. The example involves a science teacher who decided to participate in the *BT Young Scientist and Technology Exhibition*, an annual competition for encouraging interest in science in secondary schools (formerly known as the *Aer Lingus Young Scientist Exhibition*). The teacher acknowledges that his motivation for becoming involved with this event was in the first place personal, in that he welcomes the opportunity to interact with the students outside of the school environment, but, that it also gave him the opportunity to direct the interests of the students towards socially relevant issues. He outlines the nature of the project in the following section:

> (It)is focused on investigating radon concentrations in and around Galway city. Radon is a radioactive gas that occurs naturally in granite and can reach high concentrations in old and poorly built houses. Long term inhalation can lead to lung cancer. We are preparing a

questionnaire to be sent home in each student's end of year report that will alert families to the dangers of radon and ask them to have a test done. The results will then be collected and analysed by the students. In addition, we are having three small model houses built with varying radon protective measures, varying from excellent to terrible. These will be placed in area of known high and low radon concentrations and testing will be performed. This will give us a handle on the accuracy of the testing devices. We are trying to negotiate a decrease in the price of testing with two commercial companies. The overall objective is to raise awareness of this dangerous gas in Galway.

Each of these examples bear clear testimony to the tremendous benefits that can be gained from involvement with service learning, especially in terms of clarifying one's emerging identity as a teacher, but, also, in terms of identifying and developing capacities in the next generation of citizens who, as a result, will likely become more socially aware and committed. Ó Tuathaigh, as mentioned earlier, contends that the most challenging project facing community leaders and teachers alike in the coming decade 'will be the creation of a new inspiring language and social vision that goes beyond the valorisation of economic growth as an end in itself and as the hegemonic discourse of human endeavour and human achievement' (Ó Tuathaigh 2001, 49).

Service Learning and the Issue of Standards in Education

An oft heard criticism of service learning relates to the amount of time that is required to organise, plan and execute the various activities involved in this particular pedagogical approach. It is further claimed that there is no direct correlation between the involvement of students with service learning and their success or otherwise with respect to student performance in standards based tests (STS). Many advocates of service learning, however, contend that the benefits that students gain from involvement with service learning goes far beyond the test scores that they manage to achieve in terminal exams.

With respect to such exams, however, there is evidence from the United States to support the view that the STS scores of students in compulsory schooling do improve as a result of their participation in service learning. The Learning Indeed initiative, for example, was launched by The W.K. Kellog Foundation in 1998, as a national US initiative to engage more young people in service to others as part of their academic life[1]. This initiative has collated research on service learning that reveals the potential of this pedagogical approach as a way of enhancing academic achievement. It makes reference to a study by Scales, Blyth, Berkas and Kielsmeier (2000) on *The effects of service-learning on middle school students social responsibility and academic success* it found that:

> Compared with other students, students with substantial hours of service-learning, a lot of reflection, and a high degree of motivation attributed to service-learning, significantly increased their belief in the efficacy of their helping behaviors, maintained their pursuit of better grades and their perception that school provided personal development opportunities, and decreased less in their commitment to classwork (Scales et al. 2000, 332–358).

---

1   Further information can be accessed at http://learningindeed.org/index.html

An additional Report prepared by W. Morgan for the Indiana Department of Education, *Evaluation of school-based service leaning in Indiana 1997–98*, lends additional support for the view that there is a positive correlation between student involvement with service learning and academic success at the compulsory school level. The study analysed pre/post surveys of 220 service learning high school students from 19 different classes in a total of 10 different schools. The surveys looked at both academic performance and civic engagement. They provided specific information on hours of service and number of days skipped. The teachers filled out a separate survey, providing information about the classes and observed impacts. The findings indicated that overall GPAs were seen to improve from about a 'B' average to a 'B+' and students' political knowledge increased as well.

There is evidence then that at the level of compulsory schooling, students can benefit, both academically and socially, from engagement with service learning. It is certainly plausible then that Irish students, at both first and second levels (that is during compulsory schooling) could also benefit from such activities. Any attempt to make service learning a part of the curriculum, however, will require the active support and involvement of all participating teachers. Both pre-service, as well as practicing teachers, will need to be familiarised with the pedagogy of service learning and of its relevance to the existing curriculum. The aforementioned examples from pre-service teachers at NUIG would certainly encourage the inclusion of a service learning approach as an integrated part of pre-certification teacher education programmes.

Challenges for Education in the Republic of Ireland: Opportunities for Service Learning

The benefits of engaging with a service learning approach extends beyond the compulsory school-going levels of education. In this section, I will attempt to outline some of the major global challenges that are facing education systems in the modern post industrial era and will also suggest how service learning may help to lessen the negative consequences of some of those challenges.

It is clear, for example, that education systems across the globe are experiencing severe challenges with respect to their civic remit. Greene identifies the task of opening up spaces 'where persons speaking together and being together can discover what it signifies to incarnate and act upon values far too often taken for granted' as being one of the primary concerns of educators today (Greene 1995, 68). The limited extent to which such spaces exist in the education system of the Republic of Ireland, from initial schooling through to third level, is currently a major cause for concern. Such concern is often attributed to the examinations-driven culture that is currently pervading our entire education system. There is evidence to suggest that such a culture is not an entirely new phenomenon on the scene either. As far back as the 1970s, Dore, for example, indicated that 'the more widely education certificates are used for occupational selection; the faster the rate of qualification inflation; and the more examination-oriented schooling becomes, at the expense of genuine education' (Dore 1976). There is also much evidence to suggest that this preoccupation with examinations has accelerated appreciably over the course of the past decade. In fact, the responsibility of education 'to foster personal and social development and to further equality and respect for others' has been significantly hampered by the emergence of what Drudy refers to as 'Crude League Tables' Furthermore, she suggests that the evaluation of second-level schools solely according to examination performance or transfer to third level 'takes no account of important sources of variation between schools, such as the socio-economic intake of pupils, the uptake of additional tuition (grinds) by students or their capacity to afford grinds' (Drudy 2003).

It was very much in evidence from the earlier excerpts of the pre-service teachers who engaged with service learning that they had considerably deepened their understandings about the nature and purpose of the educational project in the Republic of Ireland, particularly at the second level. Such understandings will certainly help them to counteract some of the more negative consequences of the present pre-occupation with points/grades in education. Such understandings may even encourage them to appreciate more fully the importance of an education that "will also equip our young people to step into their future as well-rounded and well-adjusted people" (Valarasan-Toomey 1998, 52).

Concluding Comments

The education system in the Republic of Ireland is often credited with playing a significant role in this country's economic success. The close symmetry between education and economic success, however, is not without its downside. It is important, for example, not to lose sight of the fact that education should not be driven solely on economic imperatives, important as these are. My involvement with service learning has convinced me that such a pedagogical approach can help to expand our understanding as to what constitutes education, particularly at the second level.

Recently, the Organisation for Economic Cooperation and Development (OECD) Directorate for Education prepared a policy document on attracting, developing and retaining effective teachers at post primary (high school/ secondary) level. The executive summary states that there is widespread recognition 'that countries need to have clear and concise statements of what teachers are expected to know and be able to do, and these teacher profiles need to be embedded throughout the school and teacher education systems' (Directorate for Education 2005, 12). Such a recognition is extremely important, especially in the context of a schooling system where 'the most pervasive understanding of the individual which one finds in Irish education is one which defines the person in terms of fixed, or given (sometimes innate) talents, abilities or intelligence' (Lynch 1987, 107). It is very important, then, that our pre-service teachers have a clear understanding about the nature and purpose of education and participation in service learning activities can certainly be very instrumental in arriving at such an understanding.

I would like to conclude by returning to the pre-service teacher who likened her participation in service learning with the removal of scales from her eyes, so that she see can more clearly that the learning context ought to be about providing a space where each individual learner can maximise his or her potential. Such an appreciation of the educational project, in my estimation, goes to the heart of the educational endeavour. It would certainly bode well for the future if such an understanding was to become mainstreamed throughout our entire education system, from pre-school through higher and continuing education.

References

Ayers, W. (ed) (1995), *To Become A Teacher: Making A Difference in Children's Lives* (New York: Teachers College Press).

Ayers, W., Hunt, J. and Quinn, T. (eds.) (1998), *Teaching for Social Justice* (New York: Teachers College Press).

Bohan, H. and Kennedy, G. (eds.) (1999), *Are We Forgetting Something? Our Society in the New Millennium* (Dublin: Veritas).

Clancy, P. (1986, 1995), 'Socialisation, Selection and Reproduction in Education', in Clancy et al. (eds.)

Clancy, P. et al. (eds) (1986, 1995), *Ireland: A Sociological Profile* (Dublin: IPA).

Cosgrove, J. et al. (2004), *Education for Life: The Achievements of 15-Year-Olds in Ireland in the Second Cycle of PISA*. (Dublin: Educational Research Centre) [website] <http://erc.ie/pdf/P03SummaryReport.pdf> accessed online 21 July 2006

Department of the Taoiseach (2005), *Speech by the Taoiseach, Bertie Ahern, T.D., at the Conference on the Future of the Community and Voluntary Sector*. Department of the Taoiseach [website] <http:// www.taoiseach.gov.ie/index.asp?docID=2508> accessed online 10 July 2006).

Directorate General for Education and Culture (2005), *Teachers Matter: Attracting, Developing and Retaining Effective Teachers* (Paris, France: OECD Publishing).

Drudy, S. (2003), 'Crude league tables are no measure of results', in *The Irish Times*, 9 September 2003.

Fitzgerald, G. (2003), *Reflections on the Irish State: Ireland Since Independence* (Dublin: Irish Academic Press).

Freire, P. (1970, 1995), *Pedagogy of the Oppressed* (New York: Continuum).

Greene, M. (1988), *The Dialectic of Freedom* (New York: Teachers College Press).

Greene, M. (1995a), 'Choosing a Past and Inventing a Future', in Ayers (ed).

Greene, M. (1995b), *Releasing the Imagination* (San Francisco: Jossey-Bass).

Greene, M. (1998), 'Teaching for Social Justice', in Ayers, Hunt and Quinn (eds.) *Teaching for Social Justice* (New York: Teachers College Press).

Learning In Deed: Recent Research on Service Learning: Abstracts (2000). Available online at <http://learningindeed.org/research/slresearch/abstracts.html> (accessed 21/07/2006).

Lynch, K. (1987), 'Dominant ideologies in Irish educational thought: consensualism, essentialism and meritocratic individualism', *Economic and Social Review*, 18:2), 101–122.

National Service-Learning in Teacher Education Partnership (2002), *Meeting NCATE Standards Through Service-Learning: Professional Knowledge & Skills*.

AACTE: Service-Learning Issue Brief. Available online at <http://www.usm. maine.edu/servicelearning/pdf/sl%20know.pdf#search='ServiceLearning%20Iss ue%20Brief%2C%20Winter%202002'>, accessed 21 July 2006.

Ó Tuathaigh, G. (2001), 'Contemplating Alternative Relationships of Power', in Bohan and Kenndy (eds.).

RTE News (2004), *Ireland placed top of Quality of Life poll*, 17 November 2004, RTE [website] <http://www.rte.ie/news/2004/1117/print/economist>, accessed 21 July 2006).

Valarsan-Toomey, M. (1998), 'Education: are we on the right road?', in *The Celtic Tiger: From the Outside Looking In*, (Dublin: Blackhall Publishing).

Chapter 10

Service Learning's Challenge to the Educator

Mark Doorley

Introduction[1]

I attended a conference several years ago at which I had the opportunity to listen to two faculty members from the University of Wisconsin. I am sorry to admit that I don't remember their names and have lost track of the conference proceedings so that I cannot give them due credit. Be that as it may, their talk and the introductory exercise have stayed with me to this day, and really serve as the fundamental motivation for this essay.

They began by putting on an overhead a copy of a letter written by an adult woman to her young adult daughter on the day she headed off to university. The mother expressed great hopes for her daughter and encouraged her to volunteer at a local soup kitchen, the same one she herself had worked at. The mother, as a student, had a wonderful experience at the soup kitchen and wanted her daughter to benefit in the same way. After reading the letter, the facilitators asked us to write out our response to the letter and then to share our response with our neighbour. I wrote that I was impressed by the mother's desire to share a meaningful experience with her daughter. My neighbour looked at me, surprised, and expressed her dismay that the soup kitchen was still running after nearly 20 years! The facilitators went on to claim that service learning pedagogy ought to lead to structural change such that current problems are resolved.

What I attempt with the students that I work with in my service learning courses ought to lead to structural change. That is a challenge that seems beyond me most of the time. Structural change is a pragmatic art that combines lofty ideals with political realism. My students leave my class with a thirst for social justice. They finish the semester with a heart full of compassion and a desire to work for social, economic and political change. Their idealism is full blown. However, I also know that with the end of the semester, very often, comes the end of a relationship with those students. I don't know what happens to them, and I become engaged with a new set of students who slowly begin to catch that same thirst for justice. It occurred

---

1 I am writing from the context of a Roman Catholic university (Villanova University) in the USA which massively conditions my reflections in this chapter. Thus, I am acutely aware that the claims I make about education may reflect the particular arrangements in my country and in particular at my institution, and I am sensitive to the limitations of that location.

to me that simply igniting the drive for justice is not sufficient. What happens when youthful idealism meets political/cultural/social/economic reality? I began to recognise my responsibility as a teacher to work for some kind of ongoing support for students who want to work for justice, as students and in their careers. I recognise the need to support students in their thirst for justice, but also to enable them to be practical agents of change.

In this chapter, I want to share with you some reflections on that responsibility. I will begin by looking at education as revolutionary in character and at service learning as a primary pedagogical mode of enacting that revolution. I will then outline the basis on which one can identify the responsibilities that academic staff have toward students who want to work for justice. Last, I will challenge us to think about the role of universities, throughout the world, as agents of revolution.

Education as Revolutionary

What do I mean by 'revolution?' I certainly don't mean picking up weapons and violently working for social change. What I mean by revolution is a turning around, turning upside down, an undoing, of the individual biases and the structural obstacles that stand in the way of the emergence of a truly free and just society. Education is the place where this revolution begins in which not only the oppressed are freed but in which all humanity is free.

During a speech offered to members of the Roman Catholic Jesuit Community involved in Higher Education in the United States, Peter-Hans Kolvenbach, S.J., Superior General of the Society of Jesus, reminded his audience that, 'Jesuit education has sought to educate "the whole person" intellectually and professionally, psychologically, morally and spiritually.' However, the 'whole person must have, in brief, a well-educated solidarity.' He went on to say that 'solidarity is learned through "contact" rather than through "concepts"', an idea he attributes to the late Pope John Paul II. He continued:

> Students, in the course of their formation, must let the gritty reality of this world into their lives, so they can learn to feel it, think about it critically, respond to its suffering and engage it constructively. They should learn to perceive, think, judge, choose and act for the rights of others, especially the disadvantaged and oppressed.[2] (Kolvenbach 2000)

I refer to this talk because I think we find here a necessary component of education as such. The notion of solidarity is of particular importance. What is solidarity? Paulo Freire, the Brazilian educator and philosopher, speaks of solidarity in the context of oppression.

> Solidarity requires that one enter into the situation of those with whom one is solidarity; it is a radical posture. The oppressor is solidarity with the oppressed only when he stops regarding the oppressed as an abstract category and sees them as persons who have been unjustly dealt with, deprived of their voice, cheated in the sale of their labor – when he

---

2   The entire speech can be accessed at http://www.scu.edu/news/releases/1000/ kolvenbach_speech.html.

stops making pious, sentimental, and individualistic gestures and risks an act of love. True solidarity is found only in the plenitude of this act of love, in its existentiality, in its praxis. To affirm that men are persons and as persons should be free, and yet to do nothing tangible to make this affirmation a reality, is a farce. (Freire 1968, 34-35)

Solidarity is built upon shared humanity. One can only be in solidarity with another human being, a person who should be free. It is not clear that one must actually be in the presence of the suffering other in order to be in solidarity with him or her. However, the incarnate meaning that is the other person in her flesh, with her eyes, with her smile, seems to be a condition for the recognition of personhood in that other. Pictures in a magazine, a documentary, the witness of one who has been 'there', these can be rationalised, ignored, denied, indeed, erased. But can the other's smile at my presence, the hand reaching out in greeting, the warmth of an embrace? Can I 'erase' these acts of freedom?[3] Face to face, person to person, freedom to freedom. To be with the suffering in their place of suffering: this is the meaning of solidarity. It is only this solidarity that will lead to a praxis that is truly revolutionary in scope.

Often there is a disconnect in students between an appreciation of a shared humanity with those suffering around them and any attempt to relieve that suffering. This disconnect occurs in the classroom because the enormity of the structural injustices that create conditions of oppression and dehumanisation is so daunting that students fail to understand that these structures are the objects of human choice. There is a profoundly ahistorical consciousness operating in my students whenever the topic of conversation turns to issues like economic justice for all people or the reworking of first world/third world economic relations. In their view, these issues are static, beyond the scope of human deliberation and choice. This is the way the world is and there is no point to attempt to change things.

Certainly this attitude can be attributed to the unwillingness of the students to advert to human responsibility for the way things are and human responsibility for the future. However, in a variety of ways, students communicate the view that structural problems are not objects of deliberation. They cannot be other than they are, so the only reasonable solution is to adjust to them. There is a way in which the consciousness of these students (and they are not unique by any means) has been formed in such a way that questions that might lead to structural change are ruled irrelevant. This de-formation of consciousness is one of the characteristics Paulo Freire attributes to 'oppressed consciousness'.

Freire notes that the oppressed experience the world as given to them, as not of their own making. The relationship between the oppressor and the oppressed is one of prescription. 'Every prescription represents the imposition of one man's choice upon another, transforming the consciousness of the man prescribed to into one that conforms with the prescriber's consciousness.' (Freire 1968, 31) The oppressed are

---

3 In Jonathan Kozol's *Ordinary Resurrections*, he makes a similar point as he quotes Reverend Overall, the pastor of the church around which many of the conversations recorded in the book take place: 'Looking into the eyes of a poor person is upsetting because normal people have a conscience. Touching the beggar's hand, meeting his gaze, makes a connection. It locks you in. It makes it hard to sleep, or hard to pray'. (Kozol 1995, 223)

not free to make their own choices and to create their own world. Since theirs is a world of prescription, the idea that the world is created by human deliberation and choice is foreign and, in fact, terrifying. Something similar can be said of today's students. The forces at work forming their consciousness are essentially prescriptive. The idea that the world in which we live, a world of which structural injustice is a massive component, is a product of human deliberation and choice is, in large part, a foreign and fearful idea. It is this sense of fear and strangeness that education must address.

In his attempts to educate the peasants of Brazil for their own liberative praxis, Freire found them to be quite distrustful of their own abilities. Having lived their lives according to the dictates of an oppressive regime, the idea that they could act in order to change their situation was often too much for them. Freire notes:

> They call themselves ignorant and say the "professor" is the one who has knowledge and to whom they should listen. Almost never do they realise that they, too, know things. They have learned in their relations with the world and with other men....They distrust themselves. (Freire 1968, 49-50)

They do not have the experience of deliberating, choosing and acting in such a way that their autonomy is affirmed and respected. Their alienation from their own power is quite intractable. It is necessary, then, to organise the oppressed and to enable them to act in such a way that their actions have the effect of transforming their world, a world that for so long was under the power only of the oppressor.

> It is only when the oppressed find the oppressor out and become involved in the organised struggle for their liberation that they begin to believe in themselves. This discovery cannot be purely intellectual but must also involve action; nor can it be limited to mere activism, but must include serious reflection: only then will it be praxis. (Freire 1968, 52)

'Finding the oppressor out' is to discover that the oppressor and the oppressed share a common humanity, that both share responsibility for the ongoing creation of the world in which they live. This is a first step toward liberation. But this must also be accompanied by action, action aimed at transformation. The action that Freire calls for is not simply acting for the sake of acting. It is action followed by reflection leading to more action. Action transforms the world in which one lives; reflection insures that this action is authentic, leading to a more humanising world.

Freire creates a pedagogy for the oppressed that liberates them from the prescriptive dominance of the oppressor and energises them into praxis that leads to the transformation of the world, the object of human deliberation and choice. The goal of this praxis is not to install a new oppressor, but to liberate all people, including the former oppressor, from the dynamic of violence and oppression. As Freire states:

> The pedagogy of the oppressed, as a humanist and libertarian pedagogy, has two distinct stages. In the first, the oppressed unveil the world of oppression and through the praxis commit themselves to its transformation.

In the second stage, in which the reality of oppression has already been transformed, this pedagogy ceases to belong to the oppressed and becomes a pedagogy of all men in the process of permanent liberation. (Freire 1968, 40)

The pedagogy that Freire creates to liberate the poor of Brazil is a pedagogy that aims to heighten human consciousness to its role in the constitution of human history. Education is the process of discovering, affirming and valuing one's historicity and the responsibility that follows upon being an historical subject.

Education ought to engage the whole human subject in the task of her existence. Education is not merely an engagement with concepts, but it is also, and in some sense, more critically, an engagement with others, the result of 'contact' with and service to those in need. The service, however, cannot be merely service. It must also involve reflection, a reflection that can enable people to be critical about the world in which the needs that the service addresses occur at all.

The students are not oppressed in the way in which Freire's Brazilian peasants are oppressed. In fact, when I have taught Freire's text and have tried to make connections between the consciousness of the peasants and the consciousness of my students, I have been condemned for belittling the suffering of the peasants by comparing theirs to the 'suffering' of students in the United States. The point of comparison I want to indicate, though, is not the actually suffering but the characteristic of 'oppressed consciousness' that I think both groups share. They share a sense that the world is beyond their control, not of their own making, something to which they must adjust. Freire's pedagogy challenges that consciousness until students, whether they be Brazilian peasants or wealthy students in the United States, come to realise that the world and its ways are an object of deliberation and choice.

The clearest pedagogical model that takes seriously Freire's challenge about education is service learning. The praxiological model functions throughout the service learning experience, it is hoped, culminating in the students' new or renewed appreciation of their responsibility as historical subjects for the world that comes into existence by their attentiveness or inattentiveness, by their intelligence or stupidity, by their reasonableness or unreasonableness, by their responsibility or their irresponsibility. Through the process of action, reflection and action, students come to appreciate the dialectical character of their existence and the ongoing challenge of living up to the demands of one's historicity.

The Basis of Responsibility

What I have attempted to describe is a classroom that exists beyond the four walls, that inhabits the whole life of the student. The service learning course is not simply a means to learn the fundamental principles of sociology, psychology, or philosophy. It is also an experience that opens doors of possibility and responsibility that cannot easily be shut again. As I noted above, once the student begins to discover and appreciate that unjust structures are the objects of human deliberation and choice, once she discovers and appreciates the humanness of the 'world', it becomes apparent that she has a responsibility to contribute to the ongoing making of that 'world'. The relationships that he or she formed in the community, the solidarity that is built up over time and shared experience, the knowledge that is gained from reflection and analysis; all this creates conditions that are truly liberatory of the student but also demanding of his/her future. But, the semester comes to an end, and this liberated and newly aware young adult is left to fend for him or herself in a political/economic/social reality that is not welcoming of those who would seek change.

Am I justified in awakening a student to the demands of justice? Am I justified to awaken in the student a desire to work for social change, knowing that the semester will soon end and our relationship will, most likely, also end? Again, the problem for me is that idealism must be tempered by realism. Unfortunately, one semester, one class, cannot sufficiently enable a student to balance his/her idealism with a sober realism. If the purpose of education is to awaken students to their historical subjectivity and thus their responsibility for the world, then the institution must make it possible for students to spend the time it takes to be idealists with realistic vision. This cannot be done unless the institution itself puts in place the academic, co-curricular, and personal resources that enable the student to arrive at a balance between idealism and realism such that they can effectively work for social change. Why am I responsible as an academic staff member to work for such institutional commitment? What would the institutional commitment look like if it existed? To these questions I would like to now turn.

Academic Responsibility and Institutional Issues

Why am I responsible? I am responsible in the same way that Dr. Frankenstein is responsible for the creature he brings into existence. I don't mean to imply that our students are monsters, but insofar as we have created the conditions under which a person emerges from the false sense of the world that so many of our students share into a world that is an object of human deliberation and choice, we are responsible to be a support and guide through that transition. Since I am the one who invited them into a vulnerable and frightening position, I must be available for them throughout the transition. For the same reason, the institution should be committed to providing the support necessary to help students figure out what it might mean for them to be committed to living an authentic existence as an historical, and so, responsible, being. Unfortunately, most institutions of higher education in the USA do not provide that kind of support. Or if they do it is done on the side, as an exception rather than as the rule.

Let me give you a concrete example. Architecture and financial allocations speak volumes about what is important. At Villanova University we have a centre for peace and justice education. In addition to peace and justice courses, the centre provides office space and support to student organisations dedicated to any number of peace and justice issues. It is to the centre that students who might awaken to their responsibility in my service learning class might go to pursue that responsibility. Ironically, it is in the basement of a residence hall! My university has a mission statement that explicitly affirms that our university is committed to working for a more just world, yet its centre for peace and justice is in a basement, at the foot of a newly renovated and magnificent school of business. I share this with you not to single out my university as the only one in the USA that does this. I merely want to point out that offering support to students to work for justice in an institution that itself falls short is very difficult. While Villanova wants to support student activism, it does not want that support to undermine or take away from other, larger, and, in the view of the administration, more significant activities/programmes.

The academic staff and, beyond that, the institution, hold the more powerful position in the teacher/student relationship. With that power comes responsibility. An invitation into a life-changing experience needs to be followed up by support as the student who takes up the invitation seeks to integrate that experience and understands its challenge. It is akin to inviting someone who does not know how to swim to jump into the river. The student knows that you know that she does not know how to swim. She trusts that you wouldn't just let her struggle, but that you would assist her. She jumps into the river at your invitation, trusting that you will take care of her, yet you go off to another challenge. There is a sense in which this is my feeling about the way things end in a service learning course. They have jumped into the river, but I have been called away to another group. Who is there to make sure they don't drown?

A key to understanding the basis of the responsibility I am detailing here is that service learning, education in general, is not, and ought not to be, a purely intellectual affair. Education is a holistic affair. It will be helpful to borrow a notion from the late Bernard Lonergan to elucidate what I mean by education as 'holistic'. Lonergan claims that our experience of the world is patterned in various ways. Many times the situation I find myself in will call for a particular patterning. At other times, certain patterns are more preferred than others by the particular person. The critical function of patterns of experience is that the pattern determines, in no small part, the kinds of concerns or questions that a person might have about the situation (Lonergan 1992). For example, when I am baking a cake, I am not concerned about the way in which the ingredients I am using have been processed, or the various interlocking systems that brought the chocolate from South America, to the port of Baltimore, to my grocery store. No, I am concerned with baking a cake. However, if I was examining the economic relations that made possible the presence of this kind of chocolate in my grocery, I may ask those questions. Baking a cake is a practical concern; understanding the importation of chocolates is a more theoretical concern. A dominant pattern of experience is what Lonergan calls the 'dramatic pattern' (Lonergan 1992).

Human deliberation and choice occur most often in the dramatic pattern of experience. This pattern is operative in 'ordinary human living'; its 'concern is to get things done' (Lonergan 1992). It illuminates the essentially artistic task of human living. Humans meet the biological demands for nourishment and sex with the dramatic demand for etiquette of one kind or another. Humans are concerned with the way they carry themselves, the kinds of clothes they wear, the jobs they perform. These are not biological concerns, nor are they exclusively intellectual concerns. However, they are mediations of biological demands and they are the demands of an intelligent actor.

These actors are in a drama that is played out before others who are also actors in the self-same drama. Each is intelligently mediating his or her biological urges in the presence of others. These others fall somewhere on a scale ranging from intimates to strangers and how one acts in their presence is determined to one degree or another by their place on this scale. Living in the drama of one's life, in the presence of others, is complex, demanding, frustrating and rewarding. However, 'the drama of ordinary living is not ordinary drama'.

> It is not learning a role and developing in oneself the feelings appropriate to its performance. It is not the prior task of assembling materials and through insight imposing upon them an artistic pattern. For in ordinary living there are not first the materials and then the pattern, nor first the role and then the feelings. On the contrary, the materials that emerge in consciousness are already patterned, and the pattern is already charged emotionally and cognitively. (Lonergan 1992, 212)

The drama is dynamic and unfolding in a dialectical fashion, both intelligently and unintelligently, both reasonably and unreasonably, both responsibly and irresponsibly. It is not static, nor is it given to the actors as an already finished product. The actor must discover that his or her role is whatever he or she decides to make it in the context of a tradition created by those 'on stage' before he or she came along and in the context of other actors who are, simultaneously and with varied degrees of candour, creating their roles.

The importance of the dramatic pattern of experience and its illumination of the artistic dimension of ordinary living is that insights into one's role in life and one's responsibility in the drama must take this patterning into account. As Lonergan so adeptly explains in *Insight,* there are a variety of ways in which the dramatic pattern can break down because ordinary human living takes place in the presence of others, it is vulnerable to any number of oversights, blockages, or strategies of denial that may not be operative in the intellectual pattern of experience in which the desire to know is pure and unrestricted. In the dramatic pattern, the concern is to accomplish things, to act, to get things done. Hence, vulnerability to the sources of unreasonable and irresponsible action increases.

Students who are engaged in reflection upon service experiences that reveal to them a world of human making that is unjust and violent are pivoting between an intellectually patterned activity and a dramatically patterned activity. When my students enter the classroom where they are 'coaching' children in literacy, they come with a more profound understanding of the obstacles that these children face in life as a result of human deliberation and choice. Insights that occur in the context of a service learning course are not occurring in isolation from the dramatic patterning of that student's experience. For example, a student may begin to understand the structural dimensions of the poverty and dysfunction of inner city public education. Because she is involved, albeit to a small degree, in inner-city public education through her literacy 'coaching', her insight is caught up not only in the throes of the struggle to understand the relations between things, but also in the throes of the struggle to understand her own role in the world. An engineering student said to me a few years ago; I don't want to be an engineer if being an engineer only adds to the suffering of people like those whom we 'coach'. Implicit in her statement is her grasp of the relationship between economic, political and social structures that have created the suffering of children in the inner city as well as the way in which her future career plans may aid and abet the continuation of those structures.

The dramatic pattern is operative in the service learning classroom in a way that it is not in the traditional classroom. It is within the dramatic pattern of experience that the subject decides who she wants to be. One does not make choices about one's role in life in the intellectual pattern of experience. One can study and understand Aristotle, Kant, Mill, or the Christian Scriptures and not alter one's role in the world one bit. Operating in the intellectual pattern does not, of itself, involve one's ordinary living. However, in service learning both intellectual and dramatic patterns are operative in a sometimes rocky partnership, producing a moment of decision and action that is otherwise not possible.

Lonergan's discussion of the insights gained in therapy is similar to what can occur in the service learning course. In therapy, Lonergan suggests that insights into one's behaviour 'must occur, not in the detached and disinterested intellectual pattern of experience, but in the dramatic pattern in which images are tinged with affect' (Lonergan, 1992, 225). The inhibitions that effect the waking behaviour of the subject are unaffected by insights that occur in the intellectual pattern. Since the inhibitions are affects that have been repressed, the insight too must occur in the context of affects and so in the dramatic pattern of experience. What are the insights that a subject has in the therapeutic context but insights whose ramifications touch upon his or her performance in ordinary living? An insight that occurs in the intellectual pattern of experience has the strange quality of seeming to be someone else's life. However, when it occurs in the dramatic pattern, it is clear whose life is involved and the stakes of adherence to one's newfound insights are much higher.[4]

It is the unfolding of the drama of my students' lives that demands that I be attentive, intelligent, reasonable and responsible for not only the service learning experiences I establish for them, but also for ongoing support of their tentative beginnings at being responsible subjects of history. The whole person is in the classroom. We have for so long thought of the classroom as one site of development, intellectual development, and the residence halls, jobs, and families as the site of moral and psychological development. However, this depends on the strained, and ultimately misguided, idea that intellectual development proceeds independent of the other two. Education is not a purely intellectual affair, and so I must be attentive as an academic to the whole person of my student. It is also incumbent upon universities to provide structures that attend to the whole student and that enable that student to integrate the various developmental tasks that education is challenging him or her to take up.

The relationship between my students and I, and between my students and their university, give rise to responsibilities primarily because education frees students from the world of their youth and invites them into a world of co-responsibility, a

---

4   In *Five Lectures on Psychoanalysis* Sigmund Freud speaks to the necessity of a patient recalling a trauma and feeling the feelings again. It is not sufficient to simply recall the incident, as if one were recalling a movie that one had seen. The patient must recall the incident and re-feel, as it were, the feelings that were aroused in the original incident. Such a re-feeling, for Freud, is key to releasing the psychic blocks that are interfering with one's normal living.

world of solidarity, a world that depends on their responsible action. This is a new and sometimes frightening world, but it is a world in which the student understands and values that her liberation is tied up with the liberation of all others. It is this that is most difficult to live with since a tempered idealism will appreciate the great distance that we must go before the full liberation of all is realised.

Since education is a freedom from the inability/unwillingness to act for a freedom to act, it is revolutionary. To be an educated person is to work for the freedom of all, to work for justice, to seek social and structural change where injustice reigns. Institutions of higher education must make it possible for all students to be educated in this fullest sense. These institutions are certainly not offering a merely academic education. As the Jesuit Superior General said, education involves our solidarity with those marginalised and voiceless people around the globe. For us to be free, they must be free.

So, what are the responsibilities for academic staff, and for an institution of higher education, to meet the demands of education?

First, the academic must herself be committed to an ongoing educational journey. There are no people who can speak from a position that is beyond question or challenge. She must become a fellow student as well as a guide. Educators can no longer pass along bits of data; they must engage in a dynamic and dialectical process with their students, such that the teacher becomes student and students can become teachers.

Second, the academic must always design learning experiences that address the whole person of the student. She should be willing to collaborate with 'student life' personnel to create learning experiences that allow the student to develop in all areas of his/her life.

Third, the academic ought to work with the community to ensure that there are plenty of opportunities for mutual bonds of affection to form between students and the members of the community. These bonds of affection strengthen the solidarity that gives rise to the thirst for justice.

Fourth, the academic ought to connect her students with the ongoing work for justice that is taking place throughout the university and the community. Students need to be nurtured by a community of like-minded people, all of whom are trying to work for change in the world that we have. It is incumbent on the member of staff to introduce her students to this community.

Finally, the academic ought to be working for justice herself, whether through her research or through active participation in social change movements. The students need a model of the integration of mind and body, academic pursuits and work for justice. The staff member's active pursuit of justice sets an example of the revolutionary character of education.

The academic who lives up to the obligations I have identified above can sometimes find himself/herself struggling alone. The institutions where academic staff find themselves are not always committed to supporting the ability of teachers to meet their obligations to their students. By and large, that is because universities have not quite grasped that education is primarily about liberation. So often universities reinforce the 'oppressed consciousness' with which students enter the university.

However, a university that does approach education as liberation can be identified by the following characteristics:

First, academic and administrative staff are actively engaged in work for justice. A research institute tailors its agenda to meet the pressing needs of the poorest of the poor, of the voiceless, the marginalised.

Retention and promotion of academic staff is linked to the participation of that person, either in research, teaching and service, in the work of justice. What this means, practically, is that an institution will not retain or tenure an academic staff member unless he or she can demonstrate his or her commitment to justice.

Third, academic staff will work hand in hand with student life/support personnel to create programmes/opportunities that will mentor students through the transition from oppressed consciousness to liberation, and from unfettered idealists to pragmatic champions of justice.

At every opportunity, through scholarly publications, courses taught, staff development, and student recruitment, the university criticises those in power, both secular and religious, who perpetuate unjust secular and religious structures in economics and politics.

Finally, the university recognises, through its rewards structure, who among its academic staff, students and administrators are most active and most vociferous in their defence of justice. More than anything else, this communicates to the university community and to the world what is held in high esteem at that university.

A University as an Agent of Revolution

At this point in this essay I realise that I have used the term revolution many times and I know that what I suggest for policy at institutions of higher education is indeed revolutionary. Let me conclude with some insight into the university as an agent of revolution. When young adults show up at the university, they come with lots of notions about what the world is like and what their place in that world is. They may be privileged people who expect the world to continue giving them what they want. They may be less privileged people who have a grudge against the world, or simply want to do what it takes to be part of the privileged class. No matter what their shape when they show up at the university, when they leave they should not be the same. They should leave the university as men and women who are fully engaged in their own history, in their responsibility to be co-creators of the world in which they are to live. It does not mean that they need to look the same, or think the same, or pursue the same careers. However, what they will share is a thirst for a world in which all people, regardless of language, skin colour, sexual identity or orientation, economic status, political affiliations, or religious affiliations, are free. Freedom is not only freedom from any type of bondage or oppression. More profoundly, freedom is for being a subject of history in collaboration with other subjects of that same history. This is what is revolutionary. To shepherd human beings into the overwhelming responsibility that is theirs as historical beings: this is the mark of the revolutionary. This does not mean that tradition has no place, nor does it mean that the past has no place. What it does mean is that educated human beings ought to be people for whom the world is an object of deliberation and choice. As such, oppression is not a necessity, be it oppression of the mind or oppression of the body. Injustice is not a constitutive element of the universe. It is the result of human beings not being intelligent, reasonable and responsible. We are those human beings who, while educated for freedom, still struggle to be free. It is a journey that only begins with one's formal education, but one which needs the nurturing that a higher education can provide.

So, those of us who work in institutions of higher education, and in no small way, those who work with younger children, make no mistake about it: You and I are about the revolution that will bring tomorrow into existence. Are we responsible for that? You bet we are. Will we shirk from it? I'm sure some of us will. The quirky thing about being subjects of history, though, is that any choice we make in this regard is a choice with consequences. My desire is to make the most responsible choice I can today, and be willing to revisit it tomorrow.

References

Crowe, F. and Doran, R. (1992), *Volume 3: The Collected Works of Bernard Lonergan* (Toronto: University of Toronto Press).

Freire, P. (1968), *Pedagogy of the Oppressed* (New York, NY: Seabury Press).

Kolvenbach, P. '*The Service of Faith and the Promotion of Justice in American Jesuit Higher Education*', delivered at Santa Clara University October 6, 2000. Santa Clara University [website] <http://www.scu.edu/news/releases/1000/koverbach_speech.html>

Kozol, J. (1995), *Ordinary Resurrections* (New York, NY: Harper Perennial Books).

Lonergan, B. (1992), '*Insight: A Study of Human Understanding*', in Frederick et al (eds.).

Chapter 11

Serving, Learning and Reflective Practice at Roehampton University, London

Jennifer Iles

Introduction

In the United States of America, service learning has been an established part of the curriculum since the 1960s. Although there has been a long tradition in British higher education of specialised, experiential learning courses, such as the qualified teacher training courses, until relatively recently there had not been any systematic endeavour to incorporate service-based experiential education into the mainstream curriculum (Walsh 1994, 13). The Roehampton University, formerly known as the Roehampton Institute, was one of the first institutions in Britain to address this formerly neglected area in higher education and since 1993 it has adopted service learning as part of its general undergraduate programme.[1] On average, the course now attracts about 30–40 students every year.

Roehampton University initially became involved in the provision of service learning in 1992 when a group of students came to study here from various universities in America on an exchange programme run by the International Partnership for Service-Learning and Leadership (IPS-L), based in New York. Our links with the IPS-L remain to this day and we continue to receive students from the United States.

Higher Education and Civic Engagement in the United Kingdom

Today, significant changes have taken place in higher education in Britain. In 1997 the National Committee of Inquiry into Higher Education's Report, *Higher Education in the Learning Society*, known as the 'Dearing Report', specifically addressed the issue of experiential learning and emphasised how community service learning provides one of the most effective ways of providing key skills and capabilities which not only prepare graduates for lifelong learning but also contributes significantly to their employability (Annette 2003). The report, together with the promotion of 'active citizenship' and the encouragement of volunteering to support community organisations by the New Labour government, have prompted a considerable upsurge of interest and support for this type of educational approach

---

1   As a natural development of its undergraduate service learning programme, in 1997 Roehampton validated an experiential Masters in International Service.

and an increasing number of institutions are now offering students an opportunity to participate in programmes of this type. As Hall et al. note, in the UK there has been progressively more talk of a 'third mission' for universities, which alongside their traditional roles of teaching and research, connects them with their local communities through knowledge transfer, education and business partnerships (Hall et al. 2004, 35). In his letter to HEFCE in 2000, the then Secretary of State for Education, David Blunkett, promoted volunteering as being: 'intrinsically beneficial to all concerned, and integral to the development of generic skills among students as well as higher education's wider responsibilities to local communities' (Blunkett 2000).

Roehampton University and Service Learning

In the service learning course offered at Roehampton University, students are required to make a substantial commitment to service. They can register for twenty, thirty or forty credit modules and the number of hours they spend at their placements depends upon the number of credits they are taking. A twenty credit course requires a total of 120 hours; thirty credits requires 180 hours; and forty credits requires 260 hours. Continuity and longevity are beneficial for both students and agencies. For the students, a considerable obligation to their placements enables them to experience significant insightful and meaningful encounters. For voluntary organisations, which are often short of volunteers, the training that they are frequently required to offer recruits can be expensive in terms of resources and staff, and this may lead them to be apprehensive about taking on students who are unable to commit themselves for sizeable periods of time (Hall et al. 2004, 43). Students do not receive any credit for their agency work. Rather, assessment is based on the production of a service placement file which consists of a variety of written assignments: a non-assessed journal which charts their experience and progress; a set of critical incident papers in which they have to objectively analyse a challenging situation at their placements; a profile of the placement agency and its relation to the wider society; and lastly a concluding paper which explores the links between service, academic learning and personal development.

Service learning is multi-disciplinary and as such it can be integrated into a wide variety of academic disciplines. However, as Enos notes, it lends itself particularly well to the sociological field, which has always embraced community engagement as well as addressing the structural causes of social problems (Enos 1998, 8). By providing students with the opportunity to use their service experiences to acquire a deeper understanding of social problems, service learning is lifted beyond functioning only as charity (Herzberg 1994:308). Simply having students do charity encourages the notion that they do service *for* disadvantaged people rather than seeing it as an activity carried out *with* them (Parker-Gwin and Mabry 1998, 278). There is more to service than just making students feel good. At Roehampton, service learning is located within the sociology programme in the School of Business and Social Sciences. The course though, is also available to students across the rest of the University's schools – Arts, Education and Human and Life Sciences. The weekly lectures and seminars are based around ideologies which have underpinned the shifts in responsibility for welfare and the meeting of human needs. Four different ideals are discussed: social equality; freedom of the individual; communitarianism; and mutual aid. By basing the lectures around this subject matter, all the students on the course will have had contact in both their daily lives and their placements with some of the debates discussed in class, whatever their academic background. As Giddens points out; 'most of the debates that occupy people are sociological debates now. They are about crime, cities, families, sexuality, individualism, social solidarity, the limits of industrialism, the changing nature of work... Because such topics are so widely discussed, to some degree they lose the sense of being a separate endeavour called sociology' (Giddens 1998, 73).

Conceptions of Reflection within Service Learning

In addition to the academic content, of course, at the heart of service learning at Roehampton, is reflection. All the papers that make up the placement file require a measure of this vital component, particularly the journals and the critical incident papers. And yet, as Moon notes, the concept of reflection has been theorised and approached in so many diverse ways by various theorists that it may appear that the term encompasses a range of human capacities rather than just one (Moon 2001,2). Even though in academia reflection is now being used extensively in a range of contexts in learning, this lack of definition can make the achievement of reflective thinking difficult. For many, Moon observes, it remains a somewhat mysterious activity (Moon 2001, 1).

One major theoretical approach to reflection comes from John Dewey, whose educational and social philosophy has been very influential in the development of experiential education (Giles and Eyler 1994). In his work, *How We Think: A Restatement of the Relation of Reflective Thinking to the Educative Process*, Dewey described reflective thinking as 'a kind of thinking that consists in turning a subject over in the mind and giving it serious and consecutive consideration' (Dewey 1933, 3). For Dewey, reflective thinking should be guided by scientifically rational choices: 'By putting the consequences of different ways and lines of action before the mind, it enables us to know what we are about when we act. It converts action that is merely appetitive, blind, and impulsive into intelligent action' (Dewey 1933, 17).

Fendler comments that Dewey's idea of reflective thinking signified a triumph of reason and science over instinct and impulse (Fendler 2003, 18). It is also future-orientated in that he saw it as a way of exercising the imagination toward future possibilities. Reflection requires the individual to imagine what would happen in a situation if (x) were to happen or alternatively, if (y) were to occur. For Dewey, it is a type of forethought which: 'deliberately institute(s), in advance of the happening of various contingencies and emergencies of life, devices for detecting their approach and registering their nature, for warding off what is unfavourable, or at least for protecting ourselves from its full impact...' (Dewey 1933, 19).

Dewey's philosophy influenced the development of several theories about how individuals construct knowledge through experience. Kolb (1984), for instance, is well known for his cycle of experiential learning. In this model a continuous cycle of concrete experience, reflective observation, abstract conceptualisation and active experimentation, bring about learning, change and growth. As Stanton et al. remark, Kolb's cycle is useful because it highlights how the skills of observation and recording are key to students' reflective experience (Stanton et al. 1999, 161). If students are to take charge of their own learning, these are the kind of skills that they need to learn and use. However, both Moon (1999) and Stanton et al. (1999) contend that although it is a useful teaching tool, Kolb's cycle of continuous learning oversimplifies what is actually a very complex activity. Also as Moon points out, Kolb suggests that reflection appears to be part and parcel of the practice of observation, and this apparently occurs *before* a person has actually learnt anything (Moon 2001, 3). This seems to contradict the common-sense idea of reflection as being part of the processing of material already learned.

Another strand contributing to our understanding of reflection comes from Schön who focussed on reflection in professional knowledge. His books, *The Reflective Practitioner: How Professionals Think in Action* (1983), followed by *Educating the Reflective Practitioner: Toward a New Design for Teaching and Learning in the Professions* (1987), both focused on reflection in the context of professional practice. As Fendler remarks, however, there is a fundamental tension between Schön's discourse on reflection, which is understood to be intuitive and practice based, and Dewey's more positivistic, scientific approach (Fendler 2003, 19). Schön identifies two types of reflection: reflection-in-action (thinking on your feet) and reflection-on-action (retrospective thinking). In opposition to Dewey's belief in logical reasoning and 'consistent and orderly thinking' (Dewey 1933,48), Schön emphasises that it is the value of uncertainty which is a helpful aspect of professional reflective practice:

> A practitioner's reflection can serve as a corrective to over-learning. Through reflection, he can surface and criticise the tacit understandings that have grown up around the repetitive experiences of a specialised practice, and can make new sense of the situations of uncertainty or uniqueness which he may allow himself to experience (Schön 1983, 61).

In order to make sense of these different approaches, Moon pulls these various ideas into a common-sense summarising model, which has proved useful in explaining and introducing reflective activities to students at Roehampton University. She also realistically suggests that reflection (as both a surface and a deeper process) is basically a simple practice but with complex outcomes (2001:4). Although in the past Kolb's cycle was utilised to introduce students to reflection, mainly because much of the literature on experiential learning is based on his model, its vagueness inhibited a satisfactory explanation of the reflective process.

Yet as Moon surmises, while some students find reflection easy, and will just 'take to it', others tend to struggle with it. Some students are simply naturally more reflective than others (Moon 2001, 10). For example, in a critical incident paper written by a student who worked as a classroom assistant at a school for disabled children, she relates her experience of being bitten by a child but stops short of any meaningful exploration of the episode: 'Before I knew it, this totally dependent, defenceless young child bit me. I was startled by the incident more than anything else...I initially felt shock when this happened to me. Looking back it was not a big deal at all'.

However, many of my students have reported that reflection has indeed helped them to see and evaluate their learning, see the consequences of their actions, and their responsibility to their clients and their organisations. As one commented: 'perhaps as a society we have lost touch with the value of contemplation'. Also, importantly, many realise that in the world outside of academia, circumstances and events are rarely clear cut and unequivocal in nature:

> Service learning taught me that in real situations there is ambiguity whereas my academic study had equipped me for rules... Service Learning involves an element of chaos; there is an element of complexity not present in model-led learning...This can be a hazardous journey.

Another wrote:

> I believe the course and my placement raised issues around my self-perception, which I am still working on. To engage in service learning required me to develop a mode of thinking which embraced uncertainty, doubt and all its discomforts.

Another essential component of the course is to introduce students to the values of service learning. The course at Roehampton University begins with readings from Kendall's *Combining Service and Learning: A Resource Book for Community and Public Service* (1990), namely Sigmon's *Principles of Service Learning* and Stanton's *Service Learning: Groping Toward a Definition*. Initially many students are unable to grasp the full import of Sigmon's three principles of service learning in which he suggests a philosophy of reciprocal learning (Stanton 1990, 66). While they may understand what the author says at a surface level, at this stage of the course many of them have not yet had much experience of serving and learning in their placements, and they often comment in their written work that they did not really see the true significance of his ideas until later in their service. Crucially, though, it introduces them to the notion of service itself – that they are not just taking a module that offers work experience, but they are there to learn and serve in their communities. Both articles prompt discussion about the idea of service, so that students start thinking about giving to the community, rather than using it solely for their own benefit. The premise that both providers and recipients of service should be empowered can prompt useful reflection about the quality of their experience. One student, working for a support agency for victims of crime, wrote:

> I liked Sigmon's views on what service learning can and should be. I tried to apply his ideas to[my agency] as an organisation. In theory, [the agency] is intended to help the receiver, but whether it actually accomplishes this or not is almost solely dependent on the volunteer. In thinking about my own time here, I can think of a number of occasions when I might have been able to do more for someone, but any number of reasons prevented me from doing so. ...This raises the question of whether volunteers should be more answerable for their quality of service – but the problem with increasing scrutiny

of volunteers is that they themselves my react adversely, and they always have the option to simply walk away.

Another student, writing about her first week at a school for disabled children described her initial reaction to the notion of mutuality and reciprocity in learning and serving:

> He sputtered again and I felt huge gobs of spit and tiny globules of apple and yoghurt still left in his mouth from lunch as they hit my face… I knew I was here to serve, that Thomas was a "client", was supposed to dictate the service and that I, through serving, was supposed to help become, as Sigmon (1979) suggests "healthier, wiser, freer, more autonomous"…. Thomas, autonomous? …And then Thomas' father entered, startling me out of my thoughts. …I saw the overwhelming love that this man had for his son, damaged, unpromising, whatever negative words I could think of, they didn't matter. …Seeing this simple act of a parent collecting his child from school…was an enormously evocative moment for me. [It] dispelled any questions about these students' worth…. These children are…worthy in every way as much as anyone else, yes, they have incredible depth and power – because look at the love they inspire… And starting from that position of love, I am much more equipped to serve properly, to openly respond to the client's cues and needs, and to learn myself.

Other readings from Kendall's work which are used at this early stage are Illich's paper, *To Hell with Good Intentions* and Cruz's article, *A Challenge to the Notion of Service*. Both articles challenge students' perceptions of themselves as volunteers. Often, as students, they are unaware of their class position in society and of power they may unwittingly exert on their clients. In seminars we look at how their clients, such as the homeless, or children in a care home, might perceive them, possibly as comfortably-off people who can afford not to work for a number of years. The controversial piece by Illich in particular, in which he advises students to: 'Come to look, come to climb our mountains, to enjoy our flowers. Come to study. But do not come to help' typically generates much discussion (Illich 1990, 320). Although his arguments are tailored specifically for those who embark on service in developing countries, they are based on a much broader argument, namely that they in fact 'serve' out of very selfish motivations and that as privileged outsiders, they can wreak havoc by coming into a world they know nothing about. This work though, does strike a chord with many students who eventually concede that it contained valuable cautionary advice, as one confessed:

> I certainly see myself in this description…. I am a sort of service learning archetype: a young, educated, privileged person entering a world of people profoundly different from any he/she has ever known, hoping to "do some good". Like most, I found it hard and painful at times, but emerged fairly triumphantly, feeling that I have grown and matured. Looking through Illich's eyes, this maturation seems very self-conscious and almost cheap… At the beginning, I found myself exaggerating the hardships of it – both to others and in my own head.

The student then perceptively rightly points out that in both American and British cultures, we are taught to assume that what you like the least is often best for you

– 'no pain, no gain'. As she says, 'there is virtue and purity in self-sacrifice and suffering'. But she goes on to acknowledge, however, that if the focus is really on the client:

> ..then the issue of my suffering, my virtue, is irrelevant. After all, I'm hardly more helpful if I'm miserable; I may be somehow improving my soul, "bettering myself", but perhaps at the expense of those people I'm supposed to be helping.

Illich's article has undoubtedly proved to be a useful conduit for some meaningful reflection about our notions of serving in the community. Because of its confrontational content, it readily facilitates discussion among the students and prompts them to start thinking seriously about their endeavours at their placements, and why they have really wanted to take the course in the first place. It also challenges them at the start to rid themselves of having a 'white knight' attitude where they may see themselves as philanthropic, altruistic people, here to share their largesse with the have-nots (Everett 1998, 301).

The students are then steered towards the sociological content of the lectures by an introduction to Wright Mill's (1970) ideas about the use of the 'sociological imagination'. His ideas are an excellent channel for steering students towards a sociological understanding of social problems and to distinguish these from individual troubles and failings. Although a few students may struggle at the beginning of the course with some of the academic issues discussed in class, the adoption of a sociological engagement with their experiences on site appears to have a positive impact on their ability to gradually gain a greater awareness of the structural sources of inequalities that effect the lives of many of their clients. A sociological understanding of their society, together with the reflective component of the course, are the means by which they are continually drawn back to critically explore the structural forces that produce social problems. A psychology student who worked as a carer in an HIV agency, wrote in his concluding paper:

> In reflection, perhaps what the incident demonstrated to me was how individuals are possibly pushed into an underclass by society rather than falling into one as a result of a conscious lifestyle choice. With the case of both HIV and AIDS especially there can be issues around being socially alienated.... I have become aware through dealing with clients with HIV and AIDS ... of the associations made by society between poverty, immorality and illness.

Some are able to understand previously learned material in new and different ways and adopt a critical self-awareness. A sociology student noted that:

> While writing the paper I felt quite resentful of supporting, however tentatively, the Neo-Liberals, and this made me think that my inclination to write from within the Marxist and Critical Theory perspectives is somehow automatic, like a reflex. I must examine this partisanship, because support for a perspective must be freely chosen rather than dogmatic if any academic advancement is to be made.

Community Placements and Service Learning

The other side of the coin with service learning are the placements themselves. Through Roehampton's location and the longstanding links of its constituent colleges with their local communities, it has been possible to offer students a wide choice of agency experiences in the London area. In the past, students have worked in hospitals, schools for children with learning disabilities and behavioural problems, shelters for the homeless, care homes for the elderly, prison visitor centres, crime prevention units, youth offending centres, refugee centres, HIV/Aids centres, Citizens' Advice Bureaux and many more agencies. As the course accepts students from most programmes available at Roehampton University, the variety of community placements that students can pursue is very broad. There are several ways in which placements are found. Some students prefer to find their own and for the course in general, this is beneficial, because they add to the pool of existing placements. Others either request some degree of assistance, or have their placements wholly arranged for them. At the beginning of the semester all the agencies are contacted by telephone and sent further information about the course.

However, placements come and go. An agency which has been used satisfactorily for many years may suddenly fold up and disappear, or through a change in management, may stop accepting volunteers for one reason. As Hall *et al* commented, the world of volunteering and the voluntary sector is complex and enigmatic (Hall *et al* 2004, 47). Whilst most students are able to carry out useful work in their placements, from time to time there are problems. Although in an ideal world, service learning experiences should be reciprocal and transformational to both student and placements, this is not always possible. Not every service experience, Stanton realistically observes, is a roaring success (Stanton 1990, 255). On occasion, there have been a few agencies that have not made satisfactory use of the students. For instance, one student at a prison visitor centre was routinely sent out to the supermarket to buy the manager's personal shopping. On the other hand, some students throw away rich opportunities to learn. One who worked as a classroom assistant consistently undermined her teacher, believing that she had a better understanding of the children. For a while she caused unnecessary confusion in the class and the headmaster was called to sort the situation out. No further students have been placed at that school. Sometimes there are personality clashes, sometimes students are simply not managed well by their mentors. One student carried out such good work in setting up a research project on behalf of her agency that her mentor appeared to feel threatened by her initiatives. However, students are encouraged not to change their placement. When they begin their placement experience students may often complain they are not fulfilling their potential. For instance, when a service learner wanted to leave his placement as a classroom assistant at a school for the deaf during his first week, it was because, 'the teacher didn't listen to his advice'. But students are encouraged to give their placement time so that they can start settling in and finding their feet. Although they may begin at what they consider low-level duties, often after a few weeks they are given work which has more responsibility and is of more interest to them.

As all students are different, they opt for different levels of engagement. Some are more suited to working in community organisations that offer the more traditional types of experiences, such as serving meals at homeless shelters, while others want to get involved in the social action type of organisations that directly challenge injustice and inequality. Although Evans et al. assert in their paper, *Community Organisations as Civic Education and Social Change Partners: A Three-Tiered Model of Service-Learning*, that 'serving meals, tutoring and painting houses does little to challenge injustices or to teach students and volunteers about the larger social and political context', even these types of activities offer plenty of scope for students to move to deeper levels of understanding about their society and become active, politically engaged citizens (Evans et al. 2004). For several years now Roehampton has sent students to a local organisation that offers a variety of services to the residents of a nearby council estate. A student who was manning a juice bar for teenagers on the estate, heard that the organisation's work with the isolated elderly was in jeopardy because of council cuts to its funding. In a critical incident paper she wrote:

> I was really shocked when I was first told what was going to happen... It made me angry to think that someone from the council had judged this as a "low priority"....This fired me up to do something about it. ...As well as getting many people in the area to sign my petition I also took part in the protest which took place outside Wandsworth Town Hall. It was the first real protest I had been on.... I felt I was doing something which proved a point to the council, that we will not let elderly people be treated this way.

Although students are rarely the primary agents for change, and as Parilla and Hesser state, in most cases, sites have more influence on students than students do on sites, they can still make useful contributions to their communities (Parilla and Hesser 1998, 318). In addition, not all students conclude their contributions to their agencies when the course ends. A number of them continue to work in their placements after the module has ended, and some have gone on to be offered permanent paid positions.

Conclusion

To conclude, service learning is ideally suited to help students reach beyond their personal experience and to understand issues in terms of the larger social context (Parilla and Hesser 1998, 324). By providing them with an experience to speak from, the students will often comment that their placement work has enabled them to gain in self-knowledge and confidence and that it has helped them to 'find their voice' (Everett 1998, 306). Yet, as Howard perceptively comments: 'as a relatively new and dilemma-filled pedagogy academic service learning is not for the meek' (Howard 1998, 28).

It is a demanding experience which requires serious commitment from students, both academically and outside the university campus. For academics too, it also requires substantial commitment as students often need considerable guidance to develop their insights into the sociological nature of their lives. Every year, the numbers of students wanting to take the course increases, and this in turn increases the time investment required to administer the module, identify suitable service sites, make site visits and read course work. But the trade-offs are more than acceptable. Students report that through being exposed to the reality of what they are studying, their learning is expanded far beyond the home and classroom. In addition, as they progress in their work placements, they often develop valuable expertise at their sites about a wide variety of topics which they then share with each other. Although service learning poses many challenges, it is a highly rewarding course because it provides students with a unique opportunity to bring together not only academic knowledge and work experience, but also compassion and empathy.

References

Annette, J. (2003), 'Education for Citizenship and Higher Education', *The First Annual Higher Education & Community Partnership Conference*, 15 April 2003 (Middlesex: Institute for Community Development and Learning, Middlesex University).

Blunkett, D, (2000) 'Higher Education Funding For 2001–02 And Beyond', Higher Education Funding Council for England [website] <http://www.hefce.ac.uk/news/hefce/2000/funding.htm>, accessed 16 June 2005.

Cruz, N. (1990), 'A Challenge to the Notion of Service', in Jane C. Kendall et al. (ed).

Dewey, J. (1933), *How We Think: A Restatement of the Relation of Reflective Thinking to the Educative Process* (Boston: D.C. Heath).

Enos, S. (1998), 'The Campus Compact: A Resource for Sociology and Service-Learning', *Footnotes – Newsletter of the American Sociologist Association*, December 1998.

Evans, S. et al. (2004), 'Community Organisations as Civic Education and Social Change Partners: A Three-Tiered Model of Service-Learning', [website] Peabody College of Vanderbilt University <http://people.vanderbilt.edu/%7Escotney.d.evans/pubs/Evansetal032404.htm>, accessed 16 June 2005.

Everett, K. (1998), 'Understanding Social Inequality Through Service Learning', *Teaching Sociology*, 26:4, 299–309.

Fendler, L. (2003), 'Teacher Reflection in a Hall of Mirrors: Historical Influences and Political Reverberations', *Educational Researcher*, 32:3 16–25.

Furco, A. (1996), 'Service-learning: A balanced approach to experiential education', in Taylor (ed.).

Giddens, A. (1998), *Conversations with Anthony Giddens* (Cambridge: Polity Press).

Giles, D. and Eyler, J. (1994), 'The Theoretical Roots of Service-Learning in John Dewey: Toward a Theory of Service-Learning', *Michigan Journal of Community Service Learning* 1:1, 77–85.

Hall, D. et al. (2004), 'Student Volunteering and the Active Community: Issues and Opportunities for Teaching and Learning in Sociology', *Learning and Teaching in the Social Sciences* 1:1, 33–50.

Herzberg, B. (1994), 'Community Service and Critical Teaching', *College, Composition and Communication* 45:3, 307–319.

Howard, J. (1998), 'Academic Service Learning: A Counternormative Pedagogy', *New Directions for Teaching and Learning*, 73: Spring, 21–29.

Illich, I. (1990), 'To Hell with Good Intentions', in Kendall et al. (ed.).

Kendall, J. et al. (ed.) (1990), *Combining Service and Learning: A Resource Book for Community and Public Service* (Vol. I) (Raleigh, NC: National Society for Internships and Experiential Education).

Kolb, D. (1984), *Experiential Learning: Experience as the Source of Learning and Development* (New Jersey: Prentice Hall).

McCullough, A. et al. (1997), 'The Sociologist on Placement', *The Irish Journal of Sociology*, 7, 99–110.

Mills, C. W. (1970), *The Sociological Imagination* (Harmondsworth: Penguin).

Moon, J. (1999), *Reflection in Learning and Professional Development* (London: Kogan Page).

Moon, J. (2001), *Reflection in Higher Education Learning*, *PDP Working Paper 4*, Higher Education Academy [website] <www.heacademy.ac.uk/resources.asp?process=full_record&section =generic &id =72> accessed 8 February 2006.

Parilla, P. and Hesser, G. (1998), 'Internships and the Sociological Perspective', *Teaching Sociology* 26:4, 310–329.

Parker-Gwin, R. and Bavry, J. B. (1998), 'Service Learning as Pedagogy and Civic Education: Comparing Outcomes for Three Models' in *Teaching Sociology* 26:4, 276–291.

Schon, D. A. (1983), *The Reflective Practitioner: How Professionals Think in Action* (Hampshire: Ashgate).

Schon, D. A. (1987), *Educating the Reflective Practitioner* (San Francisco: Jossey-Bass).

Sigmon, R. L. (1990), 'Service-Learning: Three Principles', in Kendall et al. (ed.).

Stanton, T. (1990), 'Service-Learning: Groping Toward a Definition', in Kendall et al. (ed.).

Stanton, T. et al. (1999), *Service-Learning: A Movement's Pioneers Reflect on Its Origins, Practice and Future* (San Francisco: Jossey-Bass).

Taylor, B. (ed.) (1996), *Expanding Boundaries: Serving and Learning* (Washington, DC: Corporation for National Service).

Walsh, C. (1994), 'A Service-Learning Programme in Great Britain', *NSEE Quarterly*, Summer: 13.

Chapter 12

Civic Youth Work and Implications for Service Learning – Lessons from Northern Ireland

Ross Velure Roholt and Paul Smyth

Service learning is a relatively new phenomenon across the UK. In Northern Ireland universities have only begun the process of integrating service learning into courses. This is unsurprising given the history of conflict and the ongoing tension and separation between communities. Historically, higher education provided a safe space, an oasis, from the violence defining many students' neighbourhoods and towns (McKeown 1984). Universities withdrew from the communities around them, either because of, or in spite of, the impact the conflict had on these institutions. Since the signing of the Good Friday Agreement, the situation in Northern Ireland has changed. The authors believe service learning has much to offer a society emerging from conflict and working to become a more just, pluralist and interdependent democracy.

Government policy now acknowledges moving forward on the basis of 'A Shared Future' (Office of the First Minister and Deputy First Minister Community Relations Unit, 2003). For the last 10 years Public Achievement (PA) has worked with groups of young people in schools, youth clubs, and museums, supporting them to contribute to this shared future and in the international arena, with partners concerned with the issue of civic engagement in violent and conflicted societies. Since 2004, Public Achievement has managed an action research project working with local universities to develop and field test a service learning community relations and citizenship curriculum. This has been a challenge but has resulted in several insights for others wanting to integrate service learning into higher education in Northern Ireland.

This chapter describes Public Achievement's work over the past two years as a model for how universities and non-governmental organisations (NGOs) can partner to provide rich learning experiences for university students and needed support for the communities, schools, and youth clubs. We begin by describing our model – civic youth work. For us the model is grounded in an eclectic mix of theories about citizenship, learning, and young people. We follow this by describing the aim, strategy, ethos, practice and curriculum of the model. The chapter concludes by sharing what we learned about supporting universities' integration of service learning opportunities.

Origins of Civic Youth Work

The model supporting our ongoing work in Northern Ireland, developed from years of reflective practice and evaluation in Northern Ireland, insights gathered from evaluating Public Achievement[1] in the USA, and conversations with colleagues involved in similar work internationally. Beginning in 1998 as a pilot project, Public Achievement Northern Ireland, has been influenced and shaped by our local context and understandings. While we retain the strong theory of citizenship from the US model (Boyte and Skelton 1997), we have also added a theory of learning and young people. Together these three theories form the origins of our model; civic youth work.

Theory of Citizenship

Citizenship is an idea most of us take for granted; although rarely in the same ways! Much of the disagreement is over whether to emphasises rights (a legalistic definition), or responsibilities (a social definition). One thing is certain – citizenship is a contested concept (Gorham, 1992). The lack of a definition creates a challenging situation for programme designers. The controversy over the definition is unlikely to go away because differences exist also in practice and citizenship depends on context. This insight provides an alternative way of understanding citizenship; it is an accomplishment (Storrie 2004). For our model, citizens engage in political action.

We organise citizen actions into two basic types, governmental and civic. We see both of these as political and recognise politics as having both a public and a private understanding (Shanley and Narayan 1997). Citizens participate in the wide range of activities as required for governments to be democratic (for example, vote, run for office, policy consultation) and citizens also contribute to the civic good (e.g. find solutions to community problems). Combined these describe the 'work of democracy' (VeLure Roholt 2004). When people engage and accomplish civic and political actions they are supporting the work of democracy and ensuring it continues. They are citizens.

Northern Ireland complicates this understanding of citizenship in two ways. First, democracy and citizenship remain contested and there is much cynicism regarding these terms. Not surprising, most understand these terms within the divided and contested world in which they live. Second, the history of public life in Northern Ireland, particularly under prolonged periods of 'Direct Rule' from Westminster, created a lived experience more aligned to 'Subject' than 'Citizen' (Smyth, 2001). Missing is the experiential and practical understandings of democratic citizenship.

Civic youth work aims to address this by supporting alternative forms of politics and citizenship, grounded in the theory of 'public work' (Boyte and Skelton 1997). The term is not easily transferable to Northern Ireland as it brings up images of

---

1   Public Achievement is a youth civic engagement initiative founded by the 'Centre for Democracy and Citizenship' at the 'Hubert H. Humphrey Institute of Public Affairs' and additional information can be accessed on their work at http://www.publicachievement.org.

water service and refuse collection, but the idea still provides a strong foundation for a renewed sense of democratic citizenship. Public work is 'work done by a mix of people whose efforts result in products of lasting importance to our communities and societies' (Boyte and Skelton 1997, 12). The emphasis is on the people themselves coming together across divisions (race, ethnicity, religion, gender, sexual orientation, age) to co-create something of lasting value. Citizens figure out what one's 'world' is like (be it school, neighbourhood, community, nation, or world), their place in it, and how one, with others, can effectively act within it. However, this figuring out must be undertaken intentionally, explicitly, and continuously (Hildreth 2000). People are producers (or creators) and not consumers of democratic work (Boyte and Skelton 1997; Smith 1982). Citizens are participants.

Civic youth work is a way of supporting young people in this process. Public Achievement groups in Northern Ireland have completed many different civic actions (for example, recycling campaigns for their schools, educational campaigns on violence and bullying, raised money for charities). All of these remained focused on 'creating something of public value' (Boyte and Skelton 1997, 16). In Northern Ireland 'public value' can be defined in many ways. PA integrates basic principles of community relations by defining public value as supporting equitable relationships and recognising the wisdom and creativity that can only emerge out of diverse populations (Eyben, Morrow and Wilson 1997). These cannot be created without working on 'real stuff' and 'keeping it practical' (Sherman 2004, 53). Public value cannot be created otherwise.

The focus in civic action is on practical problem solving (Boyte and Skelton 1997). It requires "going out to the neighbourhoods in which we live, as an organised force to find solutions to community problems" (Lynn 2005, 41). Action without investigation is ineffective. To solve problems in their community, group members learn as much as they can about their community and how to get something done within it (Van Benschoten 2000, 16). Researching the local area, learning about problems and figuring out solutions to these are easier when group members talk to each other and people from outside of the group. Citizenship is built on dialogic civility (Arnett and Arneson, 1999). These conversations enlarge our understanding of community and facilitate our entry into other communities, to visit or belong. As the group talks with others in order to research, plan and implement a civic action, they quickly learn 'who cares?' and 'why is this an important issue?' (Boyte and Skelton 1997, 16). By doing so, civic action raises individual and group 'critical consciousness' (Freire 1970). As they work on an issue, they learn more about the social, cultural and political structures that often prevent peace-building and democratic work from happening. Doing so they also learn how they too can make a difference by working through and overcoming these challenges.

This theory of citizenship informs our model. In this model, citizenship is a process and not an age based social role. People have to accomplish citizenship by joining together to solve community problems (through either formal or informal politics) in ways that respect and support a shared future and result in creating something of lasting value for everyone. The model, civic youth work, joins this theory of citizenship to a theory of learning.

Theory of Learning

To inform our model, we borrow insights found in experiential and informal education, service learning, and situated learning. Four ideas about learning have been used extensively in the design and practice of our model, including understanding learning as a social activity, the importance of conversation and dialogue, reflection and context.

The theory of learning begins with John Dewey (1900) and his emphasis on connecting learning to the lives of (young) people and the value of engaging in real world issues. Dewey described learning as more than accumulation. It must also inform and deepen our understanding of who we are and how we want to live our lives. It allows us to act more intentionally to craft the world we live in and our self within it. Education allows us to recognise choices and provides us with the courage to make choices based on inquiry and reflection. Working with real world issues and problems, he found, to be one of the most useful ways to enhance learning. Contemporary problems surrounding us can be a rich source for learning and provide important evaluation of the relevance and usefulness of what we are learning. It also reminds us that learning is an interactive process.

The way we learn is through conversation and dialogue with others (Smith and Jeffs 1999). Experiential education's emphasis on doing and reflecting are typically joined to doing these activities in small groups, allowing the individual to benefit from the diversity of opinions of others (Malekoff 2004). This is also true with service-learning. These are most effective when the service and reflection are done in diverse groups (Eyler and Giles 1999). All of these point to the value of understanding learning as more than a cognitive activity. Learning occurs between people.

Encouraging conversation and dialogue also supports learning (Smith and Jeffs 1999) and engaging in dialogue provides the opportunity not only to learn but also to teach others (Freire 1970). The richest educational experiences are those where people act as both teachers and learners: in the process they learn both the latent skills and talents they have to offer, in addition to the talent and skills of other group members. Furthermore, dialogue and conversation are critical for reflection.

Reflection deepens and enriches the learning available from experience (Eyler and Giles 1999) and it creates the possibility for this learning to be illuminated, discussed and transferred. Reflecting on an experience discloses learning: noticed, it can be discussed and expanded upon. Experiences are powerful educational tools but only when they are connected to concepts and opinions and reflection makes these connections possible by encouraging group members to talk about what just happened and its significance. Finally, reflection allows the learning that results from experience to be transferred to other contexts. Without reflection this transfer is unlikely.

We often treat learning and education as separate from any context. In Northern Ireland, schools and universities, for years, attempted to be an oasis from the context surrounding them, in spite of the many ways in which the conflict impacted on the lives of staff, faculty and the institutions themselves (McKeown 1984). 'Situated learning theory' (Lave and Wenger 1991) encourages us to see how learning is joined to context. They cannot be separated and we have found this to be especially true of youth civic engagement. Citizenship always has a local flavour. It cannot be learned outside of this real and local context (Brown et al. 1996). The importance of context also refers to a learning approach. Learning within a real context provides benefits that often teachers or students can predict. 'People who use tools actively rather than just acquire them, by contrast, build an increasingly rich implicit understanding of the world in which they use these tools and of the tools themselves' (Brown 1996, 23). Learning how to use and do something is very different from learning about (Bruner 1996), so that when the learner is required to accomplish meaningful (useful and important) tasks within a real context that has real consequences, overall learning is enhanced (Brown 1996). While often unacknowledged, context plays an important role in learning.

This is clearly the case in Northern Ireland where young people are born into a conflicted and divided society. Although the level of violence has dropped significantly since the signing of the 'Good Friday Agreement' in 1998, many young people still live in communities on political 'interfaces' where there are high levels of tension and fear, and sporadic outbursts of violence. Many young people also live in families that have been directly affected by the violence and where the trauma of injury and bereavement still impact significantly on family life. Public Achievement's internal evaluation (VeLure Roholt 2005) revealed how this 'culture' of violence, has become part of young people's everyday lives. It affects how they live, learn and, of most concern, has become normalised, with many young people not describing instances of physical bullying, abuse and intimidation as forms of violence. Ignoring this context prevents students from learning how they can participate it its transformation. Context plays an important part in learning.

These four insights into learning guide the everyday practice of our model, which emphasises real world tasks on an everyday problem chosen by the group. The model includes a group facilitator, called a 'coach', who plays a dual role: questioner and participant. The following theory of young people further clarifies the coach's role.

Theory of Young People

Age is not equated with an ability to contribute: 'From an early age, youth have much to contribute' (Cahn and Gray 2005, 27). Still, when talked about, young people are described by what they lack (delinquent, emergent, future citizens, and so on). In Northern Ireland young people are often described as either victims or perpetrators of the conflict (Smyth 2004: Hanson 2005) and scholarship, internationally, has focused on trying to change this image of young people and realised that they are 'community assets and important contributors' (Sherman 2004, 50). Now, however concrete programmatic changes and supporting practice are required.

We are continually surprised by how little youth, even those in universities, are invited to contribute, even though young people have enormous skill and talent. Typically, we only invite young people to volunteer and while volunteering is a valuable and worthwhile contribution to our shared future, but is not the only way young people can contribute. The experiences of working with young people in Public Achievement and scholarly work on young people within philosophy

(Matthews 1992), psychology (Way 1998), geography (Aitken 2001), sociology (James, Jenks and Prout 1998), anthropology (Danesi 2003), cultural studies (Lesko, 2001), youth work (Jeffs 2001), and social work (Checkoway and Richards-Schuster 2003) provides an alternative theory of young people, one emphasising possibility, opportunity, and agency.

We begin with a simple statement: 'Young people are citizens now!' Implicit in this statement is an alternative understanding of young people to that presented in biopsychosocial theory, commonly referred to as developmental theory. The category of young people, youth, adolescent is not 'natural' but rather historical, sociological, and cultural (James, Jenks and Prout 1998; Rogoff 2003). Who they are depends on when and where they are asked.

Young people are filled with possibility. There has already been much work to re-imagine young people as evaluators (Checkoway and Richards-Schuster 2003), researchers (Christensen and James 2000), philanthropists (for example, YouthBank UK), entrepreneurs (for example, Young Enterprise), educators (Phillips, Stacey and Milner 2001), philosophers (Matthews 1992) and leaders (Wheeler and Edlebeck 2006). This is only a sampling of the roles young people are capable of fulfilling and the contributions they can make. Our model emphasises the importance of remaining open to the possibilities emerging from group members and do not assume that someone cannot do something because they are too young.

Given that infinite possibilities exist for what young people can do, how do we allow these possibilities to emerge and flourish? Opportunity matters and possibilities emerge when the right situation is created (Sherman 2004, 52). Opportunities and possibilities are joined. Who young people are does indeed depend on the opportunity they are provided (Connolly and Healy 2004). Being offered the invitation and support to participate in new opportunities is critical for young people to discover and share their talents and skills.

This goes beyond citizen and democratic work. Who we are and what we know is joined, but not determined, by the experiences available to us and the support we are given. Recognising the importance of opportunity and how it connects to possibilities challenges how we work with young people. Rather than focusing exclusively on teaching or developing the individual, energy also needs to go into creating environments for youth participation (Ferman 2005). In our attempts to 'develop' them, we often forget that they also have agency and, given the supportive environments, can facilitate their own development.

Programmes are often created because young people are delinquent, out-of-control, apathetic, disengaged, or deficient. Missing is the basic understanding that young people cannot be 'fixed' without their participation: for things to change they must be involved (McLellan 1996). Rather than attempt to teach them something, an alternative is to ask what they want to learn. Rather than expect them to master specific skills, ask them what they want to be skilful in.

Young people want to participate in new and challenging ways. Increasingly we learn that 'youth want more than voice and more than programmes. They want specific roles and ways they could contribute' (Cahn and Gray 2005, 30). Civic youth work offers a model for creating meaningful and often new ways for young people to contribute to their communities. This model supports the following understanding of young people:

- Young people do not always want to participate in pre-determined, already known ways. They want ownership of the processes for their participation:
- Their skill and talent is not related to their age:
- Each young person should be understood as an individual and met personally.

This is the only way we can learn who they are and what they want to do.

In the next section, we move away from theoretical discussions and begin to connect these ideas with the concrete practice of civic youth work. As we illustrate, these three theories are woven throughout the practice in real and meaningful ways.

Describing Civic Youth Work

Now we move on to describe how we put these theories into practice. This next section describes the aims, strategy, ethos, practice and curriculum of the civic youth work model.

Aims

There is one overall aim, to invite and support young people's participation in the work of democracy and peace-building. This participation relates to practising democracy in the group, although the model also aims for young people to 'practise democracy in all areas of one's life' (Van Benschoten 2000, 304). The focus is not on learning a particular set of knowledge, skills, or attitudes, rather to support their participation in and facilitation of democratic processes. Civic youth work creates the right conditions for young people to experience and practice democracy.

Strategy

The strategy includes three parts: the group, the coach and an approach. Civic youth work is about groups of people working together to solve problems (Boyte and Skelton 1997). Group work is a powerful learning tool, it allows us to see what skills and talents we possess by noticing what skills others have. Often other group members are the first ones to notice that we do have something to contribute. Because each member has something to offer, the group can get much more done together than they might working alone.

The strategy includes a 'coach', who facilitates group reflection and evaluation of what they have done and plan to do, while supporting conversation and dialogue between group members and encouraging the group to talk with each other about difficulties. They also notice group accomplishments and, when appropriate, share these. Finally, the coach ensures group members remain safe in the group, by intervening when necessary to assist in resolving conflicts and re-enforcing group norms.

Finally, the strategy includes a problem solving approach based on action research (for example, Koshy 2006). It begins with the group discussing and learning about personally important local public issues. These issues are then investigated, using either traditional or more experiential research methods. Problems associated with the issue emerge and are discussed by the group, until they identify a problem to work on. Throughout, the process moves between trying something, thinking about what they did and planning further action. Often groups go through this cycle many times in responding to a single problem, although not always. It is a fluid process of moving between action and reflection (Koshy, 2006). The approach is most effective when adapted to fit the group's inertia. In the last stage of the cycle, all of their work is evaluated by the group. Many groups take lessons learned from the evaluation and begin work on another community issue.

Ethos

The spirit of the work remains uncertain, safe and democratic. To truly practice democracy the end cannot be determined. This includes not only the outcome of the work but also the issue of focus, the plan, the roles people have within the group, group membership, meeting activities, and on and on. Everything remains open to negotiation and compromise. The group has power and control over what it does and how it does it.

This does not mean the group can choose to mistreat or harm others. Ensuring safety is critical for the success of the work. The coach and other group members create group rules/norms during the first weeks and coaches guarantee everyone is treated with respect and feels safe in the group. In most groups, the members insist that this be a rule for everyone in the group.

Knowing when to step in and when to step back is a constant struggle for most coaches. Maintaining safety is non-negotiable. Almost everything else is negotiable. What the group does and how it does it remains their choice, as long as it does not violate their or others' safety. While frustrating for the coach, it is necessary to allow the group latitude. Figuring out that nothing will happen on their project unless they choose to act is an important insight and such lessons are not easily learned. Some groups require greater patience from the coach, but rarely does a group decide not to work at all on a project they feel is important and where they have the power to determine what they will do and how.

Practice

The overall daily practice focuses on community problem solving and group building. Groups at any place within the strategy will be community mapping, conducting research, brainstorming possible ways of taking action, discussing and creating a plan of action, and taking action. For this to occur, there are other practices that often need to be facilitated.

Working in a group is not a natural activity and requires practice. There are a number of activities created to build a group, increase trust, improve communication, and encourage group decision-making. What the group needs to support its joint work cannot be known until after the group has formed and each group is unique with specific strengths and weaknesses.

Over the last two years, we investigated what practices make it more likely that group members and coaches will experience the process as being successful. The following eight were found to be important:

1. Supporting Action Projects: the coach supports young people to create an action project and encourages them to share their talents.
2. Using Appropriate Language: making sure everyone understands what is being said and what ideas people are tying to communicate is part of the daily practice.
3. Facilitating Democracy: for democracy to flourish it must be facilitated. This looks different in different groups but most young people talked about learning to ask open-ended questions and negotiating roles and responsibilities along with deadlines.
4. Inviting Collaboration: accomplishing the group project requires the group to work collaboratively.
5. Responding to Conflict: all groups will experience conflict. Part of what goes on during the group sessions is responding to and resolving conflict.
6. Reporting Progress Publicly: to contribute requires that the work be made public. Successful groups are those that practice this skill and regularly share their progress with others.
7. Evaluating Activities: from session reflections to end of project evaluations, successful groups try to learn from what they are doing to determine what worked and why.
8. Celebrating Achievements: successful groups take time to celebrate what they have accomplished.

The practice within these groups is diverse and rich. This makes for a meaningful experience for those involved, but remains a challenge when we try and train coaches.

Curriculum

Through funding by the United States Institute of Peace, the Community Relations Council for Northern Ireland and the Department of Education in Northern Ireland, staff at Public Achievement conducted an action research project to create and field-test a training curriculum for democratic civic youth work and this is now complete. The curriculum provides information and opportunity to build capacity in the eight practice areas described above. We found successful training adheres to the same principles and practices that we expect from the coaches and in PA groups. It remains embedded in action research. Training is intentionally designed to provide an initial experience of the practice and then asks training participants to explore ways they can create this with other groups. When possible, real situations are created and reflection is used to deepen understanding of several or all of the practice elements.

For example, one of the first training sessions of the curriculum presents a problem for participants to solve in small groups. The issues that arise in the training are almost identical to those in practice. After the group has worked for a while, we stop the activity and begin to reflect on what happened. Guiding questions include:

- What was it like for you to work on solving this problem?
- What emotions did you have during the activity?
- What did you learn about working in a group?
- Who were the leaders in your group? Did any situations arise because of their leadership?

As we work through the experience of problem solving, the participants themselves share how the activity could be improved. Surprisingly most of their suggestions continue to reinforce the eight practice elements.

Community and University Partnerships for Learning

This civic youth work curriculum is the final product of a two-year collaborative project. Within months, the design encountered challenges and had to be adjusted. This experience illustrates the challenges and opportunities for creating service learning partnerships with institutions of higher education in Northern Ireland. In this section, we discuss this experience and the lessons we learned.

The Project Design

The original design included working with ten students in teacher training and ten students in youth work training programmes, each year, for a minimum of two years. The core activity was action research. Students were to be trained in civic youth work and then paired up and supported to work with a group of young people in various settings. As they worked with these groups, they would meet regularly in seminars to reflect on their experience and how useful the training was for their ongoing practice. From these conversations and with their participation, additional training sessions were to be created and past training plans re-designed. Each year an internal evaluation, interviewing both university students and young people, would provide further insight into the strength and weaknesses of the training.

This is not what happened and recruiting university students to participate was extremely challenging. In the first year, only university students already working with Public Achievement for various reasons, participated in the project. The training occurred, but not as originally planned. The only aspect of the original design that remained was the evaluation that occurred each year as the project cycle reached completion.

Challenges to Community/University Partnerships

Over the course of the two years, we considered how we would have designed the project differently. The changes in the design relate to three major unanticipated challenges with the original design, including: the culture of Northern Ireland universities, the presence of gatekeepers, and general student attitude towards service activity.

Over the last 30 years, universities distanced themselves from what was happening on the streets and in the lives of many of their staff and students, and became aloof and 'detached' from the context. This culture adds a particular challenge to forming partnerships with universities. They have no institutional history or memory and relatively little experience of connecting and working closely with communities. This became evident in this project, as many university faculty and staff did not understand service learning and the benefits it provides to both the university and the surrounding communities. This is in spite of the fact that universities have had significant and well publicised difficulties because of the growing student numbers in areas of Belfast and Derry, and tensions between this student 'community' and the longer-term residents. Much of our efforts during the first year were directed at explaining the value of the project for students, but many of the faculty remained skeptical of the educational value of such experiences.

Second, access to university students, we found, requires permission from gatekeepers. These individuals have enormous autonomy in deciding whether we can share opportunities with students. Over the last 18 months several gatekeepers refused to share our project with students. From their perspective, the academic programme was too intense and time-consuming for the students to participate in a non-accredited project. Participation in this project was not a decision the student could be allowed to consider.

Finally, when we met with and talked personally to university students, all wanted to know what compensation they would receive if they participated. Only those activities that provided them with an additional accreditation or financial compensation were attractive. Very few seemed interested in participating in an additional learning opportunity, and even less wanted to contribute freely to surrounding communities.

Individually each of these could be overcome and, in part, many of these conditions were responded to and worked through, although together we experienced them as insurmountable. It is unlikely that this culture will change without the institutions taking the lead, both in the community and the university. We have seen the beginnings of real change within the university structures and the academic offerings in teacher training and youth work. For it to be expanded and sustained, leadership from both sectors need to continue pushing for increased and improved collaboration.

Lessons Learned

These challenges do not make creating partnerships with universities impossible. We continue to build strong relationships with universities in Northern Ireland because we need their participation for a shared future to flourish. This experience has redirected our efforts. Building a solid relationship with key and interested staff and faculty is now our primary aim. Creating effective bridges between the universities and surrounding communities depends on faculty involvement (Checkoway 2001). Sometimes, this means we support the work a faculty member finds important even if it does not fully fit within our own mission. Doing so has resulted in benefits that we could not have anticipated.

Building effective partnerships is not easy, the mistakes we made in this project highlight that good intentions do not create good partnerships. The project aimed to recruit students to participate in a project unknown to most students, in programmes that required them to already commit substantial number of hours each week to community-based work. Rather than ask students to commit additional time beyond what universities required, we became a site for them to complete and reflect upon these university requirements. In response, we have increased the number of students we support on placements and internships, and even provide undergraduate dissertation supervision to several students each year. This created additional work for our organisation but also provided us with participants for the project. We began to realise that if we wanted the university to work with us, we had to work with the university.

Finally, we are working on accrediting the curriculum we developed for civic youth work. While not included in the original design, an accredited curriculum benefits both our organisation and participants. It provides us with a structured connection to universities in the area, one that will not falter if the people involved currently leave the project, and it makes the work more enticing to students.

Conclusions

For the last two years, Public Achievement has been evaluated at the end of the programme cycle. Regardless of the evaluation focus (young people, coaches, partners, and so forth) the programme, like most service-learning, is talked about as providing a powerful learning experience and teaching participants how to 'get something done'. Our programme has allowed participants to recognise citizenship as more than voting and politics as something more than political parties. Our service learning project provided an opportunity for participants to create public value as they learned about politics, social change and working with young people. In a divided and contested society, learning how to create public value – products that benefit the whole society – should be a basic experience for all university students. Producing this outcome consistently requires a great deal of energy, time and commitment.

Service learning increases the difficulty because for these learning experiences to be successful over the long term, they require partnerships between multiple organisations and groups of people. A service experience grounded in theory was not enough. A training curriculum joining theory and practice was insufficient. Service learning requires a commitment from multiple partners.

Our experience on this project might raise questions as to why we continue working with universities at all. For us this is simple, if youth work and teacher practice is going to change, and we believe that it must for a shared future to become a reality in Northern Ireland, the training colleges in youth work and teaching need support. It is no longer responsible or acceptable for universities to remain isolated from the surrounding communities or for community organisations to refuse to work with universities. The conflict has subsided and now begins the task of creating a culture, both in institutions and society at large that recognises and responds to this new reality. Universities with all the public resources and privilege they represent, have an added responsibility to shape a new future for Northern Ireland and to set Northern Ireland up as an example to other troubled parts of the world that do not have either the resources or the political consensus to create a society that engages and values all its citizens. Service learning has been an effective approach in supporting this work elsewhere, and we believe that Northern Ireland could gain much through embracing this approach, and appreciating the wisdom present in our young people and the communities in which they live.

References

Aitken, S. (2001), *Geographies of Young People: The Morally Contested Spaces of Identity* (London: Routledge).

Arnett, R. and Arneson, P. (1999), *Dialogic Civility in a Cynical Age: Community, Hope, and Interpersonal Relationships* (Albany, NY: State University of New York Press).

Boyte, H. and Skelton, N. (1997), 'The legacy of public work: Educating for citizenship', *Educational Leadership, 54*:5, 12-17.

Brown, J.S., Collins, A., and Duguid, P. (1996), 'Situated cognition and the culture of learning', in McLellan.

Bruner, J. (1996), *The Culture of Education* (Cambridge, MA: Harvard University Press).

Cahn, E. and Gray, C. (2005), 'Using the co-production principle: No more throwaway kids', *New Directions for Youth Development, 106*:4, 27-37.

Checkoway, B. (2002). 'Renewing the civic mission of the American research university', *Journal of Public Affairs, 6*, 265-294.

Checkoway, B and Richards-Schuster, K. (2003), 'Youth participation in community evaluation research', *The American Journal of Evaluation, 24*:1, 21-34.

Christensen, P. and James, A. (2000), *Research with Children* (London: RoutledgeFalmer).

Office of the First Minister and Deputy First Minister, Community Relations Unit (CRU) (2003), *A Shared Future: A Consultation Paper on Improving Relations in Northern Ireland.* (Belfast: Community Relations Unit (CRU), Office of the First Minister and Deputy First Minister (OFMDFM)).

Dewey, J. (1916). *Democracy and Education* (New York: The Free Press).

Eyben, K, Morrow, D and Wilson D. (1997), *A Worthwhile Venture, Practically Investing in Equity, Diversity and Interdependence in Northern Ireland* (Coleraine, Northern Ireland: University of Ulster).

Eyler, J. and Giles, D. (1999), *Where's the Learning in Service-learning?* (San Francisco, CA: Jossey-Bass Publishers).

Feerman, B. (2005), 'Youth civic engagement in practice: The youth VOICES programme', *Good Society Journal, 14*:3, 45-50.

Freire, P. (1970), *Pedagogy of the Oppressed* (New York: Seabury Press).

James, A., Jenks, C. and Prout, A. (1998), *Theorising Childhood* (Cambridge, UK: Polity Press).

Jeffs, T. (2001), 'Citizenship, youth work and democratic renewal', *Scottish Youth Issues Journal, 2*:1, 11–34.

Hanson, U., (2005). *Troubled Youth? Young People, Violence and Disorder in Northern Ireland* (Belfast, Northern Ireland: Institute for Conflict Research).

Hildreth, R.W. (2000), 'Theorising citizenship and evaluating public achievement', *PS: Political Science and Sociology, 33*:3, 627–632.

Lave, J. and Wenger, E. (1991), *Situated Learning: Legitimate peripheral participation* (Cambridge, UK: Cambridge University Press).

Lesko, N. (2001), *Act your Age! A Cultural Construction of Adolescence.* (New York: RoutledgeFalmer).

Lynn, A. (2005), 'Youth using research: Learning through social practice, community building, and social change', *New Directions for Youth Development,* 2005:106, 39–48.

Malekoff, A. (2004), *Group Work with Adolescents: Principles and Practices*, 2nd Edition. (New York: The Guilford Press).

Matthews, G. (1992), *Dialogues with Children* (Cambridge, MA: Harvard University Press).

McKeown, C., (1984), *The Passion of Peace.* (Belfast, Northern Ireland: Blackstaff).

McLellan, H. (1996), (ed.), *Situated Learning: Multiple Perspectives* (Englewood Cliffs, NJ: Educational Technology Publications).

Nitzberg, J. (2005), 'The meshing of youth development and community building', *New Directions for Youth Development,* 2005:106, 7–16.

Phillips, T., Stacey, K., and Milner, J. (2001), 'You're a peer what?! Clarifying the roles of peer supporters, educators and researchers for youth consultants', *Youth Studies Australia, 20*:4, 40–48.

Rogoff, B. (2003), *The Cultural Nature of Human Development*, (Oxford: Oxford University Press).

Shanley, M.L. and Narayan, U. (eds.) (1997), *Reconstructing Political Theory: Feminist Perspectives.* (University Park, PA: Penn State Press).

Sherman, R. (2004), 'The promise of youth is in the present', *National Civic Review, 93*:1, 50–55.

Smith, M. and Jeffs, T. (1999), *Informal Education: Conversation, Democracy and Learning* (Ticknall, Derbyshire, UK: Education Now Publishing Co-operative Limited).

Smith, M. (1982), *Creators not Consumers: Recovering Social Education*, 2nd Edition. (Leicester, UK: NAYC Publications).

Smyth, M. (2004), *The Impact of Political Conflict on Children in Northern Ireland* (Belfast, Northern Ireland: Institute for Conflict Research).

Smyth, M. and Thompson, K., (eds.) (2001), '*Working with Children and Young People in Violently Divided Societies – Papers from South Africa and Northern Ireland*', 215–230 (Derry Londonderry, INCORE/the United Nations University and the University of Ulster).

Smyth, P. (2001), 'From Subject to Citizen? The role of youth work in the building of democracy in Northern Ireland', in Smyth, M. and Thompson, K., (eds.).

Van Benschoten, E. (2000), 'Youth-led civic organising: Countering perceptions of apathy and redefining civic engagement (a conversation with Joel Spoonheim of the Active Citizens School)', *National Civic Review, 89*:4, 301–307.

VeLure Roholt, R. (2004), *Contesting Youthhood, Crafting Democratic Citizens: Young People doing the Work of Democracy* (Minneapolis, MN: University of Minnesota).

VeLure Roholt, R. (2005), *Evaluation of Public Achievement Sites 2005* (Belfast, Northern Ireland: Public Achievement).

Way, N. (1998), *Everyday Courage: The Lives and Stories of Urban Teenagers* (New York: New York University Press).

Wheeler, W. and Edlebeck, C. (2006), 'Leading, leadership, and unleashing potential: Youth leadership and civic engagement', *New Directions for Youth Development, 2006*:109, 89–97.

Chapter 13

Place Matters: Partnerships for Civic Learning

Nan Kari and Nan Skelton

Introduction

Campus-community partnerships have the potential to generate multiple resources for public work. Among them, an increased pool of contributors, technical assistance for community-based research, new opportunities for funding, and rich contexts for civic learning. Purposes vary. Partnerships can be short or long term, narrowly focused on a specific project or more broadly framed around community improvement. Relationships between institutions of higher education and community organisations or neighbourhoods are complex and must bridge distinct cultural contexts. This chapter tells the story of the creation and sustenance of a project co-created by neighbourhood groups and several institutions of higher education in St. Paul, Minnesota. The journey over the past ten years illustrates common challenges, tensions and the potential benefits of campus community partnerships.

Campus Community Partnerships

The Jane Addams School for Democracy (JAS) was founded in 1996 to create a space for democratic education for new immigrant families and students from local colleges and the University of Minnesota. It was designed as a democratic organisation, one that could serve as a vehicle for public work and social change. Inspired by the early settlement traditions begun at Toynbee Hall, in East London, the Jane Addams School reflects the democratic philosophy of Jane Addams, a leader in the USA settlement movement who believed that classroom environments in and of themselves could not ensure civic learning.

JAS resides in the *between*, a metaphoric location that bridges the neighbourhood with the academy. This intercultural space found at the intersection of colleges and neighbourhoods creates rich opportunity to deepen our collective understanding of how diverse people work together for common purpose. JAS was founded by a neighbourhood settlement house and two institutions of higher education with the conviction that the textured stuff of a neighbourhood – its history, geography, accomplishments and problems, and especially its people – creates an essential context for civic learning and public contribution.

Over the past decade, partly in response to growing public scepticism about the enormous public investment in post-secondary education, leaders in higher education in the USA have taken seriously broad questions of public accountability and effectiveness, especially in educating citizens for a global age. How institutions work *with* the public and contribute *to* the pubic lie at the heart of much of this discussion. National education associations, foundations, universities and colleges have launched a myriad of symposia, research efforts, high-level commissioned reports, and on-the-ground projects. In 1999, for instance, more than 300 college presidents and deans signed the *Presidents' Declaration on the Civic Responsibility of Higher Education*, a National Campus Compact document that called for a recommitment of higher education institutions to their civic missions.

> How can we realise this vision of institutional public engagement?....It will require our hard work, as a whole, and within each of our institutions. We will know we are successful by the robust debate on our campuses, and by the civic behaviours of our students. We will know it by the civic engagement of our faculty. We will know it when our community partnerships improve the quality of community life and the quality of education we provide. (Ehrlich and Hollander 1999, 4)

In 2000, the Kellogg Commission on the Future of State and Land Grant Universities issued a letter to the public called *Renewing the Covenant*. This report, the culmination of an extensive national study about how to renew land grant missions, was written with a sense of urgency that America's success in a changing world hinges on a recommitment of these institutions to public engagement.

At the University of Minnesota in 2000, President Robert Bruininks instituted a permanent university-wide Council on Public Engagement (COPE), a high level committee charged to ensure integration of civic learning and public engagement throughout the institution, reflected in classrooms, faculty and staff work, and in partnerships with Minnesotans outside the university. COPE's purpose is to transform the institution's culture so that it becomes a publicly engaged university.

These initiatives, in their many iterations, form an important backdrop to the practical on-the-ground work of forging effective partnerships between neighbourhoods and higher education institutions.[1] They help highlight and fuel a national conversation that draws attention to the largest questions of education – how people learn to participate fully in a democratic society and how institutions can transform their structures and cultures to reclaim their civic purposes. The experiences of the JAS have helped shape some of this work. In a 2004 study, for example, COPE named the university's partnership with JAS as one of several effective models for civic learning. In 2005, National Campus Compact identified Macalester College,

---

1   See also *Higher Education for the Public Good: Practical Strategies for Institutional Civic Engagement and Institutional Leadership that Reflect and Shape the Covenant between Higher Education and Society*, a report prepared by Scott London from the National Dialog Leadership Series, Monticello, Minnesota, June 2002; *Democracy, Civic Participation and the University: A Comparative Study of Civic Engagement on Five Campuses,* by Susan A. Ostrander published in the Non-profit and Voluntary Sector Quarterly, vol. 33, no. 1, March 2004.

another academic partner, and JAS as one of eight exemplary campus community partnerships in their research effort, commissioned by the Knight Foundation. These opportunities have encouraged critical reflection on the politics needed to create and sustain reciprocal relationships between higher education and neighbourhoods.

Jane Addams School for Democracy and the West Side Neighbourhood

JAS is not a public school (belonging to the school district) nor is it a stand-alone 'bricks and mortar' school; it shares space with the neighbourhood high school. It is perhaps best understood as community education in its most robust sense – a school built by a diverse group of people for their self-education.

Participants today include people from two to eighty years of age – immigrant families, college students, faculty, and others. They speak at least four languages – Spanish, Somali, Hmong, and English. Two evenings each week, 150–200 participants gather in one of five learning-circles organised by language: the Spanish Circle, East African Circle, Hmong Circle, a Teen Circle, and a Children's Circle. The Children's Circle includes children and youth, most of whom are English speaking. JAS provides a highly participatory setting where immigrants and students alike learn how to manoeuvre in a self-directed, reciprocal learning education environment. The school's broad aim is to create and maintain a public space where ordinary people – immigrants and non-immigrants, adults, youth, and children – learn from one another and engage in the exciting and challenging work of learning to be a fully contributing citizen in a democratic society. Since many activities taken up by participants occur outside evening gatherings, the work of JAS is not limited to two nights per week.

From the beginning, founders of JAS argued that place matters and that understanding one's context is essential to effective civic learning. When people establish connections to a place, they learn its geographic spaces, its idiosyncratic stories that make it unique, and they build relationships with people who live there. As these connections deepen and commitment grows, people view community issues with a different lens, one that reflects their self-interests.

St. Paul, Minnesota and the West Side Neighbourhood

The story of the JAS is closely tied to its neighbourhood roots. The West Side is a discrete, geographically bounded neighbourhood in St. Paul, Minnesota with a population of about 16,000 people. Its clear demarcation promotes clarity about the community, unlike many less well-defined, contiguous urban neighbourhoods. 'West Side Pride', a mantra repeated frequently by residents young and old, expresses the strong affiliation many associate with the neighbourhood. Indeed, people who have long since moved from the area often retain their West Side identity.

The neighbourhood's topography shaped its early history. An extensive river frontage and system of caves formed in the river bluffs drew industries like breweries, quarries, and manufacturing plants. The topography also divided the neighbourhood into two distinct areas – the Flats, the industrial and working class part of the neighbourhood and the Upper West Side, located on the top of the bluffs where more affluent people lived. Frequent flooding of the low-lying land discouraged residents, mostly immigrants, who had settled along the river. In the 1960s, an urban renewal project demolished the housing in the flats to build a levy, requiring its residents to move. Today much of that riverfront property is considered prime land for development, and the neighbourhood and city council are in discussion about a proposal for high density, upper end housing that could dramatically alter the face of the community.

The West Side, sometimes called the Ellis Island of the Midwest, prides itself as a portal of entry for immigrants dating back to the mid-19th century. Over the years many immigrant groups have settled in the neighbourhood, producing a rich cultural diversity that has long been a source of identity and pride. More than 70 public art murals, sculptures and public gardens visible along its streets, inside churches, schools, and on outer walls of local businesses express the neighbourhood's cultural history and portray its leaders. Its cultural festivals draw thousands of people from throughout the metropolitan region. In 2006, Latino, Hmong and East Africans (mainly Somali people) represent the dominant immigrant communities residing here.

The Founding

In the spring of 1996, leaders from the College of St. Catherine and the University of Minnesota (Centre for Democracy and Citizenship at the Humphrey Institute of Public Affairs) approached Neighbourhood House to explore interests in shared work. The faculty at the College of St. Catherine had redesigned the core curriculum and wanted to experiment with a more active, student-centred pedagogy. Frustrated by the structures that organise and constrain reform in higher education, faculty and student leaders sought opportunities free of these structures to develop practices in active learning. A community-based setting could provide an alternative learning environment for students and faculty. The University of Minnesota had strong interests in finding concrete ways to rebuild its institutional civic culture and land-grant tradition. One facet of that work included building reciprocal community relationships to engage students, faculty and non-university people in addressing public problems. Neighbourhood House leaders wanted an opportunity to experiment with the recovery and potential adaptation of earlier, more democratic practices of settlement work to their current model. They also sought innovative, more collaborative ways to work with immigrant groups who used the facility. Hmong people expressed urgency in needing to prepare for the USA citizenship test, which meant learning one hundred history and civics questions in English. With the 1996 Welfare Reform Act about to be enacted, Hmong families would lose their government assistance if they remained non-citizens. Spanish-speaking immigrants were interested in improving their English language skills especially as it related to work environments and entrepreneurial activities. The importance of Neighbourhood House as one of the original supporting institutions cannot be understated. The programme director (a co-founder) helped college and university personnel make connections with leaders in the Hmong and Latino communities so that the planning process included a more diverse group.

As the various groups' and organisations' broad interests were embedded in the vision and design of JAS, the supporting institutions could invest resources and energy in the enterprise and used the opportunity to experiment with innovations. Although organisational interests varied somewhat, all saw the benefit in working with community members to strengthen the West Side neighbourhood.

Three sponsoring institutions gave birth to the Jane Addams School, including Neighbourhood House, the College of St. Catherine, and the University of Minnesota. As JAS resided within the 'parentheses' of a network of supporting organisations that related more directly to the JAS than they did to each other, JAS developed an independence and identity of its own; it has been able to broker relationships between campuses and the neighbourhood in many different ways. This scaffolding proved an effective way for JAS to maintain accountability to the community, to foundations, and to its collaborating institutions, while ensuring creativity and shared ownership. The arrangement gave greater flexibility for fiscal administration while allowing JAS to link into existing institutional infrastructure, like budget systems, human resources and technology, without having to carry the full cost of developing and maintaining its own infrastructure.

Building and sustaining relationships among three organisations, two of which are not physically located in the West Side neighbourhood, was challenging work. The strength of individual connections with home institutions and the ability to build networks and secure resources has been a factor affecting the level of investment by any one institution. As JAS leaders have moved out of key roles at the College of St. Catherine and Neighbourhood House, these organisations' relationships have weakened, although some shared work continues. In time, other neighbourhood organisations and colleges have stepped in, while the University of Minnesota's involvement, especially through the Centre for Democracy and Citizenship, remains strong.

The partnership with the University is not a formal or legal contract. It is, however, a serious learning covenant in which the community has agreed to contribute its 'place', knowledge, questions and talents to a learning relationship with people from the university, who in turn agree to contribute their knowledge, questions and talents. It is through this reciprocal agreement, and the work associated with it, that an authentic learning community forms. When this happens, new knowledge, new practice, new ways of organising are created. The authorship is co-owned, and that is critical. JAS and the larger neighbourhood have flourished under this arrangement.

Although community-based research was not a priority in the beginning, new and interesting opportunities have emerged and members of JAS and others involved in the larger neighbourhood have undertaken a variety of action research projects, providing a fertile ground for graduate students and faculty interested in community research.

Building other Campus Community Partnerships

Although establishing and maintaining relationships is time consuming, JAS leaders recognise the benefits from investment of multiple organisations and continue to seek ways to grow the network of partners, both in the neighbourhood and with local colleges. In 2006, graduate and undergraduate students from eleven area colleges and universities participated at JAS. However, to say that JAS has a partnership with each of these institutions would be inaccurate. Yet it is student involvement that often provides the opening for a working relationship with institutions.

New relationships between JAS and institutions of higher education have developed organically and with different levels of intensity. They rarely begin in administrators' offices. Typical campus-community partnerships form around a specific task, for example to seek funds to tutor children in reading; to bring community youth on campus; to establish community clinics, and the like. Often impressive publications showcase the partnership and its outcomes. Though productive, these partnerships are often one dimensional, particularly when the responsibility for building and sustaining the relationship falls to a few designated people, for example, someone on campus and a 'partner' in a community non-profit. In contrast, JAS builds relationships with colleges 'brick by brick' in multidimensional ways with many involved: through shared research, curriculum development, faculty development, student work study and internships.

In its largest framing, we describe JAS–college/university affiliations in terms of shared public work to co-create a better common life. Although people do not usually initiate partnerships based on an abstract idea, the power of public work as an animating concept becomes evident when people see concrete products resulting from a shared effort. When Macalester College and JAS, for instance, planned and convened a symposium on reconceptualising citizenship at the college, new citizens from JAS gave short public reflections and helped facilitate roundtable discussions with college students. Through this successful event that brought visibility to JAS and the college, a more textured, multidimensional sense of partnership began to emerge. In another example, the JAS strengthened its partnership with the College of St. Catherine when Hmong women, experienced with textiles, co-taught a seminar with a professor in a course on socio-cultural components of clothing. Classes were convened both on campus and at JAS. In both instances, the public work gave visibility to a beginning partnership, which opened opportunities to explore ideas and initiate new endeavours in multiple areas.

We have learned that robust partnerships in which many people claim ownership must be stitched into the structures and practices of JAS and the academic institution. When many people are connected in multiple ways and when they make their shared work public, the relationship reaches a tipping point that reveals an authentic college-community partnership. Students play important roles in this process.

Students come to JAS in many ways: as service learners affiliated with a variety of courses from public policy to textile design to philosophy; they participate as interns able to contribute 10–20 hours per week; others use JAS as their work-study assignment. The latter two ways, especially, require an established relationship with career services or service learning offices on campus, which sometimes becomes a starting point for a more formal institutional relationship. In other instances, students come with their instructor, who includes the time spent at JAS as part of the class requirement. The advantage to this arrangement is that the academic shares the experience with her/his students and can better facilitate integration of experiential learning with course theory. On the other hand, the required participation takes away student choice, which sometimes leads to resistance and a sense that the experience is an imposed assignment. This runs counter to the JAS philosophy that people are active learners not recipients of someone else's plan and direction.

Generally, the students who come through work study, internships, and AmeriCorps or VISTA positions, form the core group of highly engaged people who shape the day-to-day work along with the JAS organisers. Many in this group have bi-lingual ability and assume important roles as language and cultural translators. They play an essential bridging role between JAS and their home institutions.

Faculty involvement also provides an entrée to institutional partnership. A growing group of faculty members have integrated the JAS experience with their course work, and offer it as one of several semester-long community learning options. Others who staff service learning and work study centres also encourage student involvement on a regular basis. These ongoing connections lay the groundwork for deeper institutional relationships.

Civic Learning through Public Work

Public work, understood as a serious sustained effort done by a diverse mix of people in public to create things of lasting value, frames civic learning at JAS. Public work defines citizens (regardless of legal status) as active, co-creators of a common public life. Thus in this framework, people are neither clients nor passive recipients. Public work is different than citizenship expressed as community service where the power dynamic flows mostly one way. It is also different from programme delivery where professional staff create programmes to address problems or deficits. Public work implies a particular kind of everyday politics where everyone can participate. It recognises diverse self-interests and the importance of relational power, even with people who may have strong disagreement. It also assumes that ordinary people think about large ideas and make meaning of their worlds. Though this assumption goes against the grain of most political theory, meaning making is itself an important political act and essential to vibrant democratic life.

In ten years, JAS members have engaged in several public work efforts with significant positive outcomes. Early on, JAS immigrant participants struggled with finding ways to have influence in their children's education. In 2001, JAS clarified an agenda to improve learning for children through community improvement and educational reform that involved a radical shift in agency: the whole community is responsible for the education of children, not just the schools. Along with several other West Side organisations, JAS leaders launched an organising initiative called the *Neighbourhood Learning Community* (NLC), which incorporates a public work philosophy and approach based on the idea of shared responsibility for the education of children across an entire neighbourhood. JAS has helped to bring together a network of community businesses, nonprofits and individual residents to co-create a culture of learning in the West Side neighbourhood. This culture-making effort has increased citizen involvement in public school issues, heightened visibility of learning experiences in non-school settings, deepened many groups' connections to the neighbourhood and each other, and it has begun to establish useable pathways between the community and its schools.

After five years, more than 2,000 children, youth and adults have engaged in innovative community-based learning opportunities, often designed and led by parents. The following examples give a flavour of the public things created with support of the NLC:

- The community organised a free neighbourhood 'trolley' or bus that circulates regularly during the summer and after school throughout the year to connect children and adults with learning sites in the neighbourhood. This is significant because accessible, free neighbourhood transportation does not exist in the city.
- Parents working with educators helped design and participate in professional development seminars to learn how to present projects in a way that animates children's curiosity and uses the neighbourhood as an important site of learning. This self-development effort, inspired by the Reggio Emilia approach to democratic education, has sparked the beginnings of a neighbourhood-based education institute to prepare parents and other neighbourhood adults to lead an innovative after school and summer programme for children.[2]
- *All-Around-the-Neighbourhood* is a project-based series of learning opportunities designed to help children and youth build connections with places and people in the community.
- In another related project, teens have roles as paid apprentices in neighbourhood businesses and non-profit organisations. More than 30 adults have mentored neighbourhood youth as they explore career interests and make public contributions through their work in the *West Side Youth Apprenticeship Project.*

---

2   Reggio Emilia, is a city in Northern Italy where over the past 40 years, educators and parents have developed a body of pedagogical thought and practices through early childhood centres. In this democratic philosophy, teachers, children and parents are all central to the learning project, which itself is the subject of continual study. Reggio inspired educators assert that learning is an ongoing process of constructing, testing and reconstructing theories. In 2004, Reggio's travelling exhibit, *The Hundred Languages of Children,* was displayed in the basement of the St. Paul City Hall, where many from the West Side NLC and JAS had opportunity to view it. Inspired by the approach to democratic education and its embrace of place, West Side parents and other NLC leaders formed a partnership with the Minnesota Children's Museum and a group of Reggio inspired educators to help develop a series of workshops for community leaders to introduce the pedagogy and process of documentation. At the end of summer 2005, the Minnesota Children's Museum presented an exhibit, *Creating a Culture of Learning on the West Side,* which helped make children's learning in the summer programme visible and public.

These and other neighbourhood generated and 'owned' projects are tangible efforts that suggest the beginnings of a shift in culture. They also generate a power base for larger organising work focused on school reform, an ongoing work of JAS and its partners and residents of the West Side.

Civic learning linked with public work implies a particular kind of learning, one that embraces an open-ended, collaborative inquiry process, which contrasts with the syllabus-driven learning characteristic of most college courses. This kind of learning involves the co-construction of knowledge from multiple sources – lived experience, theoretical and academic fields, as well as cultural knowledge. This 'whole-hearted' learning acknowledges the fullness of the learner's experience. In this way, JAS offers a learning community of the richest kind. With the conviction that learning is political, people take up important issues in a real life context, examine personal bias, look at familiar situations through alternative lenses and, in the process challenge old ways of thinking and being. For many students, the JAS environment offers a poignant contrast to the more familiar classroom-centred experience. Sara Carpenter, who in 2001 was a senior at Macalester College, described her experience in this way:

> People like me can be blabbermouth college students who think they have answers because we read something in a book. The space at JAS asks you to consider what other people are saying – to consider other voices, others' knowledge, whether from books, theory or experience, as legitimate sources. I learned to take up the role as listener, which required me to also examine my role as talker. The two [roles] need to engage each other. Before coming to JAS, when I would have conversations with people in student groups at school, it seemed more like a listening-talking exercise where you would argue your point without listening too much to what others were saying, except to find the flaw in their argument. This meant we kept saying the same thing over and over again. What others said didn't have much impact on me. At JAS, because we have to listen so hard to really hear what others say, arguments can change…and it has become easier for me to let it happen, to admit I'm wrong about something without seeing it as a bad thing. This is learning. If you're going to learn something new, then you have to be willing to change your mind about it. It is also a political skill.[3]

Such learning invites a serious engagement and, sometimes, playful encounters that can turn old ways upside down.

Challenges

Limits of Current Partnership Language

How people conceptualise campus-community partnerships matters. The framework defines roles and expectations; it carries assumptions about power and knowledge; and it influences the nature of the relationships formed among people and between organisations and higher education, thus shaping the processes and outcomes of the shared work. Forming and sustaining partnerships between neighbourhoods and

---

3   Sara Carpenter interviewed by Nan Kari, 09/10/2001.

institutions of higher education are complex, multi-layered, political endeavours. Too often the language used to describe it over simplifies the process and hides the politics of negotiating diverse interests and differences in power.

The universal categories used to describe the partners and the players, who include academics/faculty, student, community organisation, and community member, builds artificial boundaries that can limit how people experience power, reciprocity and co-creation. Perhaps more importantly, they impede the ability to cross borders and to exercise legitimate authority. When, for instance, we talk about academics and community members, does this imply that academics must remain on the outside, apart from the community? If we talk about teaching and learning, does it follow that the college-affiliated people are the teachers and the community members the learners? Does the 'doing' happen in the real world of neighbourhoods and the 'meaning-making' inside the academy? And are there public purposes for college-community partnerships that go beyond contributing knowledge and people to address unmet needs in the community? We would argue that the dominant framework and the 'short-hand' language implies a hierarchy that privileges theoretical knowledge and professional credentials, assigning academics and other professionals to the top rungs and community members and students to the bottom.

Too often academic discussions about campus-community partnership focus on how to get faculty members to value community based learning; how to lead classroom reflection sessions that help students stitch together theory with their real world observations; and how to rework the promotion and tenure system to reward action research and community involvement, often referred to as faculty service. While all viable questions, this frame puts the conversation squarely inside the academy, which then limits who participates in creating a different vision about what is possible.

Constraints of a Helping Framework

A second, related problem is the dominant helping framework that many students and faculty carry with them to their work in communities. College students often experience a 'cultural clash' when they first come to JAS. Reflective essays written at the conclusion of the experience for their course work can reveal dramatically different interpretations of what appears on the surface a common experience. This is where the public work frame makes a difference. Students, and sometimes academics, frequently think of work in community organisations or neighbourhoods as an opportunity to 'give back' in acknowledgment of privilege, or as a venue to gain first hand knowledge about societal problems. Too often their contribution is foremost on students' minds. On the other side, community organisations, struggling with scarce resources and growing demand for service, often welcome volunteer help to fill the gap. Indeed, neighbourhoods undertaking significant redevelopment projects or schools seeking to improve children's reading embrace these examples of campus-community partnerships. But these conceptions of partner roles constrain possibilities for true reciprocity, an element important to sustaining partnerships. An organising model offers an alternative. What distinguishes an organising approach from a service model? The following chart summarises:[4]

Table 13.1   Organising model versus service model

	Service model	Organising model
Why	Fix problems of 'the others'	Build power through networks
How	Implement programmes/projects (often short-term, need-based)	Develop leaders (builds capacity, slow work)
Who	Individuals and clients	Institutions, organisations, communities, groups
Results	Activity: projects, reports, studies (is time-bound)	Action: leads to change, builds capacity, can transform people and institutions (happens over time)

Although these two models fall along a continuum, the service model tends to be more one-directional, the expert uses specialised knowledge to evaluate the problem and develop an intervention (often programmes), usually with input from the recipients or clients. This approach understands power as somewhat static, and it can be hidden. An organising approach, which is far less efficient, takes time to discover people's interests, build relationships, and develop leadership that can catalyse and sustain change. Power, understood in more fluid terms, is visible, at the centre, and openly negotiated. Rather than a focus on programmes, learning is emphasised. Any serious, sustained change whether in communities or institutional settings, including higher education, requires political knowledge and skills.

JAS promotes a balanced give and take at the partnership level and among learning partners at the individual level. If our primary task is to build a vibrant and diverse community of learners, then to invite students, faculty, or for that matter, partnering institutions to primarily 'help' immigrants become citizens is a philosophic mismatch. This is not to say that students and faculty don't make significant contributions as learning partners with non-native English speakers. But a helping frame carries assumptions about roles and power, often unexamined, that counter the egalitarian democratic environment we aim to create and sustain. As students tend to be familiar with the service framework and the primacy of academic knowledge, tension arises when they encounter the JAS culture, where we ask newcomers simply to find membership in a diverse community.

In the early years JAS struggled to find ways to help newcomers negotiate the dissonance many experience as they try to find their way in unfamiliar territory, where norms and expectations are slightly different than anticipated and roles not immediately clear. At first we were inclined to pre-empt student discomfort by easing

---

4   A version of this chart was presented by Sister Judy Donovan of the Industrial Areas Foundation at the Kellogg Forum on Higher Education for the Public Good, June 4–7, 2002.

them into a different set of expectations. That is, we tried to 'fix' their uneasiness with explanations and solutions, only to realise that experiencing culture differences and finding one's way through the discomfort into community membership is likely one of the key learning experiences at JAS.

Negotiating Knowledge Creation

Striking cultural differences with unequal power relationships typically characterise academic and neighbourhood cultures, particularly as it relates to knowledge creation. Academic environments teach processes such as literature review, research, writing, and presentation as paths toward knowing. Non-academic settings often incorporate other sources of knowing. JAS, for instance, emphasises the importance of lived experience discovered through storytelling and dialogue as viable routes to new knowledge. Local history and cultural knowledge also contribute new angles to problem framing. Providing the space and invitation to consider multiple sources of knowledge becomes critical in building campus-community relationships.

Sustaining Partnerships

Sustaining relationships that cross borders, geographical, cultural, institutional, requires ongoing attention. Several lessons have emerged through JAS partnerships with the University of Minnesota and other academic allies:

- Learning to *build and negotiate power* when it appears unequal is essential to successful partnerships. This includes shaping a large compelling vision, recognising power resources, learning how to incorporate different sources of knowledge and creating a process for shared meaning making.
- *Collaborative work*, especially work that crosses academic and community cultures, requires a set of political skills that can be learned by faculty and non-faculty: naming self-interests; building relationships; negotiating power; communicating effectively; sharing resources are among them.
- Successful partnerships can unleash creativity and *generate new resources* to accomplish goals that no single group can achieve alone.
- Successful partnerships benefit from *experienced leaders* who have been engaged in civic efforts. They are people with a large vision, able to see connections and possibilities. They tend to be generalists who can think from interdisciplinary perspectives. They cross disciplinary borders within the university and can bridge university and community cultures.
- *Focus on mutual learning* helps to equalise power differences associated with expert knowledge. When people learn to appreciate and use multiple sources of knowledge, problem solving is enhanced and relationships deepen.
- Successful partnerships open spaces where people think together, challenge themselves, try new ideas, reflect on lessons learned. *Time* is a factor. It takes a long time to build trust and create effective working relationships with diverse groups.
- Finally we come again to the opening assertion: *continuity matters*. Communities

need to know the campus will be involved in work related to the vision for the long run even though faculty and students may come and go over a period of time.

Conclusion

Higher education students frequently talk of their sense of disconnection from community life, which the academy does not, and perhaps cannot on its own, adequately address. The emphasis on abstract theoretical knowledge creates an intellectual culture separated from knowledge gained from lived experience and cultural understanding. Young men and women, second generation immigrants especially, often express angst about their age-segregated college experience, which distances them from relationships with children and elders of their cultures of origin.

There are few places where people can establish intergenerational and cross-cultural relationships in community settings. Often these relationships, when they happen, form around tutoring or other one-way, service based exchanges. The barriers to equalitarian relationships are real: differences in languages, customs, worldviews, education and economic status. All help erect walls that impede relationships and understanding across difference. Yet the ability to work with diverse groups of people in public for public purpose in a real context is at the heart of civic learning. To ensure an authentic democratic education, one that nurtures the skills and attitudes for democratic participation, requires more than a selection of readings 'about' diversity or democracy. To see oneself as a public person, competent to make significant contribution, people need sustained work in real places, replete with the complexities of society.

JAS provides one such space. Often, on first impulse, students describe the JAS community in terms of cross-cultural friendships they form. Indeed, students come alive with stories of new friendships that invite participation in other's cultural traditions, and sometimes they make transnational connections with family members. Indeed, these powerful, and often sustained friendships form the glue that keeps people involved over many years, well beyond college graduation.

But the public dimension of community and its place can be equally powerful. That there is a larger 'we' matters. The broad vision to engage people as active agents in a shared public life cannot be achieved through a focus on individual relationships alone, regardless of the depth of personal reward or transformative power. It is this larger public community that forms an important context for civic learning for students, faculty, and immigrant families when the academy and communities collaborate.

References

Ehrlich, T. and Hollander, E. (1999), *Presidents' Declaration on the Civic Responsibility of Higher Education* (Providence: Campus Compact).

Kellogg Commission (2000), *Renewing the Covenant: Learning, Discovery and Engagement in an New Age and Different World*, 6th Report. (Washington DC: National Association of State Universities and Land-Grant Colleges).

London, S. (2002), *Higher Education for the Public Good: Practical Strategies for Institutional Civic Engagement and Institutional Leadership that Reflect and Shape the Covenant between Higher Education and Society* (Monticello, MN: The National Dialog Leadership Series),

Ostrander, S. A. (2004), 'Democracy, Civic Participation and the University: A Comparative Study of Civic Engagement on Five Campuses', *Non-profit and Voluntary Sector Quarterly*, 33:1, 74–93.

Chapter 14

Service Learning as a Shared Developmental Journey: Tapping the Potential of the Pedagogy

Brandon Whitney, Julie McClure, Alissa Respet, and Patti Clayton

Introduction

Service learning can be a powerful vehicle for advancing civic engagement in higher education, in large part because of its intensely reflective, critical nature. This chapter is an embodiment of this essential characteristic of the pedagogy, and it is the product of in-depth individual and collaborative reflection, not on service per se but rather on the nature and evolution of the particular service learning experiences of students at an institution of higher education in the USA. The four authors, who include two alumni, an undergraduate, and an academic staff member, have all been involved in service learning over several years with gradually increasing levels of contribution, investment, responsibility and ownership. Reflection on this involvement has enhanced our understanding of how and why we have found service learning to have extraordinarily powerful outcomes. Together, we have undertaken, and are still engaged in, a shared developmental journey that has transformed us, our relationships, our fellow students and academic staff/faculty, and our service learning programme itself. In this chapter we examine the student dimensions of this mutually-transformative journey, drawing closely on our personal experiences, in an attempt to give a student voice to the developmental potential of service learning.

The Benefits of Service Learning

Service learning has been shown in the literature to be beneficial for all groups involved, including students, faculty, institutions and communities (see Eyler et al., 2001). However, for the purpose of this article we will focus on the benefits for students. Astin et al (2000) have documented stronger outcomes in academic performance, writing ability, values, choice of a service career, and plans to participate in service after college among service learning students than among students who participate in service alone. Eyler and Giles (1999) have shown positive impacts of service learning on personal development, interpersonal skills, social responsibility, tolerance, and learning. In our experience with service learning at North Carolina State University, we have witnessed these and other outcomes. Additionally, we have come to understand Service learning as a valuable *process* as well as a way to achieve desirable *outcomes*. Specifically, we have realised that an important quality of service learning is its ability to foster and facilitate a powerful developmental process. In other words, we see the potential benefits of service learning as deepening and expanding over time, as students become ever more engaged with the pedagogy and, through it, with one another. The most important outcomes of service learning are related to growth and this growth need not plateau, but rather, can continue through ever higher levels of transformation. Practitioners, therefore, might well ask, as we have; 'How can the developmental potential of service learning for students be fully tapped?'

We understand service learning to be most fundamentally a relational process focused on capacity building and grounded in the principles of 'servant leadership' (Greenleaf 1970). All participants (minimally students, academic staff/faculty and community partners) are engaged in relationships not only of reciprocity, in which all contribute and all benefit, but of mutual learning, growth, and change. Our programme therefore focuses on a range of interdependent learning outcomes; emphasises the careful use of critical reflection and thoughtfully designed integration of service experiences with course content in order to generate learning and growth; and seeks to nurture relationships with an eye to their transformative, not merely transactional, potential.

The Shared Experience

It is our belief that we have, at times, been able to fully tap the developmental potential of service learning because we understand and engage with the pedagogy as a developmental process and one that focused on the growth of all involved. We have come to call this approach to the pedagogy a 'shared developmental journey'. Our own experiences with service learning embody this approach. Through participation in an initial service learning course the three student authors experienced the general student outcomes that Astin, Eyler and Giles document. Each took engagement with service learning beyond participation as students enrolled in courses: becoming leaders, scholars, and change agents within the community that is our campus' service learning programme and became 'co-creators' of the programme. The fact that our engagement with service learning has gone far beyond initial roles as students in courses is due in large part to a pervasive commitment to student-academic staff/faculty co-creation throughout all dimensions of the programme. Hierarchical interactions between students and academic staff/faculty were traded for egalitarian and collaborative relationships, with the result that all not only worked better together but grew together as well. Working in this way, with students, academic staff/faculty, administrators, and community partners, the service learning programme director grew in her abilities as a teacher, mentor, leader, scholar, and change agent. On many levels, the context of our involvement with service learning has been that of a powerful mentoring community, with each of us contributing to others' growth. Mutual transformation through a process of co-creation in the context of a mentoring community is a powerful framework for the relationships that are at the heart of service learning.

Through this shared developmental journey our understandings of and approaches to learning, leadership, personal growth, relationships, and citizenship have been transformed. In order to explore the question posed above regarding how to tap the developmental potential of service learning, we open with three individual student stories, describing the personal multifaceted experiences with service learning. We then examine the connections between and most significant outcomes of these experiences. Having made the benefits clear as we progress, we conclude with a brief discussion of the challenges involved in such an attempt to approach service learning as a shared developmental journey.

Student Stories

We begin by introducing ourselves and sharing an overview of our experiences with service learning as students, highlighting particularly important moments in our growth. Notice in each of our stories the progression in responsibility for, and ownership of, our service learning experiences over time.

Julie McClure, 2005 Graduate of Biological Sciences, North Carolina State University

From first grade through twelfth grade I participated in Girl Scouts, so I had a strong history of service before entering college. During my first year at NC State when I applied for admission to a leadership and scholarship programme, I was given a reading from Robert Greenleaf's 'The Servant as Leader' and asked to explain how my leadership style related to his idea of servant leadership. Through this early exposure to Greenleaf, I began to see the potential interconnectedness of service and leadership, which had been distinctly separate endeavours in high school.

During my sophomore year I took my first service learning course, a seminar that examined leadership and ethics within the changing landscape of science, technology, and society in the twenty first century. I was excited about having service opportunities which was a project that involved assisting a high school [second level] teacher in the integration of project-based learning into his course – built-in to our course and about using it as a vehicle to enhance my knowledge and skills regarding leadership. This course was unlike any other I had taken, in many ways. For example, everyone was expected (by the professor and other classmates) to come to class fully prepared to contribute meaningfully and what each person thought about a reading and how it connected to our experiences drove class discussion. Because of this responsibility and a pervasive focus on critical reflection, I grew intensely as a person, student, and leader. On one occasion when we were reflecting on a reading by Parker Palmer and were asked to evaluate our roles in our service learning projects in terms of how willing we were to take risks with the potential for failure; a light bulb went off in my head when I realised that I hate risk, not only within this project but in my life as a whole, in large part because I fear failure.

After completing this course, I decided to continue and deepen my involvement in service learning, so I took a second course which prepared students to serve as 'Reflection Leaders' (peer leaders who partner academic staff/faculty and support the reflection component of service learning, through facilitating out-of-class small group reflection sessions). I served as a reflection leader for a course on nutrition and began to consider a future in that academic field. I remember a powerful reflection session when two students who were working with the 'university dining' (catering unit) to publish a brochure on healthy meal options on campus were told to avoid mentioning unhealthy options available on campus. The students were convinced that it was untruthful and unfair not to tell students what to avoid, and from class material they knew they could perhaps best meet their goal of eliciting behaviour change by highlighting the worst options. I invited the students to take the perspective of university dining, whose goal is to provide students with desirable food, partly in order to make a profit and sustain their operation. We considered the possibility that while potentially useful in affecting student behaviour; it might be contrary to this organisational goal to represent any dining offerings in a negative light. I could sense the black and white of truth and lies, right and wrong, melting into shades of grey. The students were beginning to see their projects, and their lives, as dependent on perspective and complicated by the reality of trade-offs.

I began to see the potential of service learning to impact our institution when I participated in a number of conferences on the theme of the engaged university in 2004 and I participated in workshops, met community partners, and spoke to over 350 people about the range of engagement experiences available to students on our campus. I worked on the development of a reflection component in our campus' alternative spring break' service learning programmes and became the student member of the programme's research team. The research developed enabled us to develop a tutorial to assist students in learning to learn through reflection; I implemented the first version of the tutorial with students taking a new version of the nutrition course, which I had helped to revise and for which I was serving as reflection leader. As we shared the process of developing and conducting research on this work at national conferences, the tutorial grew beyond being a tool on our own campus and became a method of improving the quality of reflection on other campuses. I continued to take advantage of opportunities to share our work and co-author a chapter for *Students as Colleagues: Expanding the Circle of Student Leadership in Service Learning* (Zlotkowski, Longo, and Williams, forthcoming) and presented at multiple service learning conferences. In that chapter, I noted that 'Never before have I felt so in control of my own education or so much a part of the learning and growth of others' (Clayton and McClure, forthcoming). This sense of empowerment and responsibility has translated into significant professional development. As a sophomore, I planned to become a practicing physician, but my journey with service learning taught me that sometimes one can make more of an impact working on the macro level and to think in terms of systems of causes and effects. Consequently, while I still see the need to treat illnesses and injuries, I believe more strongly now in the role of prevention through education and policy interventions and have thus begun graduate studies at the School of Public Health at University of North Carolina – Chapel Hill, studying Nutrition.

Brandon Whitney, 2005 Graduate of Biological Sciences and Political Science,
North Carolina State University

I was privileged to be a part of several enrichment opportunities as an undergraduate, many of them emphasising leadership, scholarship, and/or service. Each in its own way exposed me to new people, places, and ideas that pushed me to challenge myself. Before becoming involved in service learning, I had spent a summer in Italy painting, a semester in Ghana taking classes and volunteering at an orphanage, and a summer conducting ecological field research, as well as considerable time working in and volunteering with our campus community service office.

I first heard of service learning through my scholarship programme when I learned from a peer about his self-designed service learning project in Siberia and I hatched a plan to create my own similar project for the spring and summer of my junior year. I wanted to explore the fields of ecological conservation and international development, to gain practical experience in community-based work, to gain insight into my future academic and career choices, to continue travelling and I wanted to work with the service learning director, who had mentored my friend while in Siberia. A seminar in ethics helped me to reframe tough questions about global poverty and the environment in terms of the ethics of sustainable development. I created and then undertook a seven month, self-designed service learning capstone project in Ecuador, exploring the normative underpinnings of sustainable development while working in the field, evaluating potential solutions to issues facing local communities, and engaging in service with local people and scholars. The service learning director and the ethics professor, served as mentors and were integral partners in my project, supporting the development of a curriculum and a tightly integrated reflection framework, and providing feedback on my written reflection.

This experience in Ecuador was a transformative journey and more an emotional, intellectual, and psychological one than a physical one. I had never been so engaged with a subject before as I could tie my learning to real experiences in the community and consciously channel my own personal development with great clarity of purpose. I saw my mentors engage with my own connections between academic material and my experiences in Ecuador, themselves taking new perspectives and exploring new questions. This dialectical process, based on content and experiences that I had crafted for myself, was a more powerful way to be a student than anything I had been involved in before. In retrospect, I view my capstone project as the 'gateway' through which I first understood self-directed learning, including, especially the power of service learning as a teaching and learning strategy that is uniquely able to tie personal development and civic involvement to student learning.

Back on campus, the service learning director and I decided that a *Guidebook on Self-Designed Service learning Capstones* through which we could support other students in creating similar experiences might be a useful product of my project. The way in which the service learning director and I went about working on the guidebook was completely unique in my college career as it was true collaborative thinking – something that had seldom occurred with other students and certainly not with a professor. This collaborative atmosphere in which we worked, interacting with each other as equals and colleagues in the creative process and attempting the same critical reflection that is inherent in service learning, became integral to my other leadership in the programme. When another student, approached us about a self-designed project, I began to mentor her and I knew that I was contributing meaningfully by helping another student craft an experience that might have the same results for her. Thus we began the process of student mentoring related to capstone projects; having completed her own project in Thailand, this student has begun working with other peers and contributing to the development of the guidebook.

Thus my understanding of the power of service learning matured from considering primarily students' personal growth and learning, to encompassing our ability to influence the personal growth and learning of others. Eventually I realised that, developmentally, this process is very much connected to some of the goals of the academy. This realisation came when I participated in a focus group of student leaders with John Saltmarsh (engagement scholar within the USA) during a symposium on campus, designed to explore what role we thought students played in the process of creating a more engaged campus. We realised as a group that there was little understanding within the student body at large of civic engagement and equally little awareness that, as a land grant institution, North Carolina State University had special obligations to the region and state. In some ways, the student role in the extension and engagement process within the university was only slightly visible and in others it was nonexistent. I began to think about the potential of service learning as a way to remedy this and realised that service learning could be one approach to better engage the university within our state and, especially, to connect students to this important work. Our understanding of service learning conceptualised as a developmental journey seemed well suited to support a campus intentional design of experiences that increasingly deepen an understanding of and appreciation for democratic processes. Service learning could be a very important strategy of the university as a tool for democracy and for nurturing citizens. It is this context in which I now situate service learning.

This journey with service learning has been highly instrumental in helping me plan my future. The content of the capstone, the process by which I learned with my mentors, and the scholarship opportunities I participated in, confirmed that I wanted to attend graduate school and helped me to articulate my interests. As a graduate student studying sustainable development and environmental science at Yale University, my research focuses on understanding the complexity of the conservation and development process in the context of partnerships between local communities and international organisations – particularly the way that 'expert' knowledge tends to overlook the potential change agency of the 'non-expert.' In other projects, I work to support neighbourhood groups as they develop urban green spaces and am building institutional bridges between other organisations and the university – drawing frequently on the rich understanding of partnerships I gained from service learning. I continue to work with the North Carolina State service learning programme, presenting, writing, and developing the guidebook.

Alissa Respet, Class of 2008 in Biomedical Engineering and Biochemistry, North Carolina State University

When I was required to complete a community project in high school [post primary school], I decided to focus on emergency medical technicians with a service oriented theme. The project required a portfolio, which contained several types of reflection, including a weekly journal and several larger reflection papers, along with examination of the connections between the project and academic material from a course. I now realise this was my introduction to service learning.

In my freshman year at North Carolina State University, I took an introduction to engineering class, which typically requires student groups to engineer a technical device. Wanting to get to know my new Raleigh community, I encouraged my group to undertake the service learning option instead. We created our own service project and participated in two hour reflection sessions every two weeks led by a student reflection leader. During one particular reflection session, when we were ahead of schedule in our project and had taken the week off, we began by talking about why we had not moved on to the next step of our project and I realised that this process of achieving important insights was not limited to reflecting on service alone. I found that the same critical thinking we used when reflecting on our service project could also be applied to other activities and to other aspects of my life and thus learned to apply reflective and critical thinking skills to my other classes and, more importantly, to my daily life.

The reflection leader encouraged us to consider taking on a reflection leader role, and I thought the position was a great way to get more involved on campus and support other students in having similar positive service learning experiences. I contacted the service learning director about taking her leadership course and became involved. At the end of the semester, we brought all of our learning on leadership and undergraduate education together to create a multi-year plan for college, which led me to become more involved in our service learning programme. I decided to work with the service learning director as a programme assistant, a role in which I not only participated in much behind-the-scenes work, but also had the opportunity to head up programmes within the office, recruit students, and participate in and present at conferences. The experience of planning and presenting at conferences allowed me to develop a greater understanding of our programme and the differences with those on other campuses. I realised that each campus has unique qualities and that some were potentially valuable for our own programme. As I began to see the strengths and weaknesses of our programme, I started utilising this awareness to help develop better ways to recruit students and faculty on our campus and decided to focus my future participation in conferences on learning more about these processes and on sharing our successes and failures so that others could benefit from our experiences. Exposed to diverse leadership opportunities within service learning and more aware of ways I could take on additional responsibilities, I joined the research team and began planning my own self-designed capstone project in Vienna, Austria in conjunction with a study abroad course.

My involvement with service learning continues and also informs my other activities on campus, including, for example, my work as a resident advisor in our honours village. In that role I seek to establish a similar sense of learning community and a similar commitment to leadership development, and I try to help my residents better understand the wide range of opportunities that are available to them as undergraduates. I plan to take on additional leadership roles with both the honours programme and the service learning programme, including strengthening the partnership between these two programmes, and to undertake my own self-designed service learning capstone project.

Analysis of Student Experiences

Even though these are not exhaustive overviews of experiences, it is perhaps apparent from our stories that the context of our encounters with service learning has been that of a programme deeply invested in student co-creation, in student leadership development, and in the growth of students as scholars and change agents. These commitments have been at the heart of our programme since its inception. Our experiences were in many ways enabled and modelled by student leaders who came before us and helped to formalise service learning on our campus years ago. These students created the original reflection leader role, undertook the initial self-designed capstone projects, established the pattern of student co-facilitation of faculty development and of conference presentations, and generally infused the programme with student leadership[1].

Examination of the three stories makes it apparent that each took on roles of ever-increasing intensity in terms of responsibility and ownership. In these narratives, we have been conscious to include some important moments that represent turning points in our service learning journeys: some moments show the emergence or acceptance of new qualities and others show the deepening of earlier understandings and skills. We divide our analysis into three stages or moments of change in which we move from participation in service learning to leadership in service learning and finally to an understanding of ourselves and others as involved in a developmental process grounded in mutually-transformative relationships.

Both McClure and Whitney gained an appreciation for learning as *participants* in service learning, evidenced by McClure's carrying conversations beyond the classroom and by Whitney being excited to sit down and write, both in ways that neither had experienced before. McClure mentioned becoming more self-directed in her learning, valuing learning as a collaborative process, and understanding reflection not only as a way of learning but also as a way of living. Whitney made connections between realms he previously considered distinct – knowledge and practice, service and learning, personal growth and academic mastery. Respet began to reflect intentionally on everyday life, not merely within the context of her service learning course, as her reflection leader helped her to recognise and use multiple opportunities to learn. All three participated in a kind of self-analysis, learning to

---

1   The three student leaders include Nick Haltom, Gretchen Lindner and Jason Grissom.

appreciate the value of personal development. Both Respet and Whitney highlighted that their critical thinking skills matured during the experience.

We see an important shift in focus from primarily ourselves to others, as well as ourselves and a deepening of personal growth as our journeys took us into *leadership* roles within service learning. McClure was not only able to see and appreciate complexity and ambiguity but saw the importance of helping others do so as well. The mentoring community she was fostering in her role as a reflection leader became a space in which she was able to help other students develop some of the same abilities and apply them in their own lives. Whitney achieved an understanding of knowledge co-creation and was able to extend the mentoring community already in place to include a new student, creating a mechanism to help sustain the entrance of new students into self-designed capstone projects and thus acting as an agent of systemic change within the programme. Respet came to appreciate the 'reflective-in-action' and critical thinking foci of service learning and began to value everything – both positive and negative circumstances – as learning opportunities, for herself and for others.

Finally, we tapped even more of the potential of service learning when we began *to appreciate it as part of an intentional developmental process*. As we became aware of this progression from participation, to leadership, to understanding of the developmental potential inherent in the process, we began to intentionally use these opportunities developmentally, for ourselves, others, and the broader community (particularly, the institution and the field of service learning). In this way, we each made the realisation that our understanding of service learning–as a mechanism through which we could design for change in ourselves, others, and the institution – was intimately connected to the notion of becoming agents of systemic change in our respective endeavours. We see this understanding of change agency manifest in our stories through McClure's work with the development and evaluation of a tutorial for use on multiple campuses, Whitney's understanding that service learning could function to engage our university as a tool of democracy and to nurture citizenship, and Respet's appreciation of the important process of sharing knowledge with and learning from other universities. McClure and Respet came to see themselves as valuable contributors to theory and practice both on campus and in the field more broadly; Whitney came to see the potential of the pedagogy not only to effect systemic change within the institution by nurturing civic responsibility of students, but also to produce individual change agents in the process.

Our participation in service learning was clearly a 'good' vehicle for nurturing; leadership in service learning was even 'better'; and our involvement as individuals who understood the potential for change agency inherent in using service learning intentionally as a developmental process was 'best'. We used to describe this 'good-better-best' dynamic, this process of ever-increasing mutual transformation through co-creation in the context of mentoring community, as 'going to a higher place' together. We conceptualised some metaphoric place into which we might lift ourselves and one another, collaboratively – that is, if we maximised the potential of service learning. As we wrote this article together, however, we realised that this was not only an imperfect metaphor but also one that was incredibly difficult to communicate to others outside of our shared understanding, although it functioned very well as internal shorthand. Acknowledging that the goal of 'individual-through-mutual growth' was not one that ought to reach any specific endpoint, we initially amended the metaphor to an '*ever* higher place'. But that, too, was missing something important. The fact that we knew we were pushing to better ourselves through service learning seemed to imply that we were conscious of this 'place' that we were seeking – which was not, we felt, a fair characterisation: the 'place', though we were conscious of its existence and could roughly characterise it, was not simply out there for us to find, even if it was non-static. Rather, we play a role in creating it – it does not exist independently of us and, in some ways, it is not 'ahead' of us but rather 'around' us. If a 'place' is something pre-defined and definite, then perhaps a 'space' is something created and original, and in important ways not pre-defined. It is elusive because, as we grow, it evolves. As we better understand the goals of our mutual involvement in service learning, we continually redefine the 'space' in which and toward which we are collectively trying to grow; but in so doing, as we begin to glimpse our goal, we understand that there is yet further growth to undertake.

This growth in our understanding of the processes we are involved in, like the evolution in our engagement with service learning itself, has been an extremely collaborative process. Each step along the way was supported in important ways by a network of relationships. We have each mentored and been mentored, challenged others and been challenged in our turn, given and received support. The growth of one has therefore been intimately linked to – indeed, interdependent with – the growth of another. Thus, in our experience, tapping the developmental potential of service learning involves not only a journey through increasing levels of contribution, investment, responsibility, and ownership but a *shared* journey.

Challenges of such a Developmental Approach

We sometimes hear, at conferences and other venues where we have shared earlier versions of our thinking regarding student leadership in service learning, that 'not everyone can have a leadership role' or that 'our programme does not have the resources or the room for such roles'. We believe that the important elements of student leadership in service learning may not necessarily be restricted to specific roles. Rather, they are qualities of the *process* of leadership – any student, in any circumstance, can be a leader regardless of the role in which she finds herself, if she thinks of herself and her relationships with those around her that way. Returning to our metaphor of a 'space' that supports our growth and toward which we seek to grow, we also see the continual creation, evolution, and re-creation of the spaces in which students become leaders in service learning within our programme. It is our judgment that limitations on leadership roles per se (for example due to office space or funding) need not hinder the creation of spaces in which students may increasingly experience the transformative power of service learning .

We also acknowledge the common creative tension between depth and breadth. service learning programmes sometimes focus on numbers of courses offered, community organisations served, or other quantitative outcome measures. Our focus has been more about the depth of development of those involved than about quantity.

We realise that some balance of these two foci is probably ideal and are seeking to broaden the efforts that support approaching service learning as a developmental journey to include more students.

Because of our focus on student/academic staff or faculty co-creation, student involvement in programme leadership is important if not essential. As students spend only three, four, or maybe five years at our institution (only a portion of which they are involved in service learning in many instances) we have near constant turnover in student leadership. Thus we have to design intentional mechanisms for the ongoing entry of new students into our mentoring community, preferably with minimal time required on the part of over-extended staff. We have begun to envision possibilities for current student leaders to draw new students into service learning courses and then into the further developmental possibilities that await them. We may need to create a more formal mentoring process than that which already exists so that younger, less experienced students (or even prospective students) see current student leaders in service learning in action on campus and beyond and can thus begin to envision themselves similarly engaged in a powerful community of learning, leadership, and growth.

Conclusion

We believe that service learning has an inherent developmental potential. In this discussion, we have attempted to answer the question posed in the opening of the chapter: How might the developmental potential of service learning, for students, be fully tapped? We have focused our attention on the student dimensions of the developmental process, but in doing so we have also suggested that students are not on their developmental journey alone: rather, faculty/staff and others journey with us. The stories make apparent the ways in which our growth was also stimulated and supported by the service learning director and other mentors in the programme, but it is also the case that they too grew through interactions with us; a more comprehensive examination of the developmental potential of service learning would also include the experience of other members of our mentoring community. Ultimately, students best undertake a developmental journey when those who support and mentor them are also striving for growth through the same process[2].

References

Astin, A. et al. (2000), *How Service Learning Affects Students* (Los Angeles, CA: Higher Education Research Institute).

Clayton, P. and McClure, J. (2006), 'Advancing Engagement at North Carolina State: Reflection Leader Training and Support', in *Students as Colleagues: Expanding*

---

2   The authors wish to thank Myra Moses and James Zuiches for review of and helpful comments on earlier drafts of this manuscript. We also wish to honour the student leaders and faculty/staff who came before us for laying the foundation on which our work builds as well as those who journey with us.

the Circle of Service Learning Leadership (Bolton, MA: Anker Publishing Company Inc. and Campus Compact).

Eyler, J. and Giles, D. (1999), *Where's the Learning in Service-learning?* (San Francisco, CA: Jossey-Bass Inc.).

Eyler, J. et al. (2001), *At a glance: What we know about the effects of service learning on college students, faculty, institutions and communities, 1993–2000: Third Edition* (Nashville, TN: Vanderbilt University).

Greenleaf, R. (1970) *The Servant as Leader* (Indianapolis: The Robert K. Greenleaf Centre).

Zlotkowski, E. et al. (2006), *Students as Colleagues: Expanding the Circle of Service Learning Leadership* (Bolton, MA: Anker Publishing Company, Inc. and Campus Compact).

Index